Watch My Tracer

Keith Chisnall

Watch My Tracer

Keith Chisnall

Reach
PUBLISHERS

Reach
PUBLISHERS

Published by Keith Chisnall using Reach Publishers' services,

31 Libra Ave, Honeydew, Gauteng, 1240

kchisnall@gmail.com

+27823137849

Edited by Frankie Kartun for Reach Publishers

Cover designed by Reach Publishers

P O Box 1384, Wandsbeck, South Africa, 3631

Website: www.reachpublishers.co.za

E-mail: reach@webstorm.co.za

CONTENTS

I have included some pictures in the book, which help to describe the war and the people involved in it. I wish to extend my deepest gratitude to the unknown photographers of some of these pictures. Some of these are more than 35 years old and therefore I find it difficult to identify their origins. Photographs without reference are from my personal collection. Some of the names of people have been changed and some faces covered for their own protection; however, place names are true and correct. With the passing of many years, it is sometimes difficult to place events on the exact dates that they took place. In no way do I pretend to have served with any units other than the ones I describe.

Keith Chisnall

Foreword

In his book, the author has traced his life in that wonderful country that used to be called Rhodesia. Keith Chisnall grew up on a farm owned by his parents, in the Sinoia area in the North-East of the country, which was to be the scene of bitter fighting between the Government and the Nationalist terrorist organisations of ZANLA and ZIPRA. He tells of his interaction with the indigenous peoples in the far-off areas in Mashonaland and of the cementing of friendships with his colleagues in conflict, where they endured tremendous hardships, the memories of which will last him a lifetime.

As we know, it was the best of times and the worst of times and many people on both sides paid the highest price for their separate allegiances. It was not an honest war, if there can be such a thing, but a true Guerrilla war fought with brutal hate, particularly by the Nationalist Organisations, especially against their own people.

There was enormous respect between certain sections of the African and White people and I personally experienced this when arriving in Rhodesia in 1962, having emigrated from England. My wife's parents farmed in the troubled North-East of Rhodesia. It will surprise many that even at the height of the bush war, this mutual respect between Black and White continued throughout the conflict and Keith highlights the strengths of these relationships when he joined the BSA Police and was cast headlong into a battle for his personal survival and the survival of his country.

The British South Africa Police (B.S.A.P.) held the honoured status of 'Right of the Line' in Rhodesia and was arguably the finest Police Force in the World at the time. As a B.S.A.P. Special

Branch Officer, I had the honour and great pleasure of serving with the Selous Scouts Regiment. As a young Detective Patrol Officer and typical Rhodesian 'Bushman', Keith became heavily engaged in overt and covert operations in the North-East of the country, planned and executed by small, locally-situated Special Branch units. The Selous Scouts was a Top Secret unit and most people had no idea that we were actually engaged in Pseudo Counter-Insurgency warfare until well after the fall of Rhodesia.

Likewise, and as the SB 2 i/c responsible for internal pseudo operations, I had little knowledge of what others, like Keith, were up to. We were all fighting the same war and for what we considered a just cause, and surely that is plain for all to see now after 35 years, with the total collapse of our once proud and beautiful land, Rhodesia.

Keith Samler

Supt' BSA Police Special Branch

Rhodesia

Dedications

To my buddies from the Rhodesian War: go well my friends, wherever you are; you are always in my heart.

To the two guys who were there for me in difficult times, Musa and Kenneth: you are always with me; I owe you.

To my parents: for your endless love and care; you are the very best and beyond.

To Trish, my sister, who understands my heart: thank you for your love and grounding, and for making this book possible. There are no words.

Ashley Chisnall, my beloved daughter: I love you dearly.

To Pamela (Mimi) Shaw and Maryke Hastie: for all the editing and support – thank you so much for all you've done for me.

Description of Front Cover

- Rhodesian camouflage uniform background issued to all operational men and women.

- Original Russian AK-47 bayonet.

- The distinct emblem of Pachedu: crossed rifles (AK47 and FN 7.62mm) over Matabele shield. Affixed emblem of the British South Africa Police.

The Pachedu Badge

The crossed rifles represented the mix of races, the various armed forces of the enemy, and Rhodesian Armed Forces serving in Pachedu, whilst the shield represented protection. The Police badge corroborated the fact that the primary members of Pachedu were drawn from the ranks of the British South Africa Police.

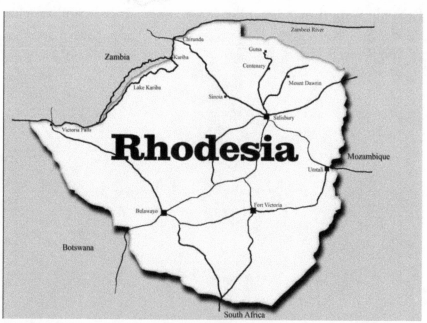

Introduction

This story is true! It is my story, based on my experiences in the Rhodesian Bush War of 1964 – 1979. Within the book are stories about units I served with, including Pachedu, Ground Coverage and the Special Investigations Section. All these units fell under the umbrella of Special Branch Control. Special Branch, or SB, was the intelligence unit of the Police responsible for internal security of Rhodesia. It, in turn, worked with all other relevant intelligence agencies such as the Military, Ministry of Internal Affairs and the Central Intelligence Organisation (CIO).

One of these units was rather special. On the surface, Pachedu didn't exist; or so it was supposed to seem 'in the books'. The operations of this mixed band of soldiers were directed from within its own internal intelligence, with partial participation from other units of the Rhodesian security organisations. There were times when the individual members of this unit were required to step outside of their chain of command, for the explicit purpose of attacking the enemy in unconventional methods; these occasions provide unique stories of their own.

With the Rhodesian armed forces stretched to breaking-point due to too few numbers, it became the norm for operational units to become smaller, for the workload to be increased and, in so doing, for the tasks to become widely more varied. The fact is there was no choice. That was how it was. The task at hand had to be done with fewer men and less support, and the intricate job of weeding out the enemy became more complex. The status quo demanded more than standard measures; thus, diverse means were employed, designed to physically and mentally decimate the enemy. Quickly we realised that it was essential to learn to handle all conditions and most importantly that, to survive, it was critical to have the total unswerving commitment of everyone.

Learn, and learn damn fast. Faster and better, or pay the supreme price. Good fortune brought us the exceptional resources of experienced people who had served in elite fighting units like the Rhodesian Light Infantry, Special Air Service, Selous Scouts and British Parachute Battalion, who gave us help and invaluable advice. Their exponential knowledge gave dynamic breadth to the troops in the evolving bush war. We also learnt from ex-terrorists, from experts in Special Branch and from local informers. Altogether, and in sync with gut instinct and stoic determination, we were able to accumulate vital skills and, in so doing, establish a covert operational unit of vast proficiency.

Within the units in which I served, we were provided with only the most basic weaponry and radio communications. However, we had the means to call in military or air support as needed – most times. These resources gave us an advantage over the enemy. Their access to reinforcements and radio communications were hampered due to their base camps being over the Rhodesian borders and far away in Mozambique, Zambia, Botswana, and Tanzania and further afield. Resupply of weaponry and manpower for them was a tough walk, over long distances, through the African bush. Only when they held the high ground were conditions in their favour but, even then, the sheer, unrelenting guts of the hardy Rhodesian forces produced tenacious opponents.

I remember someone once asked me, 'Who were the best fighters - ZIPRA or ZANLA?' Without hesitation, my curt reply was, 'They were both bloody useless.' By then, the grizzly severity of battle had given the world a different face. Gone were the early days of an idyllic youth and the free-spirit of a flaxen-haired farm child. The cornucopia of adolescent innocence had plummeted into the sheer, inhospitable face of reality.

The futility of war is clearly a dark and beastly burden that humanity bears. For as long back as we have existed, documents record myriads of stories of young soldiers who were thrust into the madness and mayhem that is mankind's warfare. Nothing, though, can accurately measure the loss of blood ... the pain ... the horror ... the wretched despair ... how the uncomplicated became the complicated! The question always remains... war is for whom, exactly? For what? What truly drives this lunacy? Who the hell really knows! All I know is that I was one of those young men. So young, in fact, that when I entered the war I had not yet developed much facial hair worth shaving.

The stories in this book are factual and the units that are mentioned existed in some of the special operations sections of Special Branch. There are some events described within these pages which, to my knowledge, have never been made public. I tender the book then as it is, sincere, and as it happened. Whilst I have no overall regret about my role in this extraordinary war, it would be true to say that, on reflection, things don't seem the same anymore. A more reconciliatory mind-set has found a place in my thinking and the raw insanity of war has a haunting, repugnant face. But, I have learnt many things.

The people in this story lived in what seemed to be a forgotten country. The Republic of Rhodesia, although seldom called that, was a landlocked terrain that lay in the midst of the Southern-African region. The country was bordered by Zambia in the North, Mozambique on the East, Botswana to the West and South Africa to the South. A very close-knit community, Rhodesians were just ordinary folk, who were thrust into the turmoil of a bloody civil war. With the scourge of warfare through all chronicled history, sadness and loss characterised the bitter intensity of these hostilities, but so, too, did the indescribable bonds of brotherhood, deep lasting connections and enduring love. What the Rhodesians did have, both black and white, was an indefinable spirit, an indefatigable will, something special, an outlook like none I have encountered since. This resilient spirit was inextricably true of a nation of 'Rhodies' - who are now scattered far and wide across the globe. Even for those who never made it through the war, their names still have life on the lips and in the hearts of all of us who remained. An enduring story about the Rhodesian War is that it was purely white against black. It is not well-recognised globally that many people in Rhodesia, both black and white, saw their peaceful lifestyle as being under attack. Both blacks and whites in Rhodesia enjoyed a far better standard of living and education than many other African countries on the Continent. Technically, the vote in Rhodesia was open to all, regardless of race, but property ownership requirements effectively denied the franchise to many of Rhodesia's black population. At that stage in her history, Rhodesia was still young and evolving, and long-term prospects for all were still good. So much so that when ZANU (supported by China) and ZIPRA (supported by Russia) launched their attacks, over 80% of the police and regular armies in Rhodesia comprised black volunteers, many of whom I had the privilege of serving with.

In the end, I left the land of my birth, forever, with ZW$16.80 in my pocket and a heavy, disillusioned heart, but the friendships and bonds I made with so many proved to be anything but ordinary. Though life has since given many of us 'Rhodies' widely different roads and homes, the memories live close ... those were extraordinary times.

When is Goodbye?

When is goodbye?
Is it in the strong handshake?
Meshed in taciturn grip?
Or in the unsaid word
so sorely riven in throats of stone?
Leaden in the final turn of heel
that masked heavy hearts
and cast us from one life into another.

Covert companion in battles fought,
Constant and vigilant in the fury of fire,
Ever-present in the sweat of furrowed brows
now long washed away by African rain.
Did farewell wait in the receding frames
within our songs of courage,
carried far into the heat of the haze
that crucified the skin and seared the soul.

Do we just melt away?
Soldiers of the bush war.
Gone.... like our ghosted footprints,
vanished into the end of day.
No trace of a time,
when once we trod,
in a beloved land ...
where young hearts became old.

Or is it, brother,
in the hidden tear
that never fell,
but lives eternal and unseen,
in every season of changing time,
in every root of every tree,
in the still valleys of Zimbabwe,
ever in the spirit....
you ... and me.

Go well .... my friend.

Keith Chisnall

Aah... the Pain

In the blackness, pain ricocheted through my body and flared into an agonising crescendo. All focus drove, at frenzied speed, to the seething eruption of nerves that converged in angry waves along my spine and chest. In a jaw-locked grimace I tried to draw breath, but my lungs failed to gain more than a blundering nano-second of oxygen. Every cell in my chest was on fire, screaming for response, but - even at the point of greatest intensity - the most overwhelming voice from raw instinct shouted, 'Stay! Do not move! Don't struggle ... be still!'

Time hung in an endless chasm. A million thoughts flashed in and out of my head, none of which made sense as to what had just happened. In the murky darkness I looked up, straining to take in what was around me. Above my head I could make out a figure. Musa! Despite the low visibility, I sensed that he was en-deavouring to reach me. I could feel my legs were dangling, but I had no true concept of my situation. My upper torso lay sus-pended, and the hollow echoes warned that a vast void yawned far below me. My rifle lay under my shoulders, wedged within a tangle of gnarled, entwined, woody roots, ironically helping to give me brace.

My eyes fastened on to Musa, following his movements so that I could be ready to shift when he got close. He moved carefully and with purpose, his boots finding footholds wherever he could. As he got close, he strove to find a place where he could best distribute his weight for balance. It was precarious. In places the soil was not secure, stones went hurtling down to who-the-devil knew where. Using what root vegetation he could for support, Musa bent down carefully. His tough grasp found its target, as he clamped on to my webbing and backpack. As best I could I lifted my body, while Musa pulled me back to the side of the shaft.

Hanging on for all he was worth, and with strength that belied his leaner stature, he literally dragged me out of the hole. With a gargantuan heave we surfaced, both deeply aware that this could easily have gone very wrong. Musa's tenacity allowed him to drag me several metres before letting go. Breathing was still difficult and the sharp air of the night stung my lungs.

I rolled over onto my side, measuredly releasing the pressure off my chest and relinquishing the cast-iron grip on my rifle; this movement brought instant awareness that the skin under my left arm had been ripped to shreds. Blood oozed from a puncture on my chest. My open hand intuitively pressed the wound and black camo paint immediately coalesced with vital fluid in bloodied, lava-like profusion.

Even as I began to take in the familiar security of terra firma, the surreal sense of falling had not left me yet. My mind went back to the open-mouthed shaft of inky nothingness that lay behind me. Whatever grand design had placed that gnarled and twisted branch in my path triggered a chord of gratitude within me. The rents and gashes its woody protrusions had inflicted on my body faded into paltry insignificance, compared to the support its shaky scaffold had so benevolently provided.

A mine shaft...? The cold fury of realisation hit me! BLOODY hell! Goddamnit! Unmarked on the map!

I lay on the chilled ground, frantically pulling my mind together, bringing it back from the spinning vortex of 'What if?' We had to move. There was no time for delay. The light would be coming; we could not afford to lose the cover of night. I figured the heavy webbing of my backpack that crossed at my chest would staunch the blood. The shredded skin would have to wait. I sat up, gingerly, and turned to push myself up. As my hands left the dust, they moved rapidly to adjust the heavy backpack and to shift the ammo belt to sit better around my waist. The spine bit back immediately! Curse! It would have to be ignored! I had no way of gauging the severity of its damage at this stage but, no matter, I could stand. The legs were good. Most important, there was no damage to the rifle!

Musa watched me from a short distance, bent down on one knee with rifle at the ready, silently catching his breath, waiting for me to recover my wits. We exchanged no words. There was no need. We could read each other's body language clearer than day! Years of fighting alongside each other had rendered excessive speech superfluous. I could sense he was concerned, but he said nothing. As soon as he saw me begin to stand, he stood up quickly, too. I straightened myself to my full height. We exchanged a look and, in that brief moment, our long-standing mutual code came to the fore. 'Watch my tracer!' - its sub-text, 'I can do this.' The message spewed out less convincingly this time but, even so, he knew I wanted to go on.

We moved straight back into formation and headed forward quietly. There was no expectation of a thank you; we both appreciated the mechanics. It was part of what we did. I would have done the same for him, anytime. Thirty kilometres stretched ahead of us to our end target, so we could not afford this unexpected hold-up.

Our two fellow team-members had been ahead. They had registered something was amiss and had returned. On seeing we were mobile, but not yet fully understanding what had transpired, they turned round again to continue operations.

Working purposefully through the bush, we wound our way ever-closer to our objective. Our window of opportunity depended on our getting there as quickly as possible. Many hours passed with no stops. Eventually, we stealthily approached the foot of a small gomo *(hill)*. This was our pre-selected vantage-point. Using the western side, so as to be unseen, we scaled up. It was 03:55 in the morning. The four of us made our way up to the hilltop and crossed rapidly to the Eastern section, so as to overlook the kraal that lay spread out below us. No sounds of life could be heard yet, emanating from the nine or so huts that appeared below us.

Musa and I positioned ourselves a little way down the slope between some granite rocks, having identified this as a good point to conduct surveillance. The other two chaps stayed up at the top, well-camouflaged in the bush surroundings. We settled in – to wait! The crisp cold of the night air, which had aided us on our journey, now started to creep into my bones. It took effort **not** to focus again on the shredded skin that had been subjected to constant chaffing during the journey. Its sharp sting again made its unwelcome acquaintance! I pressed my bloodied arm close to my body to try and keep out the cold. The blood stain across my chest had spread out across my rib-cage, but was now almost dry. Musa narrowed his eyes at me in question. In the early light, my blackened face helped hide my frown, but it did not remove the blue of my eyes, and he could read them like a fucking book! His jaw was grim, as was mine. He knew I was taking flack; but he also knew that only if it became life-threatening to our ops unit, then - and only then - would I give the order to pull out. He turned back to look over the scene below.

Musa was a quiet man, one given to introspection. His black skin was paler than many of his tribe, his eyes a little narrower, but his heart was of that of a lion. Life's mysterious workings had caused our unlikely paths to cross. I had fought beside many men, but none like him. He was not prone to sharing his inner world with all and sundry. Insights into his world must be earned and were given only to those closest to him, and most of all, only to the few trusted by him.

I shifted my shoulder against the support of the rocky outcrop; bruising racked my upper body and replied with throbbing displeasure to pressure. The first soft rays of the morning sun began to light the horizon in an orange glow. Musa shifted his webbing and cradled his rifle across his bent knees. Cockerels began to crow, setting off the few mangy dogs that slept near the huts. Someone was starting a fire. Dark smoke started to spiral indolently toward the sky. The distinctive smell of a wood fire drifted up to us in the rising temperature of the early day. Then, in amongst the scene of relative normality, came the first sign that not all was well! Instead of the smell of cooking, the acrid, sulphurous odour of burning hair reached our noses. With knotted brows we scanned intently, straining to look further and to take in detail. Shit, they *were* there. The intelligence reports of Chiweshe were ringing true.

The pungent smell took me far back to my youth. To the farm. I could remember that smell, the smell of burning hair. I was but a very young boy. A vision of the wood fire flooded back ... so many years ago ... yet yesterday!

1

The Early Days

Early morning:

My bedroom was quiet. In fact, the whole farmhouse was quiet, waiting for the breaking day. A jumble of comic books lay where they had been dropped, next to the blue blanket that was now hanging partially off the bed and onto the floor. The first shafts of the early morning sun shone softly through a narrow gap between the curtains and the unpainted cement window-sill, its rays dappled by the branches of a nearby thorny Coral tree with its abundance of bright red flowers. As I slumbered in the motionless torpor of a sleeping child, my partially-closed bedroom door suddenly burst open and Rastus, a boxer-cross Rhodesian ridgeback pup, bounded in and made an ungainly attempt to launch onto the bed. This proved to be comically unsuccessful. However, his elation at finding me still in bed inspired a renewed attempt. Despite my best efforts to evade this onslaught, his wet nose and raspy tongue made full sloppy contact with my face. Rastus was rapidly followed by the rest of the farm dogs and, in this daily ritual manner, I was wakened. My exasperation was always short-lived, however, as the promise of azure blue skies and warm sunshine beckoned. Besides, it was summer and school-holiday time!

'Breakfast!' Mum yelled from down the passage. Having orchestrated this devious method to awaken her brood, my mother was confident that all three children would soon be seated at the dining-room table. And she was right. Three tousle-haired children duly turned up for 'skoff.' Templeton, our dour house-servant, dutifully dished up the delicious, home-grown wheat porridge that he had cooked. His flat, bare feet shuffled noiselessly on the polished cement floor, while he made sure that the salt dispenser was centrally placed on the long wooden table. His somewhat tattered, but clean and starched white shirt, trousers and apron verified the fact that he was a houseboy, who worked in the boss's house. Today, there was not the usual banter at table, save for the inevitable 'Trish's look' that was disapprovingly bestowed upon me, as I enthusiastically ladled two giant spoons of sugar over my porridge and topped it off with lashing of thick, farm cream. My sister, Trish, was always the 'healthy' one of the kids, an early sign of her later vegetarianism. Older sister, Lindy, was unfazed; her true interest lay in painting and knitting, not in little brothers. My pursuits lay in a very different world - hunting and fishing; now that gave purpose to life. It was time to gulp down a glass of freshly-squeezed orange juice, excuse myself from the table and bolt for the bathroom. After the bothersome chore of brushing teeth and a cursory washing of the face, I was ready to get outside and onto the farm.

I slung my .22 pellet gun across my left arm, and headed for the back door. The gun lay long against my young body. Just outside the kitchen door was the Rhodesian Donkey, or hot-water boiler. It consisted of a 44-gallon drum lying on its side, supported by a basic brick construction, above a fire. This was the hot-water supply to the house and, in order to adjust the heat, you adjusted the burning wood pile. The garden boy, Nelson, was busy roasting a rather large rat on the coals. He had caught it by digging up a hole in the old maize field, behind the borehole. I watched him as he used his leathery, work-hardened fingers to turn the rodent over to get an even cook – blowing exuberantly on the coals afterwards to cool them down again. After a few minutes the rat was ready, black on the outside with all the hair burnt off, but inside cooked to a 'T.' Hot coals did the trick. The smell of burnt hair would stay with me forever. Nelson expertly bent the victuals backwards, effectively splitting the stomach open, and used his fingertips to rip out the roasted guts. Rastus bolted down a small morsel that he was thrown. I was offered a leg, but rapidly shook my head, 'No, thanks,' and, with fleeting turn of my stomach, took off at a pace.

The path took me on a well-worn route – down the trail through the large farm garden, past the avocado tree with the curious 90-degree branch, down the stony road with a familiar detour around the stubborn patch of starbur thorns, and deftly past the tree that housed the resident black mamba. Rastus and I happily trotted our way down towards the sheds and workshop. Barefoot, as always. There I would find Dad, who had been up since long before dawn. This was a place where all the fun things a boy could ever want on a farm could be found. Intriguing piles of old scrap farm implements, a drying shed where maize was laid out to dry (if it had become wet from late rains), tractors, trailers, a multitude of tools, sacks, mashanga (old corn cobs), even an old goat shed, now a primary residence for rats, spiders and a plethora of little folk from Africa's spectacular insect kingdom.

Farm dogs:

Rastus was a robust one-year old. He had been found as a stray on a nearby farm, after being abandoned by his previous owners. With his muscular body and strong, square face, he was a real-life Jock-of-the-Bushveld type, sandy-coloured, with a distinct ridge along his back, and an endearing personality. Rastus's closest canine companion was Jason, a strapping brindle of indeterminable heritage, with a tail that whooshed glasses off tables. Jason was boisterous, strong and solid, an outstanding watchdog. Such dogs were viewed as an enormous asset for the purpose of protection, especially during the later war years.

Work on the farm:

My father, known to all as Ted, was working industriously with the welding machine. He was bent over a plough-shear that had cracked after having hit a rock in the maize fields. With long legs and strong sun-tanned arms, 230 pounds, he stood six foot three and had intense  blue eyes. He wore an oil-stained, short-sleeved shirt with khaki shorts and well-worn Veldskoens, no socks. His shoes were standard farmer attire. Veldskoens were made from the inner part of cow hide, had thick rubber soles, and were comfortable and cheap to buy. The huge, green, John Deere tractor was positioned nearby, engine hot, with the broken plough resting precariously on a Rhodesian teak plank, strung between two empty oil drums. The tractor's large back tyres carried warmth from the sun and I drew close to their heat, whilst waiting for Dad to finish his welding. The tractor driver was crouched down, holding the plough shear steady. I had been warned before about not looking directly at the brilliant white flashes that flared from the welding-machine, but somehow there was always a compelling fascination that made peeking irresistible.

Sabow the pig hunter:

'Mangwanani!' said a voice in a low tone, startling me for a split-second.

'Mangwanani,' came my quick response as I recognised the voice. My focus switched immediately to the double-barrelled hammer shotgun that Sabow cradled in his arms with such easy familiarity. He was on his way back from a night of bush-pig hunting in the maize fields. Pigs caused untold damage to mealie crops and were regarded as a ruddy nuisance. My father was meticulously strict about guns. Sabow had been issued with 2 AAA cartridges the night before and had been instructed, in no uncertain terms, to remember that there had to be a pig for every cartridge used - no misses. Last night had been unsuccessful. Sabow greeted Dad and reported to him on the night's events and confirmed which maize lands he had been guarding. At the same time, he handed both the shotgun and two rounds back to my father. Dad queried something and then nodded. They spoke in Fanagalo – a mixed jumble of languages of Shona, Ndebele and English vernacular. This unusual language was common to all farming communities and mines of Southern Africa. The language spanned the different tribes and dialects, making communication easier. Sabow cupped his hands with respect and then turned to begin his journey back to the compound where he lived, to sleep for the day. The shotgun was old, with unsightly wire wrapped around the chamber area - just in case it blew up. All the 'blue' had worn off the gun's metal, caused by years of constant handling. The entire gun now had a well-used metal shine to it. The old, oily leather sling had no buckles left and was

attached to the gun with yet more wire. In Rhodesia, wire could fix anything! The triggers were stepped back from each other, so you could select either barrel. However, if you were in a panic, you could inadvertently pull both  at the same time and wind up flying backwards from the blast of two rounds. This feat would provide outstanding prospects of acquiring a painful backside and bruised shoulder. You had to be careful with Sabow's shotgun!

Sabow must have been 60 years old and his clothes looked as though they had been shredded by the maize mill. However, one thing for certain was that Sabow was skilled at shooting pigs.

His trick was simple, but effective. In the deep of night, he would enter the maize fields and sit quietly. Pigs are generally noisy eaters and as soon as he heard the familiar crunching sound, he would stand up and cup his ears to pick up the direction and

distance the pigs were from him. Wild pigs munch away, then stop to listen. Sabow would creep forward when the pigs were crunching and stop when they listened. You had to be about three or four metres from pigs to kill with one shot in the pitch-black night. Sabow kicked up fine dust as his old, wiry legs shuffled off across the open area between the sheds. His dusty feet were thrust into shoes that he had resourcefully made for himself from old car tyres. His big toenails, long and dirty, extended beyond the end of the shoes. These shoes were commonly called *manyatellas* and many of the farm labourers wore them. They cost nothing to make and were cool to wear. I wiped the dust off the butt of my pellet gun and wandered over to Dad, dreaming that one day I would be as proficient as Sabow with his big pig gun.

The farm:

'What can I do?' I enquired, not really asking if I could help around the workshop, but wanting to see if Dad had some bright idea about what fun activity I could engage in with the dogs.

'I've got to finish this, then go up to the lands to find the rock that caused the damage to the plough,' he answered tolerantly. 'Wait in the bakkie and we can go together.'

The bakkie was an old, green, Isuzu pickup, with rust in every panel. He turned his attention back to his welding, whilst I weighed up his suggestion and opted, instead, to take the dogs down to the slaughter slab - inquisitive to inspect the area where a cow had been shot three days previously. The labourers on the farm were issued rations of maize and beans once a week. Once a month, Dad shot a 'mombi' (cow) for the labourer's meat rations. He used a .22 Hornet, with a hair-trigger, to shoot through the cow's heart. The shoot normally took place after the cattle had been herded into the dipping-area for their weekly cleansing of ticks. Once the necessary deed was done, the farm labourers would clean out the stomach and entrails of the ration cow by ripping out the contents and draping them over a branch. A foul-smelling stew was made from the guts. They would then cut the beast into hunks and drop pre-weighed amounts into the many enamelled, metal bowls placed by others in a circle around the activity. The head was reserved for the farm foreman. It always intrigued me to see him wander off toward the compound with the large bloody head balanced precariously on top of his own head, blood dripping down his shoulders. What on earth could they find tasty about that, I would ponder? Tripe and onions was, however, my father's favourite dish. I found it repulsive. I once asked him what his favourite vegetable was and he said 'Onions, with anything.' I guess the smell and flies were enough to put anyone off, save the hardiest. Each family would enjoy a bucketful of wobbling flesh and there was inevitably much drumming and dancing in the evening, when the monthly meat ration came about. The left-over animal hide was heavily treated with salt, folded and put into the skins shed. The dogs were always in serious trouble if they were spotted entering that room. The problem was that not only were the skins valuable, but they contained residue from the tick poison that was used in the spray-race at the cattle dip. If the dogs ate the poison, they would react as if they had rabies and literally go berserk. Disorientation, frothing mouths and dizziness would make them run into trees and walls. Even licking the blood from the slaughter slab could have deadly consequences and so, as soon as I saw Rastus having a go at a dark, suspicious-looking patch on the slab, I yelled at him to get the hell away from it.

At that moment Dad called out, 'Come!' and I ran back to the green Isuzu bakkie. The dogs didn't need any encouragement. They knew the drill. A mango that I had picked earlier was pulled out of my back pocket and placed onto the middle seat between Dad and me. Pellets for the gun stayed in my pockets.

'That unloaded, boy?' came Dad's immediate question, his hands on the steering-wheel.

'Yes, Dad,' was my solemn reassurance, well-knowing that my father's approach to guns was non-negotiable.

Kephas, the farm mechanic, leapt nimbly into the back of the bakkie, having first loaded a box of assorted tools. The tractor, with its repaired plough, was already chugging off towards the lands to continue ploughing. The dogs were keenly aware that this action signalled that a 'run' was imminent, and started to circle the bakkie with tails wagging madly. We took off towards the lands. Jason consistently led the way by running up front of the bakkie, always smelling the ground for any buck spoor. Rastus preferred to pace himself alongside the right back wheel. The dogs could run for miles of tongue-lolling, ear-flapping, chest-heaving exertion, and they loved it. Periodically, Rastus had to be picked up when he lagged behind, although there was the occasional respite when we encountered a rickety wire gate that needed opening. He was not yet strong enough to complete the full distance that we usually covered. The dogs' paws were as hard as rubber from this favourite activity. There was many a time when Jason would dart off into the bush, hot on the trail of fresh scent from a buck or rat, and the bakkie would pass him by. He would then be indecisive as to whether to follow the bakkie, or pursue his target. For a second he would exhibit reluctance to discard the hunt but, soon, he would be back in his position in the front, snarling competitively at Rastus as he passed him. The sun was now well up and heating the air, as we bounded along the dusty road, past the huge orchard and onto the tree-lined dirt road leading to the lands. Blue hills could be seen in the distance, setting a scenic backdrop to the farm's 3000 hectares of rich, arable soil. This was truly a young boy's paradise and open playground. Here, he was free to just be.

Tough farming times:

The rains hadn't come yet. Ploughing of the lands was critical so as to get the seeds in - ready for the first week of November. Broken implements and equipment, like the plough-shear, were a major setback. Damage like this normally meant that the tractor drivers ended up having to plough right through the night to catch up. Spares were an expensive stock item and shops were far away. So, old tractors were stripped of their very guts, their parts harvested in order to be welded or bolted onto the other tractors. It was imperative to keep the wheels turning. Once the lands were ploughed into their long (mostly) straight lines, the drivers would change implements and lash on the maize planter. The maize planter was a strange-looking contraption. Attached to the back of the tractor, it had four small hoppers which held the seeds aloft and steadily dribbled them into the holes made by the leading wheels. An assistant would sit at the extreme rear of the implement - precariously balanced, with his feet being his only real support. His job was to adjust the hopper's height so that the seeds would be planted correctly ... and also to check when the hoppers needed filling. If the seeds were not buried deep enough they wouldn't germinate, so his job was extremely important. The John Deere planter had a special circular disk with holes for each row being planted. The disk was sized to take one seed per hole and it rotated and dropped seeds as it went, and a rear, inverted wheel built a line of soil over each row of seeds, as the tractor moved forward at a specific speed. Go too fast and the seeds would not have time to drop into the holes and would get smashed in their passage downward. The maize seed was also treated with a red powder to try and combat eel and cut-worm infestation, which could devastate a crop ... and our livelihood. Oh, how we wished for the first rains. We had no irrigation and trusted in the routine of Nature to give us the much-needed rains. Drought was a devastating event that could, and would, end our farming ventures. God needed to water His gardens and soon.

Learning to shoot:

At the end of each traversing line, the tractor driver would have to raise the implement off the ground to turn round and continue planting along the next row. In the turning procedure, some maize seeds would inevitably fall out onto the verge. Plump, grey doves greedily identified this section of the field as a highly desirable fast-food spot. With that, and together with my trusty BSA pellet gun, came my participation as a self-appointed curtailer of 'thieving bandits.' Besides, a dove could fetch 3 pennies from the local farm-labourer's kids and, if the head was sold separately, I could get a wholesome 5 pennies for the entire bird. A dove on the ground was an easy shot and just one pellet would suffice. The elegant cattle egrets, with their white plumage and bright yellow beaks, would also follow the tractors, while plundering the choice array of insects that tried to hop away. Egrets, however, were not for shooting - they didn't eat maize seed.

Fat francolins were also abundant, but they had a heavy covering of mottled brown feathers and a pellet could not penetrate such protection. A head shot was the only answer and that was a bit more difficult, as they did not stand still for long. Guinea Fowl were not only armoured with heavy feathers, but they were ever cautious and alert and you had to be skilled at stalking them. I always said that guinea fowl possess just two brain cells, one that motivates their eating ... and I couldn't remember the use of the other one. The prize, though, for a guinea fowl or francolin was well worth the additional effort and 'shupa.' The drawback was that both Jason and Rastus loved to chase them, which was decidedly unhelpful and severely thwarted my business enterprise. You had to be alone to stand a chance at bagging the bigger birds.

Python:

Dad and Kephas went to inspect the rock that broke the plough. Whilst they were busy, I took a short walk to examine some nearby thick bush, in which Jason had shown an interest.

'Daaaaad!' I screamed loudly, as the blood rushed rapidly from my face. In my curiosity, I had inadvertently come across a terrifying scene ... just six short feet inside the bushes. I retreated immediately with shock and didn't dare approach any closer. Recognising the urgency in my voice, Dad quickly came up next to me and stretched his neck to have a better look, without physically walking into the bush. In Africa, you don't just 'wander' into the bush, not if you aspire toward a long life span. Lying prostrate on the ground, under a wild guarrie bush, was a hapless Duiker, and wrapped tightly around it was the biggest snake I had ever seen in my life. A mammoth python! It had seized the poor buck in its jaws and effectively constricted it to death. I shooed the dogs away. As it hadn't started to devour the small mammal yet, the whole thing must have just occurred. Dad quickly instructed Kephas to drive the bakkie back to the house to fetch my mother - and the camera. While waiting for their return, Dad and I carefully ventured forward for a better view, but the snake showed us his vehement disapproval of our invasion of his space by breathing heavily. We paused where we were, not making a sound. The snake now remained motionless, but was keenly aware of our unwelcome presence.

'What's going on?' asked Mum, as she rushed to join us with her old Brownie camera at the ready. Her eyes widened as she took in the unbelievable scene. Dad cautioned her to hush.

'We need a photo of this, Nyoka. It's not often that you get to see a snake this big in the bush - it must be 14 feet long,' he said.

He took the camera from Mum and ushered her forward, so that she would be in the picture as well. In that instant, there was as sudden whoosh as the snake unexpectedly and angrily lashed out. Its entire focus and intent was to strike out at the nearest thing that was upsetting it – Mum's brightly-coloured dress. The razor-sharp teeth snapped shut inches from her stomach, as she lurched backwards out of the way, stumbling frantically over the rough earth, and falling in a breathless heap next to my feet.

'My God! Did you get the picture?' was all she could muster.

'Nope,' came Dad's response. 'We will have to do it again,' he said, laughing to diffuse the shock.

'Not a bloody chance!' and with that Mum took off for the safety of the bakkie, her heart pounding. We drove back to the farmhouse with scarcely a word, as the shock lingered. The 'offending' plough-breaking rock left lying in the field, had long been forgotten. Mum came to be the farms' resident snake-shooter after that, her favourite weapon being the .22 hornet rifle, and she was good at this task.

It was only 8 o'clock in the morning ... phew!

Life on the farm:

Templeton was washing the dishes in the enamel sink, whilst my mother set up the milk-separator to start making butter. Our farm butter was made from the rich, creamy milk that the milking boys brought in from the regular morning run. The separator was a series of sturdy bowls linked, one on top of the other, with a spout for the lighter low-fat milk and another spout for the heavier cream. The machine was cranked by hand and the centrifugal force would separate the heavier cream from the milk. The small dairy of six Friesland cattle kept the household (plus the dogs and cats, numerous ad hoc visitors and sickly children from the compound) in daily supply of fresh milk, with the spare cream being made into butter. Our dairy cattle were well-loved and all bore names, as did their offspring.

Salt was added to the butter and yellow blocks were smacked soundly into rectangular shapes, using two strong wooden paddles. Opaque water would squirt out. The end result was a deep-yellow block of 100 per cent pure, unadulterated, delicious farm butter. The first block was invariably destined for a firm family favourite, namely 'Templeton biscuits.' Templeton, in his intermittent role as a hard worker, was a dab hand at making these biscuits, which followed a very basic recipe, each with an obligatory glazed cherry atop. The secret ingredient was the butter. The biscuits would be wolfed down just about as fast as they were made. Oven-warm Templeton biscuits with tea - you have no idea!

The farmhouse kitchen was very simple. A bare cement floor, two wooden tables (one of which homed the milk separator), a few small cupboards and a fridge ... but at least it boasted an electric oven - and a well-used jaffle iron. Near the back door, there was a shelf that housed the so-called 'back door surgery.' An array of *muti* (medicine) including aspirin, Dettol antiseptic, cough mixture, bandages, eye- and ear-drops and tummy medicines, made up the stock. These were used for the farm workers when they fell sick. On one memorable occasion, we had been visited by John Berry, a representative for a well-known pharmaceutical company. He had been visiting all the farms in the area to bring awareness to the ongoing bilharzia problem, a serious disease caused by parasitic worms. Farmers were encouraged to provide anti-bilharzia tablets to their labour forces. Trouble arose when a rumour emerged amongst the workers that this was a ruse to make them infertile. When assembled and provided with the tablets, my father became aware that many of the workers feigned swallowing the tablets and no doubt spat them out later.

The heat of the day invited a swim. Up to the left of the farmhouse, and a short walk away, was a large, round-shaped reservoir, bricked up to store Africa's real gold ... liquid water. The trouble was that one had to first depopulate its surface of the many water scorpions that swarmed across it in bothersome numbers. By pulling enough of them out by the tail, and flinging them quickly aside, one could find enough space to plunge into the water. Unfortunately, the stinging beetles there appeared to be sympathetic to such impolite displacement of their neighbours and found ways to invade your swimming-costume, launching well-directed attacks on sensitive spots. This was, however, more irritating than painful, so the swim would continue anyway. I left the reservoir, wet and refreshed, but the water looked decidedly greener from all the slimy growth that had been churned up from the bottom. The water scorpions rapidly re-ensconced themselves and harmony was fast restored.

A short detour passed the orchard provided a delectable midday snack. Depending on the season, there was of a wide array of green guavas, paw paws, grapefruit, avocados, pomegranate, both curved and round mangoes, or irresistible mulberries. One snag about juicy mulberries is the vivid purple stains they left on the feet, hands and mouth, or worse, on clothing. These tell-tale signs were a dead giveaway of the illicit meal that would be sure to draw chastisement for a spoilt appetite.

'You've been in the mulberries again?' was Mum's rhetorical question as I entered the kitchen for lunch.

'Ahmmm...' came my mumble, as I tried to distract attention from the purple stains. 'I only walked past and ...' came my useless, non-existent excuse, all the while knowing that I was busted.

During the week, the farm labourers were awoken for work by a unique alarm system: a loud, metallic clanging. This sound came from a plough disc, suspended from a tree, that was beaten rigorously every working day by the chief, using a short piece of iron bar or 'simbi.' This was a rudimentary but effective method to waken the labour force and get the day underway. My father rose at 3:00 a.m. every day to be well-prepared for the demands that could, and did, come his way.

Terrorists start their nonsense:

When children in the farming communities reached their sixth birthday, they were sent to boarding-school. This was common in the farming communities, where distances made this necessary. As young as we were, part of our training at school included briefings on what to do if we were under terrorist attack. Certain bells signified different actions, whether it be congregating at pre-determined points, or getting under our beds in the dormitory.

In truth, our youth meant that we hadn't the faintest idea what was going on with the terrorists and why there was now such a problem. Most of us were keener on rugby than political issues. Dad often left the farm on Police Reserve duties, as he was a section leader of a stick of six men. We didn't know it at the time, but he was heavily involved in the first real engagement with the terrorists at the Battle of Sinoia. It became apparent that the security situation in our district, called Lomagundi, was becoming a problem. More and more reports were coming in, where the local population had seen or heard about terrorists. With Dad being in the Police Reserve, he would get first-hand information from Sinoia Police Station. He often spoke with Mum about these issues and of course, as kids, we had our ears pricked up whenever terrorists were mentioned. Dad was out on anti-terrorist duties more often and that started to affect the productivity on our farm. Other farmers in the area were also part of the Police Reserve and groups of men or sticks were formed to do patrols in our area. They gallantly went out on patrol wearing blue uniforms, topped with white helmets with 'Police' written on them, and armed with WWII .303 rifles. Dad had a large radio slung under the dashboard of the Isuzu bakkie and, as we went around the farm, he would listen intently to the early morning sitreps (situation reports) being broadcast from Sinoia Police Station. These sitreps were directed to the Section Leaders of the Police Reserve sticks in the area. He also had to report back to the Police Station if he had any information.

High School:

The holiday break had gone by too quickly and we were soon back at school. It was 1968. We were boarders at Sinoia High School, as the farm was too far away from our school for it to be practical for our parents to pick us up every day, or every weekend. The High School was set on the outskirts of the little town of Sinoia and was populated mostly by farming kids from around the area, including Banket, Lion's Den, Karoi, Mangula and Alaska Mine. The school was modern, by most Rhodesian standards. It housed four large hostels located on expansive grounds, all spread out some distance from each other. As children we knew no other life. We had been boarders since we were five, having started our early schooling at the local Primary School. Regulation, bland food, hard beds, uniforms, cold water and no-nonsense matrons had been our founding and our experience of life outside of the farm.

At the end of every year, the senior boys would traditionally hold 'initiation' for the junior classes. This was a testing-time for the juniors. Kangaroo courts would be staged by the seniors, and sentences liberally administered for trumped-up defaults; and it was impossible to exculpate yourself. Punishments varied, but most entailed some level of brutality - to put it euphemistically! Gauntlet was an enduring favourite. In this instance, the junior would be stationed at the doorway to the dormitory - facing inward - whilst the seniors positioned themselves on either side of the central corridor, brandishing weapons. These consisted of an assortment of cricket bats, long socks containing shoes, weighted kit bags, wire coat-hangers, batons and virtually anything that could inflict injury. The customary signal for an errant junior to start the gauntlet run was a swift crack on his butt with a cricket bat. He then had to run up and down the length of the dormitory until it was deemed that he had paid his dues. This could be as many as eight times. If, during the assault, the junior had the severe misfortune to fall, this would prolong the barrage as he would now be forced to crawl the whole way. You did not want to fall down! Bloody noses, cuts, black eyes and bruises were rife. Most youngsters ended up in tears from sheer pain and humiliation.

Another punishment was to be condemned to stand naked alongside the bank of a river that was located near the school. Here, one had to face a hail of compressed mud balls flicked from flexible sticks. Blood spattered onto the ground with direct hits. Only when one of the juniors was nearly blinded did the rules change to permit the target to stand facing away from the 'inflictors.' All told, and what with the innumerable other 'creative' chastisements designed to entertain the higher-ranking, the three weeks of initiation were unmitigated hell. For the juniors, this time could not be over fast enough. I faced initiation seven times. Perhaps my face was too boyish and my legs too thin. Eventually, and blissfully, the impending school holidays brought escape and sweet relief. Of course, as we grew older and became seniors, we were the masters of the initiation events.

There were some interesting characters at school. Frans Nell was one of these characters and what a tough guy he was. I remember we were doing homework late after supper one evening and, as Frans was not too keen on paperwork, he was fooling around with

an old bully-beef tin, trying to rip it in half. With a bit of a heave he managed to tear the tin but, in doing so, it slipped from his hand and the sharp and jagged edge of the tin cut a 5 inch x 1 inch trench through his leg. Now we were never allowed to talk or make a sound during homework time, so Frans casually tore off a few pages from his homework book and shoved them over the wound. He stopped the bleeding. Every boy within sight was glued to his actions. He never made a sound. One day, he came down with appendicitis and was rushed off to hospital to have his appendix taken out. Now, we had no idea what went on behind the curtains, but Frans said he was terrified of the nurse. We asked for further details and he said that she had pulled down his pants and proceeded to shave him, ready for the operation.

'Things happened,' said the embarrassed Frans. 'Things down there!'

'So, what then?' we barked at him for further information.

'She wacked me with a spoon!' he wailed.

We were in stitches. If we ever saw a nurse walking around with a spoon, we knew what it was for and would shudder at the thought of poor Frans and his eye-watering experience.

Frans later joined the highly-trained and professional Rhodesian S.A.S., but was killed whilst on a terrorist-camp raid in Mozambique. So young and such a waste - a loss to us all. Frans was my friend.

Kariba Dam:

The six-week long Christmas holidays began in fine form. Acres of mealie fields were planted and this allowed for a short break on my father's farming calendar. Plans had been made for a trip up to Kariba. Kariba! This was the best news. Fishing, fishing and more fishing. Kariba is a huge man-made hydroelectric dam, built in the 1950s and opened by Queen Elizabeth II of England in the early 1960s. It is located on the Zambezi River to the far north of Zimbabwe, forming a natural border with Zambia. In those days, Kariba's vast waters were not as commercial as these days and offered a glorious natural haven. It was a place you could never forget, with its magnificent panorama and spectacular, effulgent sunsets.

In preparation for our trip, Dad had the boat cleaned out and rigged with spare fuel tanks, fishing rods and a keep-net for the 'mammoth fish catch', an axe, tent, folding chairs and tools. He also loaded a monumental array of other things that meant my parents would be able to handle any problems - including vehicle breakdowns and medical emergencies. That was one indisputable trait shared by Rhodesian farmers and their wives – they could turn their hand to virtually anything; nothing was insurmountable.

My task was to fetch the earthworms. These were kept in a large, steel, 44-gallon drum, which had been cut in half lengthways and filled with compost. The worms thrived in this compost, which had been made from leftover veggies from the kitchen. To run out of worms while fishing would be a catastrophe. On our journey from the farm up to Kariba, Dad and I would travel in the bakkie, pulling the boat, whilst Mum and the girls would come in the old Ford Taunus, with all the food, bedding etc.

We set off from the farm in the very early hours of the morning. Parting instructions had been given to the house and garden staff the day before about feeding the dogs and cats, and included optimistic directives about other chores ... such as cleaning behind this and that, as well as keeping the garden spruced. Off we went in convoy, bouncing along the single, dusty, farm-strip road that would lead us to the main road linking Salisbury to Kariba. Kephas, the mechanic, accompanied us and rode in the back of the bakkie. It was dark and the headlights bounced along the rutted road. Just as Dad turned right onto the main tar road leading to Kariba, he felt something tighten around his ankles. Peering down he found, to his unexpected surprise, that a large snake had wrapped itself around his feet. Unruffled, and with true farmer tenacity, he used gentle movement to encourage it to disentangle itself so that he could reach the brake. Unfortunately, before he could open the car door, the snake disappeared up into the dashboard area. Bugger! (Which was a mild euphemism for other words that may have come to mind!)

'Not to worry - just keep an eye open for it,' instructed Dad coolly, and continued to drive as if only some trivial minor mishap had just occurred. My feet shrank immediately under my bum as I dematerialised into the back of the car seat. From then on, my awareness magnified into super-human aptitude, as I kept a sharp look-out for any protruding reptilian head. After travelling for some interminably long hours (for a child), our little convoy trundled into the sleepy little town of Karoi. Karoi was a small farming town with a couple of food stores, a Police Station, a few clothing shops and the mandatory petrol stations. This was a place to refuel and stretch one's legs. For a brief moment, all was forgotten about the reptilian intruder. Sandwiches were passed around by Mum.

The sun was just peeking its head over the hills. A lethargic petrol attendant ambled across to the petrol pumps. He nodded his head in bored acknowledgement of our request to replenish the fuel tanks and to check oil and water levels. He casually proceeded to the front of the car to open the bonnet. After a brief struggle with the latch, he bent down to locate the oil dip-stick, an action that he had repeated many hundreds of times before. At that moment, all hell broke loose. A murderous, scalded scream ruptured the quiet, like an explosion. The attendant shot back up, as if electrocuted, and the dip-stick went flying. 'Amaaiwe!' he shrieked, while simultaneously transforming himself into an aviator. To his stratospheric amazement, he had encountered our non-paying passenger. After being rendered mute from shock, the best he could muster was a rapid stabbing of his finger to point out the scandalous offender, which he had discovered all curled up next to the battery. It took a good ten minutes for Dad to remove the obstinate snake, watched bemusedly (from a safe 10-metre distance) by a clan of intrigued petrol attendants, all chattering in an excited but nervous trill. There was a collective sigh of relief as, eventually, the snake huffily left its warm spot and slithered off into some nearby bushes.

The rest of the journey was uneventful, save for an encounter with a herd of about fifteen elephants lumbering across the road. It was fortunate that the elephants were some way off when Dad first saw them, as it gave him enough time to slow down. By this stage, we had reached the windy downhill section of road that headed towards Kariba. One indisputable fact is that it would have been practically impossible to reverse the laden bakkie, with an ungainly boat hitched on the back, at sufficient speed to avoid a charging elephant. The elephants, however, were obviously intent on getting to water and didn't care to chase us this time. With that reprieve, we proceeded up the hills, closer and closer to the beautiful waters of Kariba.

We arrived at Lomagundi Lakeside, hot and tired. I just wanted to get into the fishing, but first we had to unpack, set up the 'tent' and build our camp. Lomagundi Lakeside was a rough-hewn campsite, right next to the lapping waters of the lake's edge. It was set amongst sturdy Mopane trees. There was no lawn, garden, electricity, running water or ablutions. There was also no fence to keep out wild animals – in essence, this was a wild, untamed area that required you to keep your wits about you. Everybody was assigned various jobs. Dad and I had to wrap the Hessian sacking - a loose, woven, brown cloth made from sisal - around four trees to act as a wind-break, and rig the canvas roof where the kitchen stuff was to be stored. That effectively was our camp, which was very basic. Cooking would be done over an open fire and we would sleep on stretchers under the stars. Once the campsite was set up, the next undertaking was to launch the boat into the lake. The bakkie was carefully backed down into the shallow waters and the boat eased off the trailer. Once the boat had been launched, it was moored to a rickety, wooden deck that floated on empty, 44-gallon drums. If it rained, everybody got wet - but somehow it never seemed to matter. The natural beauty of the terrain was a balm to every heart. That was camping at Lomagundi Lakeside in the late 1960's.

Len Harrison-Durl ran the campsite. To us kids, he seemed to be at least 150 years old. His worn-out clothes and droopy pipe, which dangled permanently from his sunburnt, wrinkled face,

added unflatteringly to his age. He chain-smoked and was forever bashing the old, burnt tobacco out of his pipe on the heel of
his boot. Len had a recurring problem with the local elephants,
which conducted regular night raids into his small but cherished
vegetable garden. He spent untold times chasing them off. One
night, Len was rudely awoken by great trumpeting and noises.
He rushed outside, with his torch clutched in one hand and his
trusty thunder-flashes in the other, fully intent on making himself more imposing than the raiding elephant. There, he found
a little shed, that he used for storing tools, being systematically
annihilated by four rampant young bulls. He tried to hurl his
thunder-flashes to chase them off, but it was too late. By then,
the shed had been totally flattened on one side, effectively cav-
ing in the corrugated iron roof. Len was flaming mad! His precious vegetable patch was one thing, but this unsolicited attack
on his shed was too much to accept. Nothing explains why the
elephants decided to try and destroy the shed – we thought he
had oranges stored in there - but, from then on, Len harboured
zero tolerance for elephants.

It was also important to watch out for hippo and other wild
creatures, like lion, leopard and hyena. We never had any major
problems with the animals, though, as they tended to steer away
from camping sites. The exception was 'Len's elephants', but
they preferred harassing him, rather than us. Hyena did come
out now and then, to lope droopy-mouthed through the camp
searching for leftovers. They were true opportunists, so we always had to store away all our edibles. We were mostly safe within the confines of the hessian 'walls', but sometimes we would
hear various nocturnal noises coming from visitors investigating
the dustbins and immediate surrounds. Kephas had once told us
three kids that when a bad lady dies, she is reincarnated as a hyena and that they cannot be trusted. He explained that the cack-
ling noise or laughter that a hyena makes was, in fact, the mad
women obsessed with the task of capturing new human form.
This mesmerising tale provided our susceptible young minds

with some uneasy reverie. The African cultures are steeped in a tradition of the unknown and they have many suspicions and stories wrapped around the animal kingdom.

On occasion, we would hear the distant grunting of a male leopard as he patrolled his territory, or the boisterous rumble of a pod of hippo. Their deep, distinctive huh-huh-huh would travel long distances and echo up the little river-bed that ran a little way down from the camp. Lying on my back under the black canopy of the night skies, was a time when I could truly breathe with Africa and attune to the rhythmic cadence of the stars and planets, as they followed their appointed journeys through the Milky Way. The soft radiance of the moon would bathe the lake in silver light, and the gentle lap of the waters made for a perfect portal into Dreamland.

In the morning, it was always a great adventure to check out the tracks to see what creature had visited the camp during the night. I guess the only things we really had to watch out for in our immediate camp were snakes - and some of the insects and spiders. Snakes, such as Black Mambas, were potentially lethal. A single bite from one of these deadly fellows was a highly unrecommended experience. Death could take place (especially for a child) within about 1 to 10 hours, depending upon how much venom was injected into the body and where the bite was located. We had a deep respect for the Black Mamba, whose speed and infamous temper warranted such respect.

Puff adders posed a different problem, for they tended to lie motionless on the ground. If you were not vigilant, you could easily stand on one by mistake. A strike from this fat snake was also lightning-fast – too fast to move out of the way.

Its inch-long fangs easily penetrated shoes. My father described a puff-adder bite as equivalent to holding your foot in boiling oil! The porky python, on the other hand, was a less hazardous cousin, despite the fact that they grew quite large - up to fourteen feet in length was common. They are not poisonous, but their bite leaves terrible scars. A python's teeth, all 148 of them, curve backwards. On inflicting a bite, they are unable to extricate themselves. You literally have to pull their head apart to separate them from the bite area.

Spiders were constant companions. They seemed to get into everything, and baboon spiders were the most predictable menace. They were large and hairy - with a formidable bite. To us, as children, their six-inch leg-span seemed to be tantamount to Hollywood sci-fi proportions - *humongous*, as we would say. They weren't lethal but, if bitten, a child would be very likely to talk about it for many years to come.

Scorpions and centipedes were even less appealing. The scorpions could sting like bloody hell, especially the thick-tailed ones with the small pincers. The oppressive heat of the Kariba Valley made it the perfect home for a large variety of these arachnids.

Then there was the merry band of insects. Mosquitoes made an irritating nuisance of themselves and, as carriers of malaria, were to be avoided. The smoke from the camp fire helped to keep them at bay at night, but the only real defence we had against their whining insistence were mosquito nets. The sophisticated array of creams and sprays available these days were unheard of back then. Kephas helpfully contributed with the suggestion that we could effectively keep mosquitoes away by smearing fresh elephant dung over ourselves. Whilst this may or may not have held any merit, it was never put to the test. Neither did we ever notice Kephas daubed in the stuff.

Blister beetles were a particularly interesting addition to the resident insect population. The commonly occurring ones were easily recognisable by their yellow and black colours - Nature's notorious colours of warning. If perhaps you managed to annoy a blister beetle, it 'pee'd' on you in punitive revenge! One thing you quickly learnt was not to scratch or rub the 'pee'd-on' spot - no matter how maddeningly itchy it might become. Scratching would only result in spreading the poison even further, thus making things infinitely worse. Angry blisters would flare up and quickly progress into a red sea of raw and tortured skin. Not an attractive look for the bodily-conscious.

Ground beetles had a seriously bad habit. If they were trapped or threatened, their weapon of choice was a potent discharge of poisonous formic acid from the rear. If  this spray happened to get into your eyes, you could set aside any reading material for quite a while, in order to contend, instead, with a temporary bout of tear-flowing blindness, laced with a seriously large-sized serving of pain.

All in all, the many intriguing species that inhabited this part of the world never truly invaded our space. By mutual respect, they sought to avoid us as much we avoided them. It was only in moments of inadvertent encounter that a true problem could occur. Besides, we were well-versed in the ways of the bush and knew what to watch out for. Checking clothes and shoes before putting them on, was the norm. From a very young age, we knew never to just lift up a rock or stick, without first cautiously checking to see what may have been lurking underneath it. Treading with awareness and care in Mother Nature's domain was a natural state of being.

Learning the ways of the bush:

Sabow, the pig shooter, taught me many things, as he had grown up deep in the bush, where his father had a kraal. His father had fought against the colonial invasion of Rhodesia in the 1890's. Sabow's knowledge of everything related to survival, was immeasurable. In truth, he was an early-life teacher for me - he taught me to 'read' the bush. With his quiet and wise ways, he imparted a world that was invisible to the uninitiated. His understanding of tracks was extraordinary – he could accurately identify all species, including birds and insects. He helped me understand his language and always spoke to me in Shona. Once he showed me a set of tracks by one of the water holes we had encountered, I clearly recall how we crouched next to the water and, with a small stick, he pointed out the first set of tracks and asked me what I thought had happened. I ventured that a dove had come down to drink water.

'That's right – then what happened?' he asked, pointing further along the edge of the water line. That was more difficult. A single feather lay next to marks of a scuffle.

'I'm not sure,' I said, as I looked up at him for answers.

'Look,' he encouraged, 'look carefully at that feather. See the tiny bit of skin on it – that tells you it was pulled out and did not fall out!' he continued to look intently at the tracks.

'See the depth of the dove's footprint in the water on the right,' he encouraged. 'This dove was hit by a hawk from the back left, forcing it to dip heavily onto its right leg. You can see that the two birds ended up where the mud has been churned up. The feather here was pulled out by the claws of the hawk.'

We made our way up the bank, looking for clues as we went. At the top, next to a fallen tree, was a small termite mound. There were feathers everywhere.

'This is where the hawk brought the dove and ripped off those feathers! It then ate some and likely took the rest of the carcass away, probably to its nest, with one chick inside.' And so it was! Many days and hours under the tutelage of the ever-patient and sage-old Sabow, gave me the gift and ultimately the skill of tracking in the bush.

'Look here .... A jackal has come to see if there were any pieces left; then he went off towards the hills.'

Sabow was also a master herbalist and skilled in using plants for medicine. He taught me all sorts of things to do with their use. He had solutions for a sore stomach or throat, stings, bites, cuts and all sort of other ailments. He also knew how to use plants to catch food. I remember a time that he picked a long, thick stem of thatching grass and stuck it into the mud, next to the little dam, so that it leaned over at an angle of about forty-five degrees. He then proceeded to cut a large, fleshy branch of the Euphorbia tree and allowed the white poisonous sap to drip onto the blade of his big knife. After half an hour in the sun, the sap started to dry. Sabow then rubbed the sap onto the entire stem of the grass that he had placed by the water's edge. He took a small handful of crushed maize from his pocket and scattered it around the bare ground, next to the grass stem.

'Okay, let's go back into those bushes and wait to see what happens.'

Intrigued, I waited with him, knowing to sit in silence. In a short time, the first flock of birds landed in the trees on the bank of the river. They wasted no time in assessing what was edible below and flew down to land on the grass stem. When there were five birds on the stem, Sabow suddenly stood up and the birds flew, or tried to, fly away ... but they had been firmly glued down by the sticky sap.

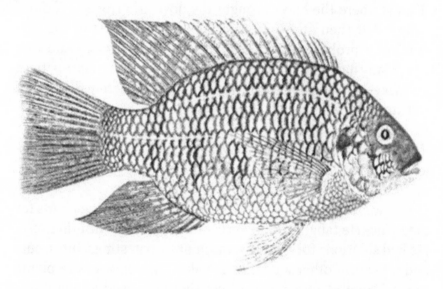

'You see what happened there?' he patiently explained. 'The birds don't want to fly straight from the tree to the food and water. They want to land on the grass first, where they feel safer.'

Sabow would cook the birds over an open fire, later. Whilst this type of thing may sound dismaying to one who is used to buying food at leisure, from fully-stocked, air-conditioned shops, it must be understood that this was how life was in a place where there were no nearby shops. Food came from the land. Life gave life. This was the age-old balance of things and the way of the ancestors.

Sabow had a trick to nail the baboons that raided the maize fields. Now, baboons were very wary and always had one or two

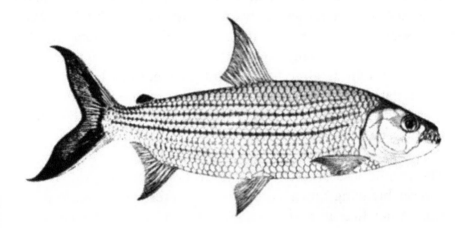

sentries looking out from the top of trees, for potential threats. Sabow had a theory that baboons could only count to three. After chasing the baboons around without success, as they always saw him long before he was able to close in on them, he came up with a plan. He seconded the help of three other friends one Saturday, and the four of them went up into the lands to look for the baboons. As soon as the troop saw the four men, they took off for the hills. Sabow and his three mates walked in full view into the maize field. After a few minutes, he sent his three mates out and instructed them to walk back to the compound, in full view of the baboons. Sabow was well-concealed. Shortly, the baboons wandered down, back into the maize, without a care in the world, and Sabow got his revenge. The system worked every time. Sabow told Dad that the baboons counted three when the four men went into the maize field and counted three when the three men left. Simple as that!

Kariba and fishing:

Fishing was great. We would catch bream, Chesa, Barbel and Tiger fish. Our boat was totally unique, unlike anything you have ever seen, or are ever likely to see. Difficult for someone to picture who never actually saw it. The boat was built up from two large, aluminium, aircraft drop-tanks, i.e. old fuel tanks. There was a flat, wooden deck, welded between the tanks, with short metal sides and a canvas sheet (in fact an old tent) rigged on top of poles, to act as a sun cover.

The engine was an old Johnson, 50-horse power, which was forever breaking down, so oars were a prerequisite backup. It was rather like an early, 'unique' version of the later popular house-boats. The boat, which Dad had made in his spare time, was appropriately and affectionately named 'Hells Bells.' There was no construction manual – only my father's imagination and the availability of scrap metal and wood found on the farm. When people came to visit, they would cry in genuine amazement, 'Hell's Bells, how the hell will that thing float?' However, we loved it. There was so much space on the boat that the whole family could walk about freely, without getting in each other's way. The engine propelled the boat forward at a sedate speed of 4 knots, not to be confused, in any way, to the saying: 'at a rate of knots.' Money did not abound, but innovation certainly did.

Dad taught me so much about fishing, and we had our favourite places where we would find the 'giant fish.' Often it was in a bay, where the thick oxygen weed gave shelter to the bream. Tiger fish would patrol up and down the open paths that hippo had forged between the underwater foliage. Another plant was Kariba weed, and was a scourge to much of the lake. It had been brought to Kariba by a Catholic Priest from Brazil and it grew in the pond by his house. When he cleaned out the pond, some of the seeds made their way into the river system that fed the lake, and that was the beginning of this plague. The weed lay like a thick, heaving, green carpet in many of the quieter waters. Catching tiger fish in the weeds was damn difficult – the wily speedsters would take off at a high rate and inevitably the fishing-line would get snagged on the trailing roots of the weeds. Worse was when the fighting fish disappeared under the boat at such velocity that it could launch an unsuspecting first-time fisherman into the water. We lost untold numbers of fish and tackle while trying to tug in the fish. Their seriously sharp rows of gumless teeth would cut through any normal fishing-line, so we had to use strong metal trace near the bait to try and stop them from breaking free. We also used spinners to trawl behind the boat in more open waters. One of the characteristics of the Tiger fish was its 'fight.' If I managed to hook one, bloody hell, it always felt like it was ten times larger than its actual weight. They would wrestle and tussle fiercely! The smaller tiger would even jump clean out of the water, like a marlin trying to get rid of the hook. If the Tiger did not jump, then I had some reasonable certainty that it was a larger one of more than five pounds. I needed a steady focus to land this predator. Once it was hauled onto the boat, I always stuck my fingers through the gills to hold it down, but nowhere near the teeth. Fingers made a poor choice of tool for removing the hook. I valued these useful digits, so common sense would guide me to use pliers for that particular job.

One of the enduring reminiscences amongst all people who know Kariba is of its magnificent scenery. In any one day, I could sit on the deck of the boat and watch hippo in the water, crocodiles sunning themselves on the banks, elephants coming  down to drink, baboons playing in the long grass, antelope, zebra and a host of bird life moving along the lake shore which included the famous Fish Eagle, whose long, haunting call became synonymous with the lake itself. Often I would see these beautiful eagles sitting aloft the dry-tree skeletons that adorn the edge of much of the lake. The trees were remnants from a time before the lake was filled and they had petrified into stark but unique formations. To grow up as a young boy in this natural environment was quite simply ... Paradise.

The bream we caught were cooked over an open fire. After the initial gutting and cleaning, my mother's technique was to wrap each fish individually in tin foil with butter, a touch of salt and a few slices of lemon. The foil parcels snuggly wrapped the fish and they then cooked in their own juices. The fresh air, sunshine and natural setting added grandly to make this eating ritual something really special.

In this rustic environment, we spent two happy weeks, fishing and boating. I often went scuba-diving, armed with a seriously strong spear gun. Whilst everybody was relaxing and having lunch on the boat, I would be diving in the waters to test my prowess. One day, Dad decided that he also wanted to try this spear-fishing lark. He climbed down off the back of the boat, bedecked in my too-small-for-him goggles. Unfortunately, the water was a bit murky from the recent rains. Once immersed in the water, he had not ventured far when a large clump of gently undulating oxygen weed morphed magically, or so he thought, into a hippo. He shot out of the water impressively, like the lift-off of a space rocket, and landed back on to the boat in virtually one superman-like leap. Breathlessly, he declared his great fortune at escaping certain death from a huge, two-ton beast. In sympathy, we all proceeded to peer over the side of the boat in search of the terrifying 'beast'. However, despite our best efforts to find it, it became increasingly clear that no two-ton monster was in the vicinity and, after this revelation, he good-naturedly endured our endless laughter and jibes ... and did not take up spear fishing ever again!

In truth, though, hippo are particularly dangerous animals. If, by chance, you did come upon one, you could be in serious trouble. A friend of mine once came up for fresh air, whilst scuba-diving, at the same time that a hippo surfaced a few feet away. Terror-stricken, he fired his spear at the beast but the metal shaft just bounced clean off the hippo's forehead. Luckily for him the hippo got just as much of a fright and took off in the opposite direction. Had it not done so, the outcome could have been fatally different. I often saw crocs in the water, green and glowing from the algae growing on them. They were commonly referred to in Rhodesia as 'flat dogs', which was something of a misnomer. They weren't a supreme problem, provided you kept a watchful eye on them and respected their space. Some of my other friends tried lying in wait under the beds of floating Kariba weed. They claimed that, in so doing, they were hidden  in total darkness and that the fish would never see them as they swam past. I tried it once ... it was an eerie experience and I had a strange feeling of being watched. I looked back into the dark depths behind me and had this vision of three crocodiles lying in the dark yonder, smiling as they summed me up for their next meal. The snap, turn and twist of a potential crocodile attack made inroads into my mind and I never repeated the 'oxygen-weed-disguise' method again.

Another chap we knew had a very lucky escape from a crocodile attack. He had been swimming around, engrossed in finding fish on which to inflict his spear-fishing ability, when one of the resident crocs, voting him as a worthy meal, grabbed one of his fins and pulled – hard! Luck, however, caused the bitten section of the fin to detach itself from the swimmer's portion and the 'swimmer' proceeded to beat a desperate escape with arms rotating faster than rotor-wing blades. He just made it to a partially-submerged Mopane tree, which he scaled in haste, complete with fins, just high enough to be out of his attacker's reach. He was then forced to wait in the searing sun, stuck awkwardly up the thin-branched tree, above a circling expectant croc, until his mates came to rescue him in their boat.

Soon it was time to go home. Between Karoi and Chirundu came the obligatory stop at the Makuti tsetse-fly hangar. This large, metal construction was specially built to accommodate cars and their trailers (or anything similar) in an enclosed environment. Once the big doors clanged shut it, was pitch dark inside and only a small amount of light emanated from a tiny window, midway down the one wall. The idea was to attract any flies to the light of the window, whereby they would meet their fate with poisons. A pungent insecticide was sprayed onto all tyres and included a squirt inside the vehicle as well. This can only be described as a breath-taking experience ... of the most unpleasant kind! The aim was an effort by Tsetse Control Operations to rid the Zambezi Valley of the rampant tsetse (pronounced tset-tsee) fly. The hot, needle-like bite of the African Glossina Morsitaris is responsible for the dreaded human Sleeping Sickness and animal Trypanisomiasis. Sleeping Sickness is a slow, wasting disease, characterised by fever and inflammation of the lymph nodes, which leads to profound lethargy and eventually to death. Tsetse flies are immediately recognisable by their large, long proboscis (designed to penetrate the toughest hide) and tendency to fold their wings completely when resting. After a friendly wave, the big doors at the other end of the fly chamber would be opened by the official and we would be free to continue out of Zambezi Valley.

The farm lay in an area of Rhodesia, which was prime maize-growing country. It was fifteen kilometres from the nearest town called Sinoia, and about 120 kilometres north of the capital city, Salisbury. The farm was called 'Hillrise' and, besides the Chisnall family itself, about 35 farm workers lived and worked on it with their families. The Hougaard, MacDonald and Flanagan families neighboured the farm. Owen Flanagan, from Njiri Farm, was also the well-known local vet - a quietly-spoken man, who was able to administer anything to virtually any type of sick animal, or handle any kind of veterinary situation. Maize, cattle, winter wheat, groundnuts, tobacco and soya beans were produced in the area. We even tried cotton one year, but it was tough farming with no irrigation. We had to trust in Nature's free gift of rain to get things right. Lew Ankers, a farmer further up the road, once fired a rain-rocket up into the air, in an effort to get water onto his crops. It must have cost a pretty penny to seed that cumuli nimbus cloud. Unfortunately for Lew, the uncooperative wind repositioned the swollen cloud above Hillrise, where it proceeded to disgorge its precious cargo and drenched our farm, instead.

The loss of the farm:

The Mashonaland region was internationally renowned for its quality tobacco. Acres of lush green leaves adorned fields over many kilometres. Picturesque scenes could be seen in the picking season, when the field workers walked en masse with long sticks (matepis) across their backs, expertly selecting leaves and then twirling them through string, onto hanging bunches on their sticks. There was a year, though, when things did not go so well for us. The tobacco barns had been filled to capacity with the laden sticks. Row upon row hung aloft, allowing the tobacco to dehydrate in the hot barns before being processed for sale. Just outside each barn was a wood-burning fire. The heat from these fires would pass into the barn via thin metal ducting and eventually would vent from chimneys. One night, disaster struck when our own barns on the farm were demolished by fire. The tinder-dry Virginia tobacco, hanging in racks on their Matepi sticks, went up in smoke when one of the sticks broke, sending the dried leaves down onto the hot flues. This was a massive loss and, once again, required a loan from the land bank to sustain our existence, until the next season would bring relief. However, it was relentless drought that was to deal the final blow of farming for us. Four consecutive years without rain took its grim toll. During that time, my father suffered from a massive ulcer from worry and was forced to undergo an operation. My sister, Trish, gravely recalls her shock at his appearance when he came to fetch us from school a few weeks later. He had shed considerable weight and his face was grey and gaunt. The lines of strain told a story. The inevitable was to take its course and, with a heavy heart, Dad sold the farm in 1969 and we had to move. Times changed for us.

We moved to Kariba. Dad started working in the tourist trade and Mum helped him out. Our small house and tiny garden, in the middle of Kariba Township, was a far cry from the large sprawl we'd had on the farm, and Mum hated it. She had left behind a beautiful, large garden, an orchard and vegetable garden, which had been tenderly created with slips and plants from many other gardens. Years of nurturing and love were lost. Whilst a precious few of the plants still found their way into the new handkerchief patch, there was no room for them all. Over the years our dogs - Rastus, Jason, Jinny, Kim - and many of our other animals, had gone home to the "happy hunting grounds" and only sweet-natured Sherry remained. But we, as kids, were growing older and were happy to enjoy the holiday atmosphere of Kariba, with its hotels, fishing, etc. I spent my holiday time tracking through the bush around Kariba. This wild area was ideal for me and was a step up as far as dangers and creatures of interest were concerned. There was a resident leopard that killed 26 dogs and 10 cats. He was so brazen that he snatched the postman's dog right off its leash, as the postman was taking his poodle for a walk. The poor dog had no chance, as the leopard had been on the postman's roof and just had to drop down past him to grab his lunch. I often saw the tracks of this leopard, deep in the riverbed below our house on the hill, but fortunately never came across it on foot. I carried a pump-action .22 rifle around with me, Dad having upgraded my weapon from air gun to gun powder. Like the old story goes, 'bringing a flick-knife to a gun fight' – my old air-driven weapon was never going to protect me. Come to think of it, the .22 would hardly have been powerful enough against a leopard anyway – but it made me braver.

Kariba was dotted with hotels and everyone in Rhodesia used to go up there to fish and have a swell time. Many folks had boats on the lake and, as we were by then heading into our teen years, good times and parties were plentiful. We had not previously had a social life of any kind on the farm, and this was all new to us. But we were in for changes.

War was imminent.

2

The Coming War

R hodesia was a young country, made up of a cross-section of different people. Immigrants from countries such as England, Portugal, Greece and South Africa had merged, to live alongside the local black people, to make a country that was known as the 'bread basket' of Southern Africa. Aside from its natural beauty, Rhodesia was very rich in minerals such as chrome, coal and gold. The agricultural sector was very productive and actively exported goods to Europe, the Americas and the Far East. Tobacco and maize were huge industries, thanks to the skill of the farming community. There were two main tribes of local people, namely the Shona and the Matabele. There were other tribes dotted here and there as well, the main difference being the languages spoken by each.

In 1965, Rhodesia ended up in civil strife, which culminated in a terrible Civil War. Most of the problems related to hunger for land, or came about as a result of power-hungry politicians. White settlers, mostly of British origin, had entered Rhodesia during the eighteenth century for hunting and prospecting purposes. Gold was a big draw card and many prospectors had wandered through the wild countryside, panning here and there. It was in the early 1890s that Cecil John Rhodes established the British South Africa Company and sent an armed force, from

South Africa, into Rhodesia, with the intent of grabbing Rhodesia for England. The Union Jack flag was raised in Salisbury - now Harare - in September 1890. From his newfound base, Rhodes (although he was the Governor of the Cape) sent a party of armed men from Rhodesia to South Africa, in an ill-fated venture known as the Jameson Raid. This all took place just prior to the Anglo Boer war of 1898-1900. His intention was to take control of the rich diamond and gold deposits lying in wait in the Johannesburg region. The region he was after was controlled, at that time, by the Boers or Afrikaners. The area was rich in gold and diamonds and Rhodes wanted it. He had already been deeply involved in the diamond mines around Kimberley, where he had made his fortune. With the new invention of the Cyanide process to extract gold, the fortunes to be made were vast.

Matabele warrior

With many of the young men out of the country on the Jameson Raid, the handful of people still left in Rhodesia were barely able to defend themselves against any attack. In fact, there were exactly 100 enlisted men of the British South Africa Company left in the country to protect Rhodes' investments. Rhodes believed that the Mashona and Matabele tribes were not up to a fight. The newly-created territory was incredibly vulnerable to attack from all its neighbours. These attacks, and the mad rush for the colonisation of Africa, could have come from the East by the Portuguese-held Mozambique or, for that matter, from the Boer-held Northern sections of South Africa. The attacks, however, came from within and the local black people of Rhodesia seized their chance to mount an uprising against the poorly-defended, remaining white settlers, in 1896. Firstly, the troubles started with the Matabele tribe to the South and West of the country and secondly with the Shona tribe to the North and East. The skirmishes that took place involved all of the immigrant white settlers, in defence. These pioneers had to pool all reserves and fight their way through this. There weren't enough rifles to go round and the speed with which the uprising happened, took everyone by surprise. Many lost their lives in this effort. My paternal grandmother's father was Captain John F. Taylor, leader of the Natal Troup, and he was heavily involved in those troubled times. He was wounded twice during the rebellion. The rebellions were eventually quelled and the country remained in relative calm thereafter. Taylor was made Commander of the Salisbury Laager during the troubles. ("Laager" was a Boer word that basically meant 'a quickly-made fort' using wagons, maize bags and anything one could use to create a protective wall around the inhabitants.) The uprising nearly wiped out all the settlers in the country, but they managed to pull through, through sheer guts

Captain J.F. Taylor with the Natal Troop Salisbury Laager

and clever tactics. A huge number of people - 10% of the local white population - were murdered during this Civil War.

After the uprising had been quelled, life got back to normal and the country started to grow at an incredible rate. Then followed the First and Second World Wars, with many of the local men volunteering for military service. My paternal grandfather, Cecil Chisnall, and his brother were soldiers in the First World War.

They ended up in the battle of the Somme in Delville Wood, where virtually their entire division was wiped out. Granddad was wounded three times. His battle scars remained as a lasting reminder of those war years. Shot through the eye, shoulder and leg, my Granddad mesmerised me with stories of battles. As a young boy growing up, I was endlessly fascinated by the family history which recorded how, at great risk, he physically carried his wounded brother out of the battle in July 1916, only to return to continue fighting and, once again, being injured. Both were machine-gun operators. They were among the few survivors of that bloody and merciless battle. I still have, in my possession, a long letter that he wrote from his hospital bed to his family which speaks of this time - his neat handwriting somehow in such marked contrast to the death-defying experiences he had. As a young boy, I was drawn to these stories and longed to test my shooting abilities ... little did I know what was to come.

In the Second World War, my father was one of the many Rhodesian volunteers. He completed his training to become a Spitfire pilot in North Africa. He wasn't proud of the fact that he had eight crashes. On one occasion, he endured an ear-shattering tirade from a spitting-mad instructor after he had managed to fly them into a deep valley and only just managed to pull up from the rocks in the valley before impacting the mountain.

Rhodesia experienced an economic depression after the Second World War but, with intrepid vigour, it soon bounced back and was flourishing, with mining and agriculture as the backbone of the economy. Politics and hunger for power at any cost, were to change all of that and, in 1965, when a number of high-spirited black people, with high political ambitions, started to vigorously embark on a campaign of insurrection against the Government, the second revolution began. There had always been political opposition to the white- controlled Government, with various smaller parties fighting for their rights. In the early 1960's, volunteers and press-ganged black people ('The Struggle for Zimbabwe'

- David Martin and Phyllis Johnson) started rounding up local people to join the struggle for liberation and skipped them across the borders to a variety of countries, including Tanzania, Zambia, Mozambique, Cuba, Libya, Russia and China, to name a few. The new recruits were trained in the use of firearms and were also subjected to political indoctrination. The trickle of people leaving for this endeavour was small, at first, but their numbers grew as the returning recruits started to indoctrinate the locals in a variety of liberation ways. These recruits were also armed to the teeth and supported financially through a huge variety of sources, including the Communist Governments, charities and local churches. Scandinavian countries poured money into their coffers. Chinese and Russian techniques of liberation were taught to the trainees and, together with fear of death in some instances, recruits started their new career as armed soldiers of the new liberation movements.

The Terrorist Groups:

African politics is always very complicated and there was much in-house fighting over the next few years between many of the up and coming freedom fighters, as they liked to be called. Two main liberation movements emerged at the end of the war that were in conflict with the white-controlled Government. Firstly, there was the Zimbabwe African National Liberation Army (ZANLA) - the military wing, and its political arm - Zimbabwe African National Union (ZANU) - made up of predominantly Shona-speaking people and headed by Robert Mugabe. Secondly, there was the Zimbabwe People's Revolutionary Army (ZIPRA), with Zimbabwe African Peoples Union (ZAPU) its political arm, made up from mainly Matabele-speaking people and headed by Joshua Nkomo. The two different factions (ZANLA and ZIPRA) came from two different tribes and, as such, their people had very different cultures and spoke different languages. There was never any love between these two groups. ZANLA was effectively sponsored by the Chinese and ZIPRA by the Russians. There were other anti-government forces, including Bishop Abel Muzarewa's small and relatively uninfluential band. Near the end of the war, Muzarewa and his small band of followers joined forces with the right-wing Smith government. Muzarewa became Prime Minister; however, the effort to convince the international countries bent on changing the political landscape of Rhodesia were not impressed by this token inclusion of black voters. It was deemed to fall very short of the 'One man one vote' option that was being generally accepted as the answer to the regions problems by the international community Ian Smith once said that Africa was full of dictators and if there was a change in government to what the international countries wanted, Rhodesia would have 'One man one vote ... *once.*'

The Pyjama Parade:

I was introduced to the conflict in the country as a young boy in a number of ways.

The independence of the Belgium Congo in 1960 caused a horde of whites to leave that country with nothing but the clothes on their backs. My father referred to them as the 'pyjama parade', as many of these refugees had hastily jumped into their cars in the middle of the night, dressed only in their nightgowns, and hot-footed it across the borders. They feared for their very lives in the newly-established, independent country, where rebels and bandits were murdering them at will. The terrifying Panga was a commonly used weapon to hack entire families to pieces. Another blood-curdling device was the sharpened spoke of a bicycle wheel that would be plunged deep through a victim's heart. This device had been used in Kenya during the Uhuru rebellions in that British colony.

Our whole family sat for days on the side of the road by the farm giving these terrified and destitute people food and water. Mum saw some pregnant women and gave them all her maternity clothing from when she had us kids. They had nothing. I don't remember much of that but my Dad, in his frank and grounded manner, brought up the chilling reality during much later conversation that this could happen to us, too. A very disturbing thought for a young mind.

Take it from me; it is inescapably discomforting to know that there are terrorists running around the land, especially given the supremely vulnerable position in which most farmers found themselves. On our farm, as with many others, we had no fence or boundary around the house. There were no burglar-bars on our windows, no security lighting, no locked doors, just an open, Rhodesian farmhouse, typical of so many throughout the country. Our primary alert of impeding danger was our trusted farm dogs. Ever-vigilant and quick to tell us when anyone approached the house, they slept in the old garage outside and had free range of the grounds. Another party in raising the alarm came from a more unusual source. At the bottom of our garden, we had a large pond. This was a favourite haunt for multitudes of romantically-inspired frogs that used it for their ceaseless courting pursuits. In this case, though, it was the sudden lack of their deafening cacophony that would call us to immediate attention. As soon as the frogs shut-up, so would we – to listen or react. And that was what we had. Dogs and frogs! Hardly the most impenetrable system ever devised ... but it sure as hell beat nothing.

Trouble was brewing. My father ran Red Section, one of the local police reserve units. This required him to frequently be absent from the farm doing his duty of chasing terrorists. More and more terror incidents were happening in our area.

Shoot them if I say so:

One night, when Dad was away on Police Reserve duties, there was a knock on the back door of the farmhouse. The dogs were going crazy. Only my Mum, the three of us kids and my Grandmother, Jean, were home. My mother woke me up by pressing the .22 Hornet rifle (the one Dad used to shoot cattle) against my chest, saying softly that it was loaded and urging me to follow her. I must have been ten years old. Her whole manner and body language told me that something was sorely amiss. I followed her down the dark, unlit passageway, struggling to understand what was afoot. Halfway down the passage we encountered Gran, who was walking back to her bedroom from the bathroom on one of her twice-nightly bathroom trips. With quick thinking, Mum hid me and the rifle behind her back in the dark passageway and let Gran continue on her mission, without alerting her to the possibility of terrorist intrusion. With Gran safely back in her room, we rapidly made our way to the kitchen. Here, in the pitch dark, my mother sat me down next to an open window. She whispered out instructions

'If I say shoot ... then shoot at those people out there!' She pointed into the darkness to the rear of the house. The whole house was in darkness to keep us out of silhouette and only a single, external light lit up some of the area near the back kitchen-door. Bravely my mother, slender in build and standing 5' 6', proceeded to open the back door and demanded of the four or five people, who were standing about twenty yards from the house, what they wanted. In the dark, there was no making out who they were. For what seemed an interminable time, I had my eye sighted down the barrel, trying to stay steady while pointing the rifle at one of the men in the group. The darkness made it impossible to keep him in clear sight, or see whether he was armed. The figures were only just visible in the dull half-moonlight, as they were outside the perimeter of the faint back-door light. I never knew if I would have pulled the trigger. I'd probably have missed anyway, as it was so dark and the group was moving all the time. One man stepped forward a few paces and explained in Shona that Kephas, the mechanic, had been seriously burnt in a paraffin-stove explosion and that he needed to get to hospital as soon as possible. Mum scarcely understood a word that he was rapidly delivering, as her command of Shona was limited to the basics of Fanagalo. I translated. The hospital was twenty miles away but, without hesitation, Mum loaded up the group and took off down the road, leaving me in charge of the house. It was all confoundedly confusing for me. As soon as the car lights disappeared around the garden trees, I went off to bed, still clutching the rifle. Poor Kephas. He had suffered extensive burns all down the left side of his body and face and narrowly escaped death. His scars eventually healed up into large keloids, disfiguring him for life.

The rebel forces were known by us as 'terrs' or 'gooks.' In a family discussion on the verandah, Dad had warned us to be ready for anything unusual or suspicious. That was why Mum has first assumed that the group had been terrorists. It was difficult to tell friend from foe in the middle of the night.

The Battle of Sinoia:

One of the first opening battles of the War took place on the 28th April 1966. Earlier, a large number of heavily-armed ZANLA insurgents had crossed the Zambian border and made their way in a south-easterly direction towards Sinoia - our local town. This large group split into two. The smaller group, composed of seven, were aiming to blow up the power lines near town. Their intentions were curtailed by the Rhodesian Armed Forces. This was a mainly Police and Air Force attack and the seven ZANLA insurgents were eventually killed in what became known as The Battle of Sinoia. My sister, Trish, remembers watching in horror as my father, dressed in his police reserve uniform and fully armed, got into the police helicopter. The nearby fusillade of gunfire exchange was loud and heated. She implored him to come back, convinced he would be shot, but through the rotor

wash her young voice was lost and she could only watch help-
lessly as the helicopter lifted and then dipped down toward the
bridge. There, the seven terrorists were pinned down by the helicopters and support groups. Police dogs were also used to flush
them out. One of the dogs died in battle, shot while in pursuit.
This was the first real battle with the insurgents; so many more
were to follow.

In Zimbabwe this first battle is commemorated as Chimurenga
Day, the beginning of the Second Chimurenga War (The First
Chimurenga War was the uprising way back in the 1890s). Three
men helped with the disposal of the bodies: a Police Reservist, a
black Police Sergeant and a white regular Policeman. The seven
were buried in termite mounds, which had been excavated by
antbears. I was told each body got its own hole. The process and
place where the burials took place was kept a secret to stop it becoming a martyrs' shrine. The seven dead terrorists were Simon
Chimbodza, Christopher Chataambudza, Nathan Charumuka,
Godwin Manyerenyere, Peter, Ephraim Shenjere and David
Guzuze.

*'We worked all night to do this secret burial. We first
took the dead terrorists from the Sinoia Police Station
in the back of a covered Land Rover. We drove out to
find a suitable site for the burial. We had to keep everything very top secret. We went back to the Police
Station and took some prisoners back to the site. They
were just ordinary prisoners, who were being held in
the police cells for things like theft, etc. We used the
prisoners to enlarge seven Antbear holes. They had
been transported to the site blindfolded. We drove in
all directions and around in circles so they had no
idea where they were. When the holes had been dug,
we took these prisoners back to the Police Station
and then took out another group and did the same
driving-around story. The blindfolded prisoners*

were then taken from the back of the covered Land Rover and told to put one body in each hole that had been dug. We then covered the bodies up using soil and drove the prisoners back to prison. The prisoners had no idea where they were, or who they had just buried. They didn't even know how many bodies they had buried as each one was done separately.'

As told to the author by one of the people who carried out the burial.

Murder of my friend's parents:

The war affected all of us. At primary school, we had to put up wooden boards against the windows every night, in the hope that this would stop grenades being thrown through them whilst we slept. The prospect of a grenade attack was not a concept that we, as young children, could comprehend. We were, therefore, never really worried and it was more of a chore to us than anything else. Later, the hostels were sandbagged and a six-foot fence was erected as a protective surround. This was also used to make a fortress for the local farmers' wives and small children who joined us in the hostel during trying times, when safety on their remote farms could not be guaranteed.

In May 1966, the shocking news came in that the parents of Nicolette Viljoen had been shot dead on their farm. This hit hard! Nicolette was in my class! We later learnt that her father, Johannes, had answered a knock at the back door of their farmhouse at 1 o'clock in the morning. Without warning, both he and his wife were summarily gunned down at point-blank range. They were dressed in their pyjamas. Nicolette's 3-year old brother, Tommy, and her nine-month old sister, Yolanda, were asleep in their bedrooms during the slaughter; that they didn't get killed was sheer luck. This group of gooks was part of the original heavily-armed ZANLA group that crossed into Rhodesia from Zambia. The first seven of this group had headed to Sinoia to blow up the power lines, where their attempts were foiled and the Battle of Sinoia ensued. This second group, led by Gumbashumba, carried out the attack on Nevada Farm. The Viljoens' brutal murder struck anger into the heart of the farming community. Heart-wrenching photos of bullet holes sprayed just above Yolanda's cot made front page news the next day and delivered a stark message that even the innocent were targets. The Viljoens were the first civilian casualties of the war. Nicolette was pulled out of school and Trish remembers her 61-year old grandmother coming to pick her up in an old truck. She describes a poignant sadness descending upon her as she watched this little girl walk slowly away from the hostel, a small brown cardboard suitcase clutched in her hand, her parents gone. She was nine years old and now an orphan. We never saw her again.

In another incident a young chap from our school, only ten at the time, had shot and killed one of the insurgents from his farm bedroom-window with a shotgun, when the farmhouse was attacked one night. He was a hero to us and he had to keep on telling and retelling us the story – every time the events and danger seemed to increase. But life moved on and, in time, the story waned as we turned our focus again to rugby and cricket.

Then another incident. A young lad had been on his farm motorcycle in the maize fields when he had been shot in his butt. Somehow, he narrowly escaped death from a barrage of AK47 bullets. It was perplexing to us that someone would wish to shoot a child; that seemed another world to us. However no answers satisfied that question and, as young boys, we continued to care more about our sport than the imploding political world around us.

Al Turl was our next-door neighbour in Kariba and one day we received the bad news that he had been killed by a lioness in the

Mvuradona Mountains, on the south bank of Lake Kariba. He had been instructing Special Forces on various art of warfare. He and one of his recruits had been sitting on a log in drenching rain one night, with their poncho raincoats over their heads. When the recruit turned to tell Al something, he saw the lioness in mid-air and he instinctively pushed Al to the side. The lioness ripped Al's chest open as she landed amongst the recruits. There was no way that a helicopter could extract Al, as it was pitch dark. The recruits ended up firing at the pride of lions throughout the night to keep them at bay. Al died as the sun was coming up and the sound of the rescue helicopter could be heard across the water.

Stretch Franklin was one of the founder members of the Selous Scouts and was killed on his motorbike, just around the corner from our house in Kariba ... what a sad loss.

Another early founder of the Selous Scouts was Dale Collet. Dale and his wife were married in our garden in Kariba. By then Dale was in a wheelchair. He had been shot and paralysed from the waist down by a terrorist in a house that the Scouts were raiding in Mozambique... but remained undaunted. Dale was one tough guy.

By the time we got to High School and had matured, we were able to understand things a bit more. Often, we heard of senior boys leaving school and joining the Air Force, Police or Army. Every year-end, the representatives of these Armed Services visited the school on recruiting campaigns. At that time, there was a National Service requirement. It was made mandatory for all white school-leavers to spend a year in one of the Armed Forces Units. By the time I left high school at the end of 1974, compulsory service had gone up to two years.

'What do you want to do after school, my boy?' Dad asked.

'After National Service, I want to join the Wildlife Department. You know I've always wanted to be a Game Ranger and work with animals. They'll only take me if I've had three years of farming or Police experience, though, so I'm thinking about joining the Police Service to kill two birds with one stone,' I responded. We had never really discussed options after school. I didn't have any friends joining me in the Police Force, as many had opted for the Army.

True to my plan, I enlisted in the British South African Police Force at the tender age of seventeen years and then had three years to complete. There wasn't much alternative for a school-leaving boy at that stage in Rhodesia's history. You either went to University and then to the army, or straight into the army, or left the country with no return ticket – those constituted your

3

Musa

In the distant tribal village, the cockerels greeted the coming early dawn. Their loud crowing stirred young Musa, as he tried to shrug off the chill under his thin grey blanket. He was curled up with his legs tight against his chest. His bed was a simple mat

on the floor that his mother had woven from the large-stemmed reed stalks that had been gathered from the riverbed down the hill from their kraal. Musa's pillow was stained brown with dirt that had resisted all hand-washings; the once-fluffy duck feathers that filled the small cotton envelope, had long since lost their buoyancy and now lay flat and did little to raise his young head from the ground.

His mother shouted an instruction to him. Musa knew well that it was time to get up. It was his job to let the cattle out of the wooden-poled boma, so that they could go and graze among the new, green, grass shoots that were carpeting the land just after the first rains. His clothes were already on him, so he didn't have to waste valuable time getting dressed; he had no pyjamas. His worn, brown shorts were too big for his small waist, having been given to him by his older brother. A thin strip of cow hide acted as his belt; he had made it himself. His shirt was a ragged blue-and-white striped one, with a single pocket on his left. He was barefoot.

It was 1965. Musa carefully stepped over his still-sleeping, older brother and stooped as he exited the pole-and-mud hut, via the small wooden-slated door. He also nearly fell over Bongi, his tan-coloured, young dog. The fresh morning air hit him, after the airless environment of the windowless hut. He drew in a deep breath and looked around for the metal water-bucket. He found it next to the maize-storage hut and, without making a sound, made his way down the familiar path to the river about 40 yards down the hill. The still morning had made the water like a mirror. He raised his hand to his chin in his reflection and growled inwardly - no hair growth yet! He then swept a few leaves from the surface of the water and scooped up as much water as he could into the bucket, careful not to touch the mud below – his mother would have something to say about that if he did. Making his way back to the big granite rock next to the kitchen hut, he put down the metal bucket and washed his face and neck as quickly as he could. The fresh, cold water woke him up. He flicked the water from his hands and looked toward the rising sun, as it began its own task of herding the morning clouds into the formations for the day.

Dogs:

Bongi was a typical African dog, with a heritage that could be traced all the way back to the Egyptians. His stand-up ears were typical of the breed and so was his curled tail, which seemed to do a full 360-degree turn arching its way back. His lips curled back in a simulated smile at his master, as Musa  bent down to stroke his head. Bongi's tail wagged in time with Musa's petting – they were the best of friends. He was a good dog, strong and with quick reactions, capable of chasing rabbits and duiker. Bongi would be closely heeled at Musa's feet for most of the day, save for the odd excursion into the bush to investigate strange smells.

The Good Life:

The cattle were restlessly moving around the small paddock. They knew it was time. Musa wandered across to the enclosure.

'What's all this noise?' he mumbled rhetorically to his favourite bull. It looked at him with its head raised. The massive Nguni bull had a mud-red, speckled colouration on its forehead, stretching between its horns. He had pure red sides and a white-and-red patchwork on his back, tail and throat. He was magnificent! In a region where the number of cattle you owned represented your wealth, this bull was highly valued. Musa reached across and stroked its head, knowingly, understanding his wish to be free of the kraal. He bent down and slid the bottom horizontal gate pole out of its position, dumped it unceremoniously to one side, and then slid out the top one. He knew that if he had done it the other way around, it would have caused problems. The eleven cattle were beasts of habit – change the routine and they become uneasy. The way was open. The cattle pushed their way through the gate, passed the boy, without instruction, and moved toward the grass on the far side of the rocky outcrop. Bongi stood back; he knew well, from previous experiences, that the cattle would have a go at him if they had half a chance. As the cattle and their minder walked, there was a gentle, rhythmic shuffle of feet and the crack of hooves on loose rocks. A metal bell rang with cheerful energy, as it hung loosely around the oldest cow's neck. The bell provided a feeling of assurance amongst the cattle. Without its hollow, metallic ring, there would be something out of the norm and they would be uneasy.

The cattle were already grazing, en route, as they rounded the first granite rocks and the sun beat down warmly, effectively clearing the early morning chills. The heavy bursts of warm, misty breath from the cattle erupted in plumes amongst the grass.

'Musa!' came a distant call from his mother – 'Breakfast!'

The boy took off at a run back to the kraal, eager to get a bowl of sweet Sadza and milk. He ran through the dew-laden grass, as it whipped at his skinny legs, and joined the worn path leading from the river. He rounded the hut, nearly knocking over his brother in his haste. He passed the maize-storage hut and jumped up onto the big rock next to the kitchen. His mother had already warmed up the solid porridge next to the fire and poured milk and heaps of sugar over it. She passed the little yellow bowl of porridge to him and he guzzled it down with his fingers, scooping up the last of the sweet breakfast and then leaning right over backwards as he gulped the remaining sugar-filled milk. With a swipe of the back of his arm, he cleaned the milk dribbles from the side of his mouth and, nodding thank you to his smiling mother, he took off back to his hut.

'Where is it?' he asked nobody, as he fumbled through his meagre belongings. As he stood up in the darkness, he lifted his trusty catapult to his chest.

'Today there are things to do!' His weapon of choice was made from the fork of a branch and the elastic comprised strips of rubber, cut with a razor-blade, from one of his brothers old bicycle tyres. The little leather strip, which held the projectile, was made from goat skin and all the parts needed to be secured were bound with thinner strips of the same rubber tyre. Small round stones were preferred and those were found near the rapids in the riverbed. The weapon had to be warmed up first, so a few, full pulls of the rubber did the trick. Into his back pocket went his beloved weapon – he knew he could hit a bird, first shot, at 20 paces.

Musa's kraal lay in the middle of a Tribal Trust Land. His nearest neighbours were half a kilometre away, where his friend Victor lived. His father had come all the way from Malawi and met his Shona mother. Musa was the second-born of their two boys. His father had died on the mines and his mother had brought up the two boys, alone. The boys were schooled at a Catholic Mission Station, where the nuns saw and noted the spirit of adventure in Musa.

Mates:

Musa headed back out to the cattle, armed with his catapult. They had moved further away from the rocky outcrop while he had been at breakfast, and he had to scoot around to the furthest

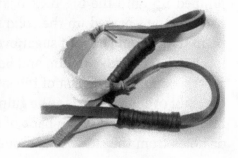

one to get them closer together. They knew what he was doing and obliged by heading together back toward the granite rocks. Having gotten the small herd more assembled, he climbed on top of the highest rock and peered up the hill to see if Victor was up and about. He couldn't see him, so raised his cupped hands to his mouth and yelled. Victor responded and the two boys ran toward each other, meeting by a huge Msasa tree.

'Mangwanani,' they said, as they greeted each other. The two friends decided on the quarry they wanted. Doves! Victor pulled out his catapult and they made their way down to the maize field near the river. It was early morning and the doves would be keen on getting their gullets filled, which would make it easier for the boys to approach them, as the doves kept their heads, down looking for seeds on the ground. Musa was first to spot three doves on the ground, just short of the maize. He loaded his catapult, aimed and fired. The small, round stone fell short, but bounced up off the ground and connected cleanly with the nearest dove's head. The others took off for the hills. The two boys ran as fast as they could to their prize. Musa held it up high with pride. His skills were improving. Bóngi jumped at his side, hoping to be part of the winnings. The boys settled down, made a fire and scorched the bird on the coals, feathers and all. They sat on their haunches with their backs to the rising sun to get warmth, while warming their hands on the fire. The bird's feathers burnt away and the carcass turned a Cajun-black in the hot coals. Victor stripped out the guts and, using his fingers, split the bird into two. The boys enjoyed their morsel as they talked about the cattle. Bongi got to crunch the head, which he devoured without a blink.

Musa brought up the issue of circumcision with his friend Victor.

'Is it sore?' he asked. Victor had no idea. He was as nervous as Musa, as both still had to go through the ritual in a month's time.

'We will be together, so that's fine and, anyway, look at all the other guys. They're okay and they are with the girls, instead of having to run around after cattle all day like us,' assured Musa, trying to drum up an air of confidence. He had spoken to his older brother. Without any embellishment, his brother had only divulged that it wasn't 'difficult.' The question therefore steadfastly remained - it was hardly a secret that there are parts of the body that are more sensitive to pain than others. Still, circumcision was a traditional passage into manhood, an initiation, and it would not be appropriate to exude blatant fear, so any trepidation was internalised. The boys knew what took place during the process. The foreskin was not removed, however; the elders would pierce the penis with a thorn from the acacia tree and, using a strong tail-hair from a bull, would thread the hair through the hole and tie it around the skin, about half an inch down from the phalanx. The hair would 'tear' through the secured piece of skin and flesh, in time, and sever both. The bull's tail- hair would decay over a few days in the process. They knew they would have to be separated from all their family members and only their male elders would tend to their needs, over the couple of weeks' ordeal. They would learn more about being responsible within the family, and a host of other issues would be covered by the advising elders, as well. Only when they reached the age of 18 years, or so, would they be classed as men. In the meantime, they would have graduated to being teenagers and boys no longer. Ummm ... a thing to ponder on. Both boys cleaned their hands by rubbing them in the fine sand. They bade each other farewell and headed for their respective cattle herds.

Fear of snakes:

Now there was one thing that scared Musa into a panic and that was snakes. This fear had started when he was a youngster. A Rinkhals had taken refuge amongst the old car tyres lying up against the wall of his hut. He had grabbed a tyre to roll it around as an imaginary toy car, and there it was. The snake had reared up and spat at him, with the venom hitting his shoulder, although he was two metres away. His mother told him that he would have been in a serious state if the venom had gotten into his eyes. Musa had had many contacts with snakes, and the cobras were his worst enemy, but one snake rose above all others in instilling dread – the Black Mamba. Musa had been plagued with dreams of snakes all his life. His first encounter with this devil had been by the granite rocks near the river. It was a huge male, measuring a commanding four metres in length. It had hissed ferociously at him one day when he'd been creeping around the rocks and bushes, looking for bird eggs. That snake would have attacked without provocation and could easily have outstripped him in speed. Finally, the men from around the area had come down to the rocks in a final bid to rid the village of this menace. Ten men had surrounded the rocks and had started by throwing rocks into the thicket, all the while simultaneously standing well back. Nobody was ready to brave a frontal attack from this ruler of the undergrowth. Eventually they'd set fire to the bushes and the snake had come out the other side, at high speed. Its head had towered above the heads of the three men, whom it had met on its way to escape. The quick-thinking men had thrown their throwing-sticks with deadly accuracy and, to their relief, had killed the snake. The celebrations had gone on all night, with the men's bravery being rewarded with tubs of locally-made beer. Whilst the event had been no laughing matter at the time, under the influence of the strong brew, they had begun to see the funny side of the whole situation and the day's drama had ended in great mirth over their cautious manoeuvres.

One day, one of the cattle was bitten on the leg by a puff adder and the bellows from the beast could be heard right up the valley. Within twenty minutes, the entire leg was swollen and eventually the neighbours came down and slit its throat to put it out of its misery. The fear of pythons was also high, as it was bad luck for the kraal if a python was found near it, so generally the plan would be to move the python away from all habituated areas. The clucking of chickens at the kraals could also attract pythons.

So, time went by in the little kraal. The rains came and went, and Musa passed through to manhood. It wasn't that bad; he had bravely told his mother about his initiation rites.

Musa's schooling days were over and his mother asked, 'So what do you want to do now that you have finished school?'

'Well, there is nothing to do in this area, so I was thinking of going to Salisbury to find work. I've passed my exams, so I can get a job anywhere,' was his confident answer.

He had no idea about the big tough world beyond his school and kraal.

New Stuff:

It was 1972 when Musa made his way to the bright lights of Salisbury, carrying his worldly belongings in a small suitcase his mother had given him for his birthday. The bus ride went on for hours and he was squashed between other folks travelling the same way. There were suitcases piled up high, on top of the old bus, and the odd goat and chicken added to the noisy orchestra of people talking and laughing as they sped on their way to the big city. Musa clutched his suitcase tightly to his chest – that's all he had in his life, plus a few dollars his mother had wrapped in a piece of newspaper for him.

'Always look after your money, my boy – put the money in your shoe, so nobody can take it from you,' came her wise words. She worried about him.

The chap he sat next to said he was going to join the Police because the pay was good and you didn't have to worry about looking for a place to live, as the Police supplied that for you.

'The Police? What do you have to do to be able to join the Police?' asked Musa with interest. The chap opened an envelope he had been clutching and handed Musa a newspaper cutting. Musa read it with concentration – hmm, now that was something to consider. He thanked the kind chap, handed him back the cutting and looked out of the dust-covered bus window as the kilometres sped past. He could not help wondering about what life was going to bring him. So many unknowns, so much to learn! Eventually he arrived in the busy and crowded bus station in the heart of Salisbury. He jumped from the last step of the bus and immediately saw his uncle, who had come to meet him. Clutching his little suitcase, he followed his uncle as they made their way through the bustling throngs of people. Musa was amazed at the activity. There were stalls where people sold oranges and single cigarettes. Barbers were busy shaving men's hair with razor blades without any handles. There were two stalls where the men were selling used car tyres. They had used a soldering-iron to carve new grooves in the already worn tyres, telling their potential clients about how many more kilometres the cheap tyres would give them. There were small cages made from chicken wire, with a dozen chickens crammed into each. Another stall sold sweets and playing cards, mahobo-hobo (a dry tasting fruit), mzanjis (a sweet tasting fruit), coka-cora (Coca-Cola), salted chicken wings and dried kapenta fish. Each stall was made from corrugated-iron roof-sheeting, supported by gum-tree poles. The noise was deafening. Musa was both confused and excited. He nearly lost sight of his uncle as he checked the price on a copper bangle that had caught his eye. Eventually the pair filtered their way out of the crowd and proceeded onto a small track, down a narrow alley. This area was a shanty town, made up of mainly immigrants from the rural areas looking for work in the commercial centre of the country. Tin huts lay in higgledy-piggledy disarray, some of more sturdy construction than others. Bits of corrugated metal and plastic sheeting kept the rain off, whilst old wooden pallets had been stripped down and the wood planks used to made great doors.

For the next two weeks Musa went out every day, making his way on foot to the city centre. He stood on the street corners with a dozen other hopefuls, waiting for someone to stop and offer him a new life. He even went door to door at the factories but, to his great distress, nobody seemed to want him. This was a huge setback.

'I am worried, Uncle,' he confided one day, as he helped to carry water from a distant tap to the shack. 'I can't find work.'

'There are many people looking for work and you just have to keep trying. Never lose faith and always remember what your mother taught you about manners,' his uncle encouraged.

Two days later, there was a commotion a few shacks down from his uncle's. It was ten o'clock at night when two loud gun shots rang out.

'Shsss,' whispered his uncle urgently. 'It's the Magandangas.'

Musa slid under his metal bed and lay motionless. There was no further action that night and the next day he asked his uncle what the story was with the Magandangas.

'Some people call them the liberation men, but the Government calls them terrorists. All I know is that I stay away from them. Either way, if you get involved with them you will be in trouble!' Musa was bewildered and didn't know what to make of all this. Everything was so different here in the city to what life was like back at the kraal, and he missed his mother's comforting support. One day when he was walking through the stalls near the bus station, he saw a man with no ears. He later learnt that the poor chap had been tortured by the Magandangas for being 'fingered' as a sell-out, or informer for the Government. That night, whilst he lay on his bed with his hands clutched behind his head, he remembered what the chap on the bus had said to him about joining the Police.

Within a week, he had applied and joined the British South Africa Police. He had nothing else to do. He stood silently, with thirty other new recruits, on the parade ground of Thomlinson Depot. The instructors ran up and down the boys' crude line, barking orders. Musa was petrified of them. He had been issued his new, smart Police uniform and was staying in a long dormitory with twenty-three other recruits. His head was shaved bald. The training was tough, but so was he, and he enjoyed every minute of it. Most importantly, he also made a few friends. He had a bit of money from his first payslip, which he halved, stashing his mother's half in a small cigar tin under his bed. He would always send his mother money, although the amount differed from time to time as his needs changed. His confidence was building again and when he wrote a letter to his mother, he exuded this confidence back to her with pride. His mother couldn't read, so he knew that she would take the letter to his old school and everybody there would sit and listen intently to Musa's adventures.

Musa spent five years working in various police stations and gained the rank of Sergeant in the process. He was diligent in his work and gained the respect of his peers. One day, his member in charge asked him if he wanted to join a special unit that could help him gain promotions in the future. It was 1977 and Musa found himself in camouflage uniform and standing next to his new friends in Special Investigations Section, far away from home in Mazoe. He knew nobody. A tall, blonde Patrol Officer came across and shook hands with Musa in welcome.

'Hi, I'm Keith, and you are in my section.'

The door to the old simple life was to firmly close and a new chapter was about to begin.

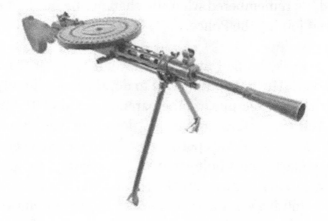

4

British South Africa Police

I was dropped off at the Police Training camp, Morris Depot, by my father. We drove through the main gate, passed two old, bronze powder cannons that stood imposingly on either side.

These were relics from battles dating back to 1897. Interestingly enough, these sturdy cannons were stolen years later, right under the eyes of the Police. The training base was bang next door to Prime Minister Ian Smith's residence. As we drove slowly down the road, my thoughts were filled with a naïve excitement at this new adventure; but an innate understanding knew that I was leaving my old halcyon freedom far behind. My raw youth gave me no insights as to what this new life would really be like, or what lay ahead. The car stopped. I jumped out and pulled my duffel bag from the back. As I walked around the car to say goodbye, my father and I, in our traditional, inimitable manner, exchanged some humorous quips.

'Don't shoot anyone on your first day,' joked Dad, giving me a light punch on the shoulder. I mocked objection. We laughed. There was a brief, poignant handshake. In a fleeting moment, his steady, blue eyes conveyed a look wherein lay every word he would have wanted to say; then he was gone.

'Bye, Dad,' was all I could find.

I watched him go, then slung the duffel bag over my shoulder and turned to report for duty, a touch subdued at our parting. Morris Depot was on a sprawling tract of land, in the heart of what was then called Salisbury. The buildings had been erected in typical colonial style, with white Victorian gables and red brickwork. Neat gardens and clean white lines on the parade grounds greeted my first day.

The police force had evolved from the British South Africa Company that had originally been owned by Cecil Rhodes. From the very beginning in a then young Rhodesia, this force was used to establish law and order. Since those days, the name had been changed to the British South Africa Police, or the BSAP as it was commonly referred to. The BSAP had an exemplary record. They ranked high amongst the premier police forces in the world. Tradition and adherence to a world of discipline and cohesion was deemed paramount.

In December 1974, there were two squads attesting as regular police. A total of 70 recruits were starting their training programme.

In addition, there were also three squads of National Servicemen who were called up for their two-year compulsory service. My force number was 9381. The fact that 9380 men had passed through these doors before me held intrigue. Where were they all now, I wondered.

At this stage I was referred to as a Cadet and, due to my age, was not officially allowed to be called a policeman. None of my schoolmates was with me at the training camp. However, long years at boarding-school (where you learn to live with every personality type and social pressure imaginable) definitely helped. Within a short time, I made friends with some of the new lads. They were equally as bewildered as I was with all the new protocols. This allowed us to form a bond. Whilst I may have been one of the tallest in the group, I was also the youngest.

It would only be after completing basic training that we could officially wear the insignia of a cadet. This was represented by a blue flash on the shoulder with 'Police Cadet' emblazoned across it. It was only in March 1975, when I turned eighteen, that I got to display one brass bar on each shoulder, showing the rank of Patrol Officer.

I met up with the other recruits, some of whom had pitched up in suits. I was grateful to be dressed in shorts and a T-shirt, so the sprint around the entire depot, with shouting instructors, wasn't too bad; however, the guys in suits struggled with that one! Once we'd had our familiarity tour, we were instructed to line up for our only one choice of haircut - a short back and sides. This was merrily accomplished with the expertise of an Italian barber in his little shop called 'The Left Right Inn'. After that, we were chased a kilometre down the road to collect kit. The suit guys had, by now, taken off their jackets. Eventually we were released to our rooms, where we plonked down our kits and relaxed for a second, before the instructors were onto us again, with demanding questions as to why our rooms were not up to standard. We had to pack away our kits in accordance with strict regulations, so we immediately had to get up again and obey those orders.

Supper that evening was a welcome relief and the grub was first class. I sleep well, in a room with three others; just like boarding-school again.

The next morning, we were up early, in our regulations PT kit, for a run around the whole depot again; just in case we had forgotten where everything was. From there, we had our first taste of the assault course, which was something that thereafter we learnt to absolutely dread: Jacob's Ladder. This was a 'mile'-high series of logs over which we had to clamber. One chap, named Thomas, who was not the slimmest of lads, struggled for weeks to overcome this course. We also learnt how high the spectator stands were at the rugby field, when we had to run up and down the countless stairs, just to have a look at the nice view from the top.

That night, things got a bit out of hand. Both new regular squads were invited to the local pub for a drink. Little did we know that we were going to be wrecked in the morning. Drink after drink was forced upon us, whilst we had to do some idiotic tricks to please the senior squads. This wasn't anything like the initiations we had at school. That was physical punishment; this was punishment of the head. I had never had an alcoholic drink in my life and to be drowned in beer made me crawl back to my room. Somehow I found it; I don't remember how! The next morning, the instructors had to hold back their smiles as a number of the recruits couldn't even stand up straight and, with an 'about turn', had to sprint off to the flower beds to continue purging the contents of their stomachs. Needless to say, these guys were quickly assigned extra PT, as they had trespassed on 'hallowed ground' - the depot's gardens.

The instructors took great pride in taking us for long runs around the local neighbourhood and, on those days, our squads started to get a rhythm going, as we beat the pavement with our running shoes. We got to bring our feet down in unison and that helped us with our marching. The instructors had an acute ability to spot the one recruit who was out of step.

Tear-gas drill was on the tutorial menu. We were thrown into our normal PT routine and, with no warning, were blasted with canisters of this horrible gas. Not funny when you are full of sweat. I think the tears induced were not only from the effects of the gas, but from the pain as well.

One of the tours we did was to the local city mortuary, where we had to watch three postmortems. This was all part of the comprehensive training we were to receive. I must say, I just couldn't handle this particular tour and joined half the other recruits outside, under the tree, where we were all violently ill. The doctors performing these post mortems were intent on teaching us everything about human biology and went to extremes to 'show' us all the information that could be acquired from these investigations.

The trip to the maximum-security prison was an eye-opener, too. There were men in there who were the biggest I had ever seen. They spent their lives pushing weights and, when we first saw them in the courtyard, they looked like a herd of buffalo. I made a mental note never to end up in there, for any reason! Looking down the spotless, shiny corridor at this mass of humanity, with their tattoos and shaven heads was, to say the least, most unnerving.

Our policy training was very intensive. We learnt what Law was all about. We had to understand the entire book on Statutory and Common Law based on the Roman Dutch System. Statutory Law covers things like murder, theft and allied crimes, whilst Common Law covered aspects such as vehicle accidents and minor offences. We did endless parades, arrest procedures, anti-riot drills and anti-terrorist training and we even learned to do speed-typing. There were lessons on radio communications, first aid and a lot of emphasis was placed on physical and endurance instruction. My undisputed favourite was rifle practice. Early on, during some of our first shooting lessons, and after I had surpassed their own scores, the instructors shouted out 'Chisnall! How the hell did you learn to shoot like that?' I did not disclose that it had come from shooting tin cans and curbing pigeon pilferage in the meal-ie-fields on the farm. In fact, I had no real idea that I had even acquired a particular skill. I had never shot competitively before, so it was as much a revelation to me as it was to the instructors.

The Police Force was steeped in many traditions, mostly based on the British way of doing things. Amongst these traditions was an early-morning wake-up summons, where a solitary bugler would loudly sound the call. He would do this while standing to attention on the parade ground, in front of the Rhodesian flag. This call would penetrate our dormitories, signalling us to rise immediately and pack our kit in a precise manner and in accordance with police regulations. The top sheet had to be turned down by exactly 4 inches and everything had to be placed in a meticulous and measured way. When there was an inspection of the barracks, our kit had to be immaculately laid out, on the bed, in an unfaltering routine. In fact, it was all so specific that, in time, we learnt to sleep like a board so that we hardly disturbed our bedding.

Shoes, boots, leggings, cap-straps, belts and the like, were all made from leather. These all had to be 'boned' to a high shine, so much so that we had to be able to see our faces in them. We were extremely fortunate in that we had a number of batmen who undertook this laborious chore. Their job was to do all the boning of the leather, to clean brass buttons, iron clothing and help with the clean-up of the barracks. The trick was to daub shoe polish onto the leather, then heat a metal tablespoon over a candle and literally melt the polish into the leather, using the back of the spoon. Then there were hours of shining with a very fine cloth. We paid them for this, but it was a seriously good investment

- save for occasions where the job was done poorly and this shoddiness would cost us dearly. The hapless recruit could wind up in detention barracks, where he would spend the whole day changing in and out of kit and being rigorously inspected on parade.

Certain aspects of my basic training were less appealing than others. The demands and pressures we were placed under were influenced by the incremental increase in terrorist activity in the country. One exception to all of this remained the shooting range. Here, I was in my own world, my inner space. The quiet preparation where mind, focus and breathing must become one, came easily to me. I had spent many hours on my back, on the farm, where my thoughts could apply themselves to this alignment. From the earliest that I can remember, the last my mother would see of me for a morning or afternoon would be the back of my tousled, flaxen-blonde hair disappearing into the fields, or turning off towards the farm hills, pellet gun slung over my shoulder. Barefoot ... and free!

I later received an award for marksmanship. 'Bloody good shooting, Chisnall' conceded the weapons instructor under his breath. This was as high a level of rapturous, congratulatory praise that he was ever likely to express. If Sabow was here now, I wondered what he would make of all of this and if he would wonder what all the fuss was about.

Whilst we were undergoing training, we were not issued with our own weapons. They were only distributed on the range. There was a reason for this. Some years previously, the bugler had been enthusiastically delivering a robust tune when one of the recruits leaned out of his dormitory window and, from 450 metres, had shot the instrument clean out of the astonished bugler's hands. The culprit piously tried to claim that he was aiming high and that he 'didn't mean it.' This useless excuse only served to fuel the formidable wrath of the hierarchy! His punishment was duly meted out – severely.

Counter Insurgence Training or COIN:

In April, both regular squads loaded all their combat gear into the back of two five-tonne trucks and headed for the mountains in the Eastern part of the country. It was bitterly cold and our new camouflage uniforms did little to keep us warm. After many hours in the back of the trucks, we arrived at our drop-off point, frozen. It was so cold, in fact, that we didn't even have to stop off for a toilet stop – everything just seemed to have shut down.

We spent two frenetic weeks rushing around in the mountains, immersed in map reading, tracking, ambush strategies, radio skills and the like. This was our short introduction to the basics of bush-warfare training! Many of us came from a farming background, which was a definite advantage. However, the majority were from the flatlands and were totally unused to mountains. Whilst we had an intrinsic affinity with the bush, we struggled with this largely unfamiliar terrain. A small 'gomo' (hill) was no problem, but damn, these giant mamas were unforgiving. This particular chain of mountains runs north to south along the eastern boundary of Rhodesia. To the east of the mountains lies Mozambique. There had been a war going on in Mozambique for as long as any of us could remember. In this region there were also ancient ruins everywhere, some of them dating back to around 1300 AD. Layer upon layer of rocks terraced many slopes, just like rice paddies. Later in my life, I took a deep interest in historical sites but, at the time, we didn't care much for the distant past. We were just desperately keen to get through the bush course. Despite our physical fitness, it was sheer hell negotiating the innumerable rocks and hurdles. Talk about stumbling blocks. 'Shit', 'Son of a bitch' and words of a more explicit nature became a standard and cacophonous accompaniment to our faltering efforts to make progress.

On one particular day, my section came across human spoor. We followed the tracks for several kilometres, as the imprint of military-style boots was clearly evident. It was also apparent that whoever had left these tracks had been simply following an open path and appeared unconcerned about leaving a trail; perhaps not anticipating the presence of Rhodesian Forces in the area. We came across what looked like a rest camp. The grass had been flattened into rectangular shapes, as opposed to oval shapes which an animal would have made. On count, we identified six sleeping-places.

Armed with this discovery, we radioed the instructors. We advised them that it was our belief we had found the first signs of terrorist incursions penetrating this area. These 'terrs' would most likely have come in from neighbouring Mozambique, which was only a few kilometres away. With the enemy infiltrating this far south into the country, there was no doubt in our minds that they were getting help from FRELIMO (the Front for the Liberation of Mozambique). FRELIMO were in an armed struggle against the Portuguese-controlled colony. We continued to follow the spoor and came across the remains of a mombi (cow) that had been brutally butchered. No local would have left a carcass like this. That was it; these grisly remnants were strong substantiation to us that these were indeed gooks. Night began to fall and we returned to base. In the end, we were not given feedback on this band of infiltrators, and we never learnt what happened to them. However, this incident gave us a damn fine early wake-up and we began to learn never to take anything for granted.

After the bush training, the trucks trundled back to Morris Depot in Salisbury. It was time to ready ourselves for the passing-out parade. The other regular squad was busy with the horses. Equestrian work had been included in their training, but as there were not enough horses to go round, this had not been incorporated as part of our squad's activities.

Passing-Out Parade:

The passing-out parade required us to wear our Number 1's. These were our best and smartest uniforms, comprising a starched shirt, tunic, jodhpurs (stiffened to a board by being ironed using soap), shiny leather leggings, spurs, leather belt or 'Sam Brown' as we called it, peaked cap and spotlessly cleaned rifle. The visual effect of a full squad, dressed in their Number 1's, is impressive and worth every effort involved in the final, painstaking preparations.

Once we were 'spit and polished', it was then necessary to make our way across to the parade ground. Trouble was, en route, it was imperative to avoid getting our boots scuffed or dirty. With no other choice at hand, the only way to do this was to engage in an ungainly 'heel walk.' Walking on heels in boots was one thing, but walking on heels in boots with spurs was quite another. Pretty much indescribable. Worse was that I wasn't used to wearing spurs; these were for the horse guys. During the parade, we were required to execute the general salute. To do this, we would have to place our right foot behind the left, in a manoeuvre that had been practised a thousand times - without spurs, though. By some unfortunate twist of fate, as we took the salute my spurs locked together. This meant that when we were required to turn right, and march past the Inspecting Officer in file, I was rendered temporarily immobile. I almost fell over in a manic effort to disentangle the infuriating restraints. It could only have been for a fleeting moment that all this transpired, but to me it felt like an eternity and, all the while, I could feel the drill instructor's eyes burning hot coals into my neck.

The well-drilled Police Band played throughout the parade. Their rousing marching-songs made my hair stand on end and filled each step we took with unrestrained pride. My family watched the parade alongside all the many other families, friends and visiting dignitaries. Nobody seemed to have noticed my mishap, which was an inward relief. Photos were taken with the old brownie camera. Smiling pictures still reflected a youthful face, but I had already grown up a lot during my time in training.

The turmoil festering in the country was still classed as a Police matter. The insurgency was not yet considered a military invasion but, rather, as a civil insurrection. Only when occasion demanded it, would the police call on the Army and Air Force. However, later when things began to seriously escalate and the Police were becoming overly stretched, the Army and Air Force came in to swell the numbers.

I left Morris Depot and spent the next six weeks learning how to drive at the Police Driving School. It was here that I first met, and employed, Kenneth to act as my batman. He was one of many indigent hopefuls who had assembled near the police quarters to seek employment. Something in his manner drew my attention. Instead of feigning a forlorn expression like many of the other aspirant workers, he exuded a positive expectation, which made him stand out from the crowd.

Kenneth The Batman:

This was the start of a very long friendship. What made for an immediate bond was his irrepressible sense of humour. Kenneth was from the Shona tribe. He had a slight build, but possessed tough, stringy muscles that were deceptively powerful. For reasons known only to him, he wore his hair longer than his fellow tribe members. He had a totally uncompromising outlook on life. His motto was 'Work hard; play hard.' One enduring bad habit was his frequent lateness for work, especially after a fun-filled week-end. I was forever giving him a verbal hammering in a vain attempt to help him develop a sense of time. The outcome was always predictable. He had an uncanny way of making me break into laughter and further chastisement became pointless. On one memorable occasion, he alluded to having been at church hence his delay. When I pointed out that no church that I knew of held public services at six on a Monday morning, he smilingly acknowledged that perhaps it had been a heavenly dalliance of a different sort that had, in fact, prolonged his arrival. He was a comic of note.

As I grew to know him, I learnt that Kenneth was fiercely loyal. He valued his job and guarded me as he would a brother. I trusted and valued him, too, and we both shared an inclination to laugh at life's absurdities.

Kenneth dearly wanted to learn to drive. By then, I had bought my first car. A third-hand Alfa Romeo 1300 cc, which he devotedly polished to a blinding shine every day. Now and then, I would drive Kenneth out to a quiet lonely road, far from possible encounters with other vehicles, and let him live his dream to drive. He relished getting behind the wheel and his smile knew no bounds. I suspected what he really wanted to do was to let his friends see him driving, but there was not a chance in hell that I was going to let him take the car away for the weekend. Besides, with his propensity to party, he was not going to get an opportunity to get creative with the manufacturer's original framework. I preferred it the way it was.

Driving was part of training:

Driving school was a happy time. There were no endless parades, or physical training disciplines. We had a lot of fun learning to drive, mostly Land Rovers and motorcycles. Most of the trainees had driven before, either on farms with the farm vehicle, or tractor, or a friend's car. Driving around town was not that easy, though. We were enchanted with the Land Rovers, but were ecstatic when some motor cycles were pulled up in front of us.

As was inevitable, the masculine inclination to experiment with techniques over-and-above the recommended ones, resulted in a number of crashes. I remember one incident where the throttle on a Patrol Officer's 250cc Honda motorcycle stuck at full speed. For a full minute, he could be heard shrieking wildly - like a castrated jackal - before fouling up, in an untidy heap, against a six-foot, diamond-mesh fence. Word soon spread through the school of his unwitting performance! To his great chagrin, he accomplished celebrity status for all the wrong reasons. In fact, to this day, recollections of his wild screaming ride still elicits a broad grin.

The skid pad was highly entertaining. Here, we learnt to control a vehicle in slippery conditions. The pad was merely a simple, large, flat, cement floor, awash with water. Vehicles were driven around at high speed on tyres with no treads. Under these conditions, skidding was guaranteed and we happily put our developing skills to the test. No doubt we did every form of vehicular 'moon dancing', screeching slide-byes and spinning circles, ever imagined. Our time at the driving school sped by and soon it was time for me to be given my first post.

New Post:

It was a hot, dry, Saturday afternoon. Detective Section Officer Winston Hart thundered into the sand driveway of the driving depot in a beaten-up, green Land Rover. He swung under a Jacaranda tree's shade and came to a halt in a cloud of dust. It was now three o'clock. I had been waiting since noon to catch a lift with him to Centenary, a little town that lay to the North East of the country.

When the recruits from 7 and 8 squads of 1974 had lined up, all the conscripts were given an opportunity to voice their personal preferences for new postings. Most were hoping for postings in, or at least, near their home towns. With little exception, virtually every man had said that he would hate to get a posting to Centenary or Mount Darwin. These two stations were positioned in the heart of the war and made up the two primary towns within a district called Operation Hurricane. As I could speak Shona, and had shown willingness to go into the operational area, there was no competition in securing my posting. I got Centenary. The other guys sighed with relief. This collective concurrence made it clear that any second thoughts on my part were not going to alter my destiny.

'Throw your kit into the Landy, I'll be back now,' Hart said as he raced toward the men's room. 'We're late and I don't want to be on the road after dark,' he hollered out as he disappeared around the building. I was bemused to notice that his words somehow inferred that it was my fault we were late.

I hoisted my suitcase into the back as detailed, and climbed into the passenger seat. There were papers everywhere, a couple of loose 7.62mm cartridges lay at the base of the gear stick, and the cab looked as though it had been through a desert dust-storm, with fine layers of dust on every surface. I knocked my knee against the grey radio slung under the dash. To fit my long legs in, I carefully had to squeeze them in on either side of the radio. The radio was large, being one of the older generation made with valves. I eased my rifle onto my right-hand side, with the butt resting on the floor plate, and scrutinised the radio, while my mind drifted to imaginings of ambushes. Kenneth was coming with me and, without instruction, he jumped into the back with his single suitcase.

Hart suddenly jumped into the driver's seat next to me.

'Hi! S.O. Hart, pleased to meet you!' he said, 'reaching out with his hand for a firm, introductory handshake. He slammed the gearbox into reverse and, within less than half an hour, we were well out of town. I was silent as we geared our way out of Salisbury and down the Mazoe hills, heading north to Centenary.

'Keep that FN handy as we go,' Hart ordered, whilst looking around into the surrounding bush. I immediately responded and worked the FN automatic rifle into a ready position, with the barrel pointing out of my door-less side. We belted along at a teeth-rattling 110 kms per hour. The journey took over three hours, pitted only occasionally with dialogue. The road was tar all the way and wound through many farming areas. I arrived in Centenary, with my hair raised on one side from the buffeting wind. Hart parked in the designated car park outside a line of prefabricated buildings, also displaying an oddly Mohican hairstyle, on his right side!

'Section Officer Cassidy is Head of Station and you'll find him across there,' said Hart, as he gesticulated towards the Charge Office. He then hurried off in the opposite direction, toward one of the first prefabricated buildings that stood across from the main Police Station. Later, I learnt these were the offices of Special Branch and Criminal Investigation Department or CID.

I ran my fingers through my hair in a vague attempt to make it respectable and then lugged my suitcase over to the main entrance of Centenary Charge office. Kenneth was on my heels. I entered the room and approached the counter; a stern-looking Constable looked up. He must have realised who I was as he promptly left the office, obviously to call somebody senior. I looked around me. The counter ran the length of the room. On the wall to the left was a large radio, with countless rows of red lights. Various pieces of A4 paper were taped to the centre section of the back wall, displaying a whole bunch of instructions. A number of these papers had pictures of 'Wanted' people. A plain, wooden bench stood to one side of the room, with a man seated on it. He had a strange lassitude, with his hands cupping his forehead.

'Welcome to Centenary!'

That snapped me out of my inspections. The greeting came from a short Section Officer standing on the other side of the counter. Cassidy, being around 5' 8, looked up at me; at six foot three, I towered above him. His Khaki tunic appeared shiny through extensive use and ironing. His belt, which was made from the same material, rode high on his bulging stomach, exaggerating the size of his rounded belly. His shiny, thin, black hair was taped across the top of his head in a futile attempt to hide his baldness.

'Constable, get PO Edwards up here and have him take PO Chisnall down to the PO's mess,' he commanded. The black constable, who had informed him of my arrival, turned to undertake this mission.

'Once you have settled in, report to my office in the morning and I'll give you a rundown of the station. Your batman can shack up with the others in the barracks.' With that, he swivelled on his heel and disappeared back into his office. Short and succinct, excuse the pun!

Patrol Officer Harry Edwards appeared. He came swiftly around the corner, bearing a huge smile. Harry had a gargantuan black moustache, which cascaded down the side of his mouth to his chin and his large nose signified his Greek decent. A jocular character! He, too, sported a shiny khaki uniform, a sure sign he had been in service for a while. He displayed a single rank bar on each of his epaulettes, indicative of a Patrol Officer, which matched my rank. He wore socks and shoes, while I, although dressed in the same uniform as him, bore boned-leather leggings.

'You'll soon get rid of those leggings, because of the bloody heat around here,' he observed.

Harry ushered me through the door. We worked our way past

the station corridors to the rear section and down a dusty path to the Patrol Officer's mess. Kenneth was led off to his quarters and we exchanged a nod as we parted.

'You can dump your stuff in this room!' he indicated cheerily. 'I'll see you later. I've got to get out to a farm to arrest some local labourer for assaulting his wife.' He left, but not without me noticing that he had a camouflage jacket in hand. Strange when it was so bloody hot!

The room was rudimentary – Spartan in fact. A single, narrow bed, with standard, police-issued bedding, took up one corner, and on the opposite side was a basic, built-in cupboard. No curtains, no pictures and no carpet! With two hands, I heaved my suitcase onto the bed and simultaneously peered out of the window onto the unadorned lawn, and beyond to an airstrip, which homed several Alouette III helicopters. Chicken-wire mesh covered the double-sided window. A Kite Spider had made its web across the window ... how nice. With Harry's words still ringing in my ears, I changed my foot attire. My suitcase was primarily full of police apparel, with very few civvies or personal belongings. Damn! I had forgotten to ask where my rifle had to be stored. With no-one in the vicinity, I didn't know what to do so I just sat around until Harry came back at 9 o'clock that night.

'Why haven't you eaten?' he enquired. The fact was that I had not even thought to eat. Within a shot, he had a light meal rustled up for both of us and we settled down in the two lounge chairs, whilst he updated me on everything. There was a lot to take in. I was to work closely with him on criminal cases and to travel around the area to get to know everybody. This turned out to be a vitally important exercise. When the war heated up, it was these very communications that provided a lifeline for intelligence-gathering and effective contact.

Centenary Police Station handled all matters relating to policing and anti-terrorism incidents within the Centenary farming area. This included the whole of the Mzarabani and Gutsa Tribal Trust lands in the Zambezi valley, both thrown in for good measure. By comparison to the area it serviced, it was a small station. Aside from Cassidy at the head, the staff included a Section Officer by the name of Brian, two Patrol Officers (Harry and I), a black Sergeant and five Constables. This contingent made up the main police station. The Criminal Investigations Department and Special Branch offices were housed in the prefabricated huts across the parking lot. That was where SO Hart's office was located. It was a well-positioned station that featured offices, accommodation for the staff, two prison blocks, a refuelling station and a large, well-tended garden, which was Cassidy's baby. Many a day the prisoners would be found, pick in hand, under the watchful eye of a constable, digging up the 'flower' beds and moving plants to some or other corner. The plants were, in fact, all indigenous, hardy, shrub types - capable of surviving extended periods of drought – but there were no actual picturesque flowers of any note. Pathways with neat verges led from one building to the next. Whitewashed stones bordered all the pathways and any other areas where you were allowed to walk. Don't get caught taking a short cut across the grass, though. No way ... Aikona!

The next morning I was up before dawn, and got myself ready for my first day. The anticipation was overwhelming. Kenneth had already taken charge of the Patrol Officers mess and had tea and a light breakfast made when I emerged from my simple room. I had exchanged my leather leggings for socks and systematically checked the shine on my brown shoes, before making my way up to meet with Cassidy. En route, I walked past the gardening contingent, which comprised four prisoners and a Police Constable. The constable was armed with a Greener shotgun, slung on his shoulder. The Greener is a single-shot weapon, which is loaded by dropping the breach, just like a Martini Henry rifle. Bloody hell, we had some old weapons in the Police Force.

'Morning, Sir,' initiated the constable.

'Sir....?' That took me slightly aback. Hmmm. In that momentary hiatus, and for the first time, I realised my rank meant something to someone. I responded and continued on my way. Within a minute, I stood outside Cassidy's door and waited whilst he and Sgt. Moyo discussed an issue regarding a crime docket. Moyo came out and disappeared down the passage. After delivering a sharp perfunctory knock on the door, I entered the office and came to attention in front of Cassidy's desk.

'No need for that here, PO Chisnall. Stand at ease.'

I didn't salute Cassidy, as he was a Section Officer. Only the rank immediately above him and beyond, to the guys with 'scrambled egg' on their shoulders and caps, were to be saluted. Cassidy briefly ran through the various duties that I was required to perform around the station. It was a short briefing and didn't differ too much from what Harry had told me the night before. I was given instructions to learn as much as possible from PO Edwards, who had been in Centenary for two years.

'Where do I keep my rifle, Sir?' I enquired.

'With you at all times after hours but, during normal working hours, it is to be kept in the walk-in safe at the station. If you go out on patrol or to a crime scene, you are to withdraw it, plus ammunition, and then return it to the safe when you get back,' explained Cassidy.

'We have our morning parade now, so make your way out onto the parking area,' he instructed, effectively terminating our first meeting. The parade was held daily in front of the two flag poles that stood outside the Charge Office entrance. The green and white Rhodesian flag was hoisted on the right, and the blue and gold Police flag to the left. On parade, the officers would stand to one side, whilst the constables and police reservists lined the other. All told, that day there were eight policemen on duty. The others were on leave, or out on patrols. After the hoisting of the Rhodesian and Police flags by Sergeant Moyo, Cassidy issued the day's instructions. Thereafter, Harry gave the instruction to dismiss; everybody came smartly to attention, completed a right turn and marched three steps, before heading off to their respective duties. Harry took me directly to the Patrol Officers room and showed me to my starkly barren desk.

'Don't worry ... that desk will look like mine after two days,' he laughed. I turned to look at his desk and was inwardly appalled to discover that its surface couldn't be seen for all the papers covering it. My eyebrows rose. You had to be kidding!

Life in Centenary started routinely. Mundane chores such as attending morning parades, uniform checks and the issue of daily instructions, were all part of Cassidy's 'running by the book' style of doing police duty. His knowledge of Common and Statutory Law was, however, enviable. Cassidy had an LLB in Law. He could quote you chapter and verse from the law books – and did! On the positive side, this library of knowledge made working for him hugely edifying. On a slightly less positive side, for those of us who were not LLB graduates, any work that was deemed not up to standard had to be repeated until acceptable. Cassidy would systematically drum the law into us. When completing a murder docket, it was necessary to type all documents in eight copies. With today's modern technology, this would have been an easy undertaking. In those days, though, it was nothing short of a confounded bloody headache. The document had to be absolutely correct, including grammar and spelling. Nothing less than 100% accuracy was tolerated. When typing on an old Olivetti typewriter through eight pages, interleaved by seven carbon pages, this became a leviathan task. One would have to exert great pressure when typing, just to get through the thick wad of pages. Previously in training, I had learnt to type with ten fingers but here it turned out to be easier to type with my two strongest fingers. Whenever dockets were being drawn up, one could hear the relentless tap emanating from either of the Patrol Officer's desks. Let me tell you, this was finger boot camp in action!

Bi-monthly visits were arranged to Umvukwes Regional Court, in order to complete the prosecution of offenders. Umvukwes (pronounced Um-vuk-wheez) was another small farming-town, based a bit closer to Salisbury. Most prisoners stayed in the temporary cell blocks at Centenary Police Station until their scheduled Court date. These cell blocks were made up of four, corrugated-clad rooms, with plain cement floors and a long drop toilet in each cell corner. In the centre of each room was a solid metal ring, suggesting that the prisoners who misbehaved, or who were considered dangerous, would be shackled by their ankles. The whole building was painted in a dull, governmental-green and had the permanent stench of human sweat. One could have a fusion of murderers, cattle thieves, rapists, assault cases or any number of different criminals to deal with. Cassidy customarily acted as the prosecutor so, if your documentation was not up to scratch, he would later have you standing before him to face the music.

The Court itself was a functional, four-walled room. It featured a basic table for the travelling magistrate, a chair for the prosecutor and a standing dock for the accused. One hot day, whilst waiting outside the courtroom in the shade of a tall bush, Harry became aware that the leaves around him looked strangely recognisable. He picked a leaf for further inspection. With profound shock, he realised that he had been standing in the shade of a giant marijuana bush. The bush, actually better described as a veritable thicket, was wide-spreading and well over eight feet tall. Harry waited until Cassidy had finished his last case and then took the dagga leaf over to show it to him. He learnt that, once a prisoner was convicted, the magistrate would hand any remaining evidence to the court orderly to be destroyed. Invariably, if the evidence consisted of seeds and leaves from drug users or peddlers, the orderly would merely throw it away outside the back door of the court room. Over time, some of the seeds had obviously germinated and had flourished into a sizable hedgerow. The local Police Constables of Umvukwes were tasked with destroying the 'plantation.' They, in turn, summoned the incarcerated prisoners to burn it all down. The grapevine had obviously worked at speed as, for once, there was no complaint or mumblings at having to undertake such labour. Witnesses also noted how the prisoners seemed remarkably content to stand in the thick haze of the redolent smoke which bellowed forth!

Sam the Tracker:

It was during my stint as a normal Patrol Officer that I got to meet some unforgettable characters. One of these was a black Police Reserve member called Sam. Sam was not a regular policeman, having never completed his training. He had been recruited into the Force for his exceptional abilities. When I first met him, he was about forty years old. Sam was a utility man, who efficaciously handled the many tasks given to him. He was frequently out on patrol with us. Late one afternoon, a prisoner brazenly bolted into the nearby maize field, trying to stage an escape. The Constable responsible for guarding that day had gone to relieve himself, giving the prisoner a perfect opportunity to make a bid for freedom. Sam was immediately called in to track down the fugitive. I joined him and we started rapidly tracking the man through the maize field that bordered one side of the station. The going was, however, no walk in the park. The field was large and it took time to work through the dense, green foliage. The mealie plants were a lot taller than we were and their tough, unrelenting leaves carved cuts into our faces and hands. The undergrowth made silent walking impossible. By then, the sun was disappearing over the hills ... and, with it, the clarity of the trail. This did not deter Sam in the slightest. He adjusted his visual by bending down to look for tracks from a lower angle, so as to better read the disturbances the prisoner's unclad feet had made in the soil. Just as dusk was ebbing away, the astonished prisoner was grabbed by Sam, as he lay curled up in a culvert on the verge of the field. It transpired that the man had not run out of the field. He had relied on the thick vegetation and the falling darkness to provide him with cover until he could get away later. He had not fooled Sam, though. This tracking ability put Sam in a league of his own. In time, his expertise became legendary. He was eventually seconded to the Police Anti-Terrorist Unit or PATU, to track terrorists.

Sam never carried a firearm, but preferred to work with a metre-long stick, which he would use to point out tracks and signs, all the while engaged in soft mutterings as he worked diligently, using a combination of instinct and skill. As a safeguard, he would have an armed watch alongside him; more often than not, it would be the senior man of a section or 'stick.' As they drew close to the quarry, Sam would use his stick to point out the direction and distance of the terrorists to the senior man. With his job done, he would then promptly disappear to the rear of the action. Very often the section leader could not even see exactly what Sam was pointing out, but they learnt to trust his information and to proceed nonetheless. Sam was always willing to lead a tracking team, but he never wanted to end up in a firefight. He was not a tall man and it was known that he sometimes disappeared between the legs of the Section Leader in his haste to get away from a battle, especially if the surrounding bush was too thick to permit his own easy exit. He had plans did Sam ... to live a long life. In one incident, Sam made a rare mistake. He had led the team of Policemen right past a terrorist, whom nobody had

seen, lying in the thick bush. It was an ambush and when Sam spotted the main group ahead, he did his normal trick of 'taking up the back seat and running' back along the route they had been on. When the battle began, Sam spotted the lone terrorist and literally jumped on him. There was much chastisement later, when the story came out that Sam had not seen the man in the bushes first. Sam was eventually persuaded to carry an FN rifle – though he never fired it.

Constable Shoko:

Constable Shoko was another interesting character. Shoko and I were nominated as working partners and you would often see us attending crime scenes together. Shoko was also from the Shona tribe, which is the largest indigenous group in this region. He was a good man. He never shirked work and was a skilled interrogator in establishing the hard facts. His intricate knowledge of the local customs was key to his successes. Nobody could pull the wool over his eyes!

An interesting event happened one day at the station. I was in my office typing up a docket for Court, when Shoko burst in.

'Ishe (sir), you have got to come and see this,' he said, as he simultaneously did an about-turn and headed for the prison cells. His tone told me that something grim was afoot, but I was totally unprepared for what I was about to see! Shoko threw open the large, steel door to the cell. The prisoner had slit his own throat with a razor blade and was lying on the floor in a pool of blood.

'Jeeeez!' It was a lot to take in. 'Get the first aid kit,' I instructed Shoko.

'Argh... don't worry too much about this fool, Ishe, he just doesn't want to go to Court! He KNOWS he did it,' said Shoko derisively, as he left to get the kit. I had a closer look at the wound and was relieved to find that, despite the noisy guttural sounds the man was making, it was not as bad as it had initially looked. I patched him up and told the night-shift Constable to keep an eye on him. As Shoko had predicted, the prisoner survived the ordeal and still had his day in Court. Shoko and I had many interesting times together.

We once arrested a farm labourer on a charge of bestiality. He was a farmer's sheep-herder. Shoko couldn't believe it. The man openly admitted his guilt to the sentencing magistrate and, to make things worse, said that 'it' was better than his wife and that he would do 'it' again. Later, Shoko's scandalised account of the accused's story to the other constables at the station, was hilarious. One would hear him clucking his distaste of this obscene behaviour whenever the subject was raised. Shoko wanted nothing to do with this case and, so great was his disgust that he wouldn't even look towards the cell where the man was kept.

Two Cartridges Is Enough:

On the political and terrorist levels, things were building up. Cassidy stated that he wanted two constables and myself to become proficient in the task of laying ambushes for terrorists. He decided that, to begin, we would randomly choose a farm and position ourselves near the farm's local compound to look out for the presence of terrorists, whose numbers were ever-increasing. Whilst this may have been a commendable plan, the part that we considered of less acclaim was where we were expected to don well-recognised police uniforms and be armed with breach-loaded, greener shotguns, for which we received a grand sum total of two cartridges each. I was also prohibited from taking my FN rifle.

'This is a Police exercise and you are to act as Policemen!' came Cassidy's sharp retort when we queried the use of the shotguns and the meagre 'stock' of ammunition.

'Make sure you have a bloody good reason to use the ammunition that you have been issued,' we were told in no uncertain terms. The fact was that quite a few good reasons sprang to mind, primarily that, had we encountered a group of terrorists armed with their traditional AK47s and machine guns, we would have had a total fire-power of six cartridges between us, with which to put up a defence that only Bruce Lee in the movies could have pulled off. Anyone further than 30 paces would have been safe from us.

Centenary was a hub of activity, with the Army, South African Police and the Air Force out chasing terrorists every day, and here we were, with our Regulation Equipment, running around as though the area was safe! After a few serious incidents in the area, Cassidy eventually capitulated to pressure and succumbed to allowing us to use FN rifles. We were still expected to wear the requisite Police uniform, but were now also allowed to wear a camouflage jacket. That's why Harry had taken his camouflaged jacket when I first arrived in Centenary. Ammunition was increased to a more robust twenty rounds per man – but the amount was still way off from being enough for a good fight, but at least the odds were somewhat better than before.

The Standoff with a Murderer:

Shoko and I were once given information by a local farm labourer that there was a murderer living in a nearby farm compound. The informer also told us in which hut the criminal was staying, so we formulated a plan. Early the following morning, dressed in our kit, we took up our firearms and departed from Centenary Police station. Arriving at the farm, we stopped the Land Rover some distance away and moved quietly down toward the compound. It was important not to spook the suspect. There was a six-foot diamond-mesh fence surrounding the perimeter and we forced open the gate at the bottom entry wide enough to allow us to squeeze through. With no further cover available, we strode purposefully down the worn road toward the hut which we knew housed the alleged criminal. Fortunately for us the whole compound was quiet, with no dogs barking. The first rays of dawn stretched across the early morning sky, as the sun started to rise over the hills in the distance. We could see quite well and quickly made our way toward the far fence, cautiously approaching the round mud-and-thatch hut, stopping just short of the entrance. Aware that our target was armed with, at the very least, a .38 revolver that he had stolen from a house in Salisbury, we also knew full well that he would have no compunction about using it.

Our mutual hand signals and nods acknowledged that this was it. Together we launched our entry, smashing down the hut door and quickly taking hold of and capturing the occupant from his smelly bed. We unceremoniously hauled him outside and handcuffed him, before his eyes could adjust to the sunlight. He was nearly naked, his hair was long and uncombed, and he stank to high heaven of unwashed-clothes and urine. On realising what had just transpired, his unshaven face leered provocatively at us and he started to yell intense abuse at us. He belligerently threatened to 'take out' our families and do other unspeakable things. During this tirade, I went back into the hut to search for evidence. The hut was dark and smelt stale but, in seconds, I found a loaded revolver tucked under the blankets that he had been sleeping on. When I went back outside, I immediately perceived a change. Something in the man's aggressive manner had triggered a volcanic rage in Shoko and his whole face had transformed. I could see him literally begin to boil, as the verbal onslaught continued to rain upon us with relentless derision. Obviously the man believed he was untouchable. As I took in the situation, Shoko suddenly seized the man, undid the handcuffs and flung them aside. He turned, removed the revolver from my grasp and blatantly placed it on the ground between them ... and stood back. His intentions were crystal clear.

An extremely tense moment now arose. The silence was both instant and deafening! For a long moment, the man took in what was in front of him: a loaded gun and a very angry policeman. The man swallowed. He was intently aware that he had every opportunity in the world to grab the gun and make a fight of it, but, clearly, he was unsure of taking on Shoko's wrath. Acutely realising that things were beyond negotiation, I gently married my hand with my Walther 9mm pistol, just in case. The seconds ticked by ... and continued, but at no stage did Shoko flinch. He just glared and his face said it all.

'Take it, bastard ... at your peril.'

Under this unflinching challenge, the man began to wither. He slowly backed down, resigned to his fate. Shoko was in control again, no nonsense tolerated. With the man safely locked into the back of the Landy, we drove back to Centenary Police Station, unable to conceal our broad grins. When we came across Cassidy, we walked coolly past him as though this was your everyday arrest but, inwardly, we were bursting to share the account with our colleagues. They would appreciate the intricacies of the incident. The arrested man turned out to be a hardened criminal, whom the police had been chasing for close to six months. Whilst we knew he had committed crimes, we did not know that he was wanted for the savage murder of eight people and innumerable armed robberies. It was immensely satisfying to know that this butcher was behind bars.

By this stage, I had spent ten months working in the Centenary area. I knew its topography like a second skin. From our daily patrols, Shoko and I got to visit, and become familiar with every farm and their layouts, as well as every Catholic mission station, store or locality that existed. We made it our business to get to know every road, every turn, and even took notes of the many footpaths that led between farms, or linked locations. We could give you the names of all the farms, the owners, the names of their head farm workers and more. We underestimated nothing and no detail was too small or unworthy to be noted. In fact, we knew the area so well that when the cardiograph people came to update their maps, they got all their information on changes in the area from Shoko and myself. Such were our records and the extent of the knowledge that we'd garnered, that even details like the width of a small bridge, or a new road, were known to us.

Keith in the Zambezi Valley

The South Africans leave:

Up until August 1975, the South African Police force had been stationed at Centenary, alongside the Rhodesians. They provided additional manpower in the effort to contain the increasing terrorism in the area. However, politics were becoming more sensitive and, with pressure from the global giants, they and other groups were pulled out, effectively severing the overt co-operation Rhodesia had with South Africa. With them went the helicopters, leaving us with diminished air power. Cassidy was not overly distressed to see them go. Some of these guys had proved to be a handful, usually due to drunken behaviour, or worse, for cases of accidental discharge of weapons in their camp. To a traditionalist like Cassidy, this cowboy-like conduct was an anathema and, in all honesty, it didn't sit well with us, either. The loss of the helicopters, however, was a blow. Consequently, the local Police were elevated to handling more terrorist incidents.

Actions increase:

The days became busier, duties amplified. Information came in that a group of five terrorists were seen staying in a small brick house about an hour up the road, which had been unoccupied for a while. We knew that we had to react speedily, in order to maximise our chances of finding them, so we grabbed up all our military gear and headed for the Landy. I knew the house well and was assigned to navigate. We stopped a few kilometres short of the house, so that we could make our way on foot and retain the element of surprise. I led the way as planned, having first instructed the Section Officer who had been left with the truck, to remain on stand-by at his radio. The night was inky black, and there was no moon. The intention was to position ourselves on the flank of the house and then radio for the truck to approach the house at speed, with its lights on full, thereby giving us a visual target of the premises. We arrived at the house and carefully, and quietly, positioned ourselves in the optimum places to control exit points and windows. The radio call went out: 'In position.' As we were the only operational team in the area, we could bypass standard radio procedure and keep things basic, without having to use identification codes. Duly summoned, the vehicle came bursting onto the scene and we readied ourselves for contact. In the next moment, the Section Officer, still going at full speed, opened fire on the house. He had a belt-fed GPMG 7.62mm machine gun mounted on the vehicle roof and proceeded to unleash it, in a full onslaught, on the cottage. A torrent of tracer rounds screamed into the house, pumping it full of holes. Within seconds, the structure was virtually pulverised. He drew to a sudden halt just outside the building, which was still illuminated by the vehicle lights. We left our positions and drew forward to inspect the results. After witnessing this single-handed attack and the relentless hail of bullets, it seemed extremely unlikely the terrs would have survived such a heated barrage. 'Bloody hell, it's like a sieve,' remarked one. Trouble was, it really was. Full of holes and with nothing inside it. No terrs, no spoor, no hit. We searched the place and it was evident the informer had lied. Whenever we received bad information to which we had reacted, we referred to it as a 'lemon.' This was a typical lemon.

Cassidy called me into his office one day. He told me that he had been asked to set up a Ground Coverage crew and wanted me to run it. Special Branch had its range of targets in respect of National Security and it concentrated on informers and the like. Ground Coverage was a toned-down version of Special Branch. My job would be to gather information about terrorist activities in the area and, in order to do so, I would need to drop my normal police work. The task would necessitate a move from the Centenary Police Station to set up a new camp on a vacant farm, using the existing buildings as headquarters for this purpose. My normal Policing days were over and I was now going to be involved almost exclusively in anti-terrorist activities for the rest of my career. I had learnt hard and fast during my stay at Centenary and the lessons I learnt from my experienced colleagues would set me right on track for my future tasks.

The incursions of terrorists, and the number of terrorist incidents, had steadily increased to such an extent that we now pushing many hours of work into military actions, rather than normal Policing. Every morning, seven days a week, we would sit at the main station radio and type out the sitreps being broadcast by all the stations, including Umvukwes, Mount Darwin and Bindura. These reports went to the various heads of departments, such as the Police, CID and Special Branch. The sitreps would contain items of information regarding terrorist-related incidents that occurred in the Operation Hurricane area, such as land mines, farm attacks, murders, etc. All this information would be discussed by the heads of departments and actions taken, where necessary. The other task that we had was the monitoring of the farm-radio network called Agric-Alert. This was a radio system whereby farmers could activate an alarm if they were under attack and also communicate with one another, or with the Centenary Charge Office. The alarm from this system was so loud it would wake us up instantly, bolt upright, and we would spring into our combat gear and head straight to the Charge Office to find out what was happening. Generally an alarm meant a farm attack, so it was serious.

5

Ground Coverage

Whistlefield Farm was specifically chosen as the base for our new Intelligence venture, mainly because of its central position in the Centenary farming area. In earlier days, this particular farm was the second farmhouse to have been attacked by terrorists and it was this attack that had initiated Operation Hurricane, which had started the so-called Second War of Liberation. Shoko and Constable Jena were included in the Ground Coverage team. As always, Kenneth, my inimitable batman, came along, too. I also had the services of two black Police Reservists to act as guards on the station, when the regulars went on patrol. The farm was located some 30 minutes up the main road from Centenary, in a Northerly direction. If you continued up on the tar road past Whistlefield, you would eventually come to the top of the escarpment which bordered the slopes of the great Zambezi River valley.

The farmhouse was of simple design and consisted of three bedrooms, a lounge, kitchen and bathroom. Two of the bedrooms were turned into offices, one of which contained the radio network. One of the first things I had to do was to establish suitable camp defences, as none existed. With some serious sweat and long hours, we dug four shelters around the inside of the perimeter fence. These were a good 7 feet deep and shaped like a cube. They would provide us with an escape under heavy artillery attacks. The roof was overlaid with eucalyptus poles and capped with a huge mound of soil. There was a sloping entrance (no steps ... easier to slide in, if under attack). Basically, we geared ourselves to rush into the bunkers if under mortar attack, but to hold our position in a small-arms attack. As further protection to the house, I came up with an idea. Six-inch girth eucalyptus poles were suspended vertically across every window, in a semi-loose format, to absorb bullets and stop rockets from being shot through the glass panes. The hanging poles would absorb the impact of bullets – well, that was the idea. Blankets served as curtains, as their heaviness would provide far better protection from shards and flying debris than light-duty material. If you soak a blanket in water and hang it up, it acts as a good bullet catcher, or so one chap had previously told me. How the hell we were going to get the blankets sodden during a firefight, with bullets flying around, was still a conundrum, but the idea still retained appeal. Besides, in light of the fact that we had no other window cover, we had nothing to lose by trying.

Every few weeks, we would run through our defence tactics. We would stage a mock attack and rehearse our procedures, so that they became second nature. Carrying our weapons, radios and medical kits, we practiced diving in to the bunkers, repeating the procedure to improve our times in both getting into position and returning fire. With speed being integral to survival, I would hound the guys to concentrate on moving at a fast pace and with purpose. On one occasion during practice, Shoko dove into the bunker - with full kit - only to re-emerge at superhuman speed – minus his kit. We were all rendered speechless at what had just transpired in front of us, but all the time Shoko was yelling blue murder. *What the hell? Were we under attack? Had he gone mad?* For a second, all was in chaos. When Shoko was able to adequately express himself, we found out that a huge cobra had obstructed his entry into the bunker. We surmised that this 'nyoka" must have selected the bunker entry-hole as his perfect winter rest. One thing for sure was that the cobra was profoundly disenchanted at Shoko's unwelcome arrival and would not budge.

Eventually we had to smoke it out. It is a well-known fact that the local black folk generally fear snakes greatly. If there is one thing that can produce a marked reduction in their facial pigmentation, it's a snake. Even after the snake had been decapitated, Shoko refused to go anywhere near the remains. There is a saying that if there was one snake, then its partner would not be too far away - which holds no truth - but it sure had Shoko occupied for the rest of the week hunting under every old tyre, brick or pile of wood that lay around.

The Mad Men:

Surrounding the camp was a 6-foot diamond-mesh fence, with four strands of barbed wire atop. In the front of the camp there was a dirt road, which led to our next door neighbour's farm. We often used to find small piles of rocks heaped in the middle of this road and could never fathom who was putting them there. We had been warned by Special Branch to be vigilant about looking out for unusual signs like these. Things out of the ordinary could represent signs left by terrorists that they had planted land mines in the road. The piles of rocks had to be cleared every time we saw them, and exasperatingly enough we had to treat each one as though there was a land mine nearby. It was only after some time, on a late Sunday afternoon, whilst I sat on the verandah of the house that I saw him. An old man, industriously collecting stones, and putting them into piles in the middle of the road. He was dressed in a dirty, tattered, brown overcoat.

'Shoko - look at what I have.' I called softly, as I simultaneously reached for my hat and headed out of the perimeter fence to investigate. Shoko was right beside me and immediately approached the old man.

'Ewe, muruquita chi panapa' (Hey, what are doing here?) he enquired, forgoing the traditional greeting. The man didn't respond, but carried on with his most urgent task. Shoko was about to re-peat the question, but stopped in mid-breath!

'Ishe, this man is mad, totally *penga* (mad). He's never going to listen to me.' With that he turned to walk back to the camp, shaking his head. I observed the old man again. Looking at his threadbare clothes, the unkempt hair and his one-pointed ob-session, it was clear that he existed in his own world. He didn't even realise I was standing next to him. Shoko's assessment was correct. There was nothing we could do to dissuade this old man's actions; obviously he had to collect stones. We let him be. Despite our new knowledge, we still treated piles of stones as suspicious. Nothing could be taken for granted; trust was a cau-tious virtue afforded only to those you knew exceptionally well. But I can tell you that whenever we came across yet another 'cannot-ignore pile of stones', we wished blight upon the mad old man whose strange world so consistently interfered with ours.

In actual fact, there were a surprising number of 'mad' men around. We were once patrolling a farm on foot and, despite our state of constant awareness, we literally fell over a body. It was a man who was sleeping next to a tree. This guy was plainly straight from the bush. He had long, grass-filled hair that fell down past his shoulders in a manner that reminded me of a Rastafarian. He wore very little, but what was astonishing was that he blended entirely into the natural vegetation - so much so that it was virtually impossible to see him. We could tell, though, that he was at peace and in total harmony with his environment. He did not speak to us, nor did we to him. We simply moved on, leaving him to his natural home. Presumably he lived off a diet of predominantly roots and fruits, probably augmented by Mopani worms and grasshoppers. His integration appeared so complete that successful rehabilitation seemed extremely remote.

A few years later, we were in the vicinity of a small village when we came across an extraordinary sight. It was a man chained to a strung wire. The wire ran between two large trees, across a distance of about 20 feet. A light chain was locked around his ankle. He must have been in his late thirties, appeared mad as a hatter, and stank to high heaven. There were metal bowls lying near the tree indicating that the family in the nearby kraal must have been feeding him, but they certainly didn't bathe or clothe him. He probably only got washed during the summer rains. Incredulously, one of the trees that served as his captive had taken on the shape of a chair and even more astounding was that it had taken on the form of his body. This must have resulted from him sitting in this 'tree chair' for probably most of his life. We had encountered many peculiar and disturbing matters in our police work and this rated as one of the most odd. The situation was complicated, though. The ways of these people may have been incomprehensible to others, but it was not always clear-cut, or as it might appear at first sight. We were not qualified to make a call on the psychological aspects of this anyway! The processes would have to take their course. Over the years, one thing I did learn was not to make hasty judgements and, as far as was possible, strive to understand why things were the way they were.

Tough farmers

Centenary had a surfeit of larger-than-life characters who farmed in the area. These farmers had invested everything they had in their land. They were tough and resilient. They worked hard … and, on occasion, many drank hard, too. One of the favoured recreational pursuits in the district was a round or two of golf at the Centenary Country Club, followed by a round, or seven, in the pub. On one memorable occasion, after finishing up their game, some of the farmers chose to stay on, perhaps a little too long! By about ten o'clock that night the numbers had dwindled, leaving only a few, including a tough, stocky chap called Angus Mctavish. Mctavish lived on a farm on the extreme

East of the District, in the corner of the Chiweshe Tribal Trust area and the neighbouring Mount Darwin farming community. Living on this remote farm, tucked away into the granite hills and thick bush, must have held challenges on many levels. Angus was well-known, also, for owning a feisty Jack Russell dog that would dive into the deep end of the swimming-pool and retrieve anything you threw in it. It was a great trick.

Now, that particular night, Angus was three sheets to the wind and was making his way back to the farm, a 20 kms journey on the meandering farm roads, when his vehicle broke down. He knew he would have to get back home, or the radio alarm would be set off by his wife and the whole area would be out looking for him. He had to walk past a number of farms on the way; most of them were about 1500 to 3000 hectares in size. He also knew that all the farmers in the area were armed to the bloody teeth and were very vigilant and alert for anything out of the ordinary. Dogs barking would be one of the warnings they would take heed of. Angus certainly didn't want his butt shot off, so he decided his best form of announcement was to start singing as he walked past the farms, hoping like heck that the residents would recognise his voice. Only problem was he couldn't remember any good songs, so he made up his own and sang it as loud as he could, with a stagger and a cough in between.

'I'm Angus Mctavish.......,

I'mmmmmm Angussssss Mctaaaaaavish.......'

That was the song and he was heard singing it all the way home. By the time he eventually reached his house, he was in huge trouble with his wife - no doubt wishing in that moment that he was NOT Angussssssss Mctaaaaaaavish.

Amongst the farmers were some who owned small planes, generally Cessna's, and they often had their own private airstrips, too. Back then, it was not unusual for the planes to fly around 1000 feet and, if the aircraft ever encountered a problem, the pilot would find the nearest open road and land. Contending with heavy traffic volumes was not one of the worries with which Rhodesians in the remote areas had to contend. A chap called Les Jellicoe had a wealth of flying experience and one day he was flying back from Salisbury, when his engine suddenly cut out. Unfortunately, when the engine cut, there were no immediate tar roads in the area and the nearest open ground was a freshly-ploughed maize field. No problem for Jellicoe ... he performed a landing with the wheels down in the mealie field – a pretty cool feat, we thought.

All of the farmers who owned planes formed part of the Police Reserve Air Wing, or PRAW, and were often called up to react to terrorist sightings. On one of the planes, we had removed the rear cargo door and installed a .303 Browning machine gun, complete with prismatic sights. This improvisation achieved effective results and was the platform for taking out a band of terrorists with one burst from the gun – considering the gunner was shooting side-on to the target and travelling at about 200 kilometres per hour, this was pretty skilful. It was also typical of the creativeness that Rhodies drew on at a time where resources were in short supply. A friend of mine in the Police called Peter Beck, was also involved in helping to make this a reality.

Jena the soccer fan:

Constable Jena was a member of our Ground Coverage Team and, as it turned out, a very brave man as well. We had come across information that a group of terrorists were frequenting one of the farms on our northern border and that they often came to join in the local soccer matches held by the labourers. They had also made themselves at home with the beer, girls and festivities afterwards. They would come dressed in civilian clothes. We undertook to find out who the labourers were going to play next, as generally it would be a team of labourers from one of the neighbouring farms. The visiting team would arrive on a flat trailer, pulled by a tractor.

The only way we were going to find out about who was infiltrating the games was to infiltrate them ourselves. Not so easy. It was common for a 44-gallon drum to be found on a tractor-drawn trailer, as it often held tools for the farm. Jena agreed to hide inside such a drum, to take with him a radio and pistol, and to travel with the labourers to the games, unbeknown to them of course. With the aid of two informers from the visiting farm, we managed to get Jena onto the trailer and into his drum. We also arranged for a PATU stick to stand by, ready to react to any information Jena was able to find. The operation went fine. Jena was well-positioned; in fact, maybe too well, as he was extremely close to the soccer field. The plan was that he would keep a look-out through small holes that we had drilled in the drum and then call us back on the radio when there was something to report. We waited and waited and eventually the radio crackled into life.

'213 Charlie, this is Jena, over.'

'Roger Jena - this is 213 Charlie.'

'Ishe, there are lots of people here and I can't see if there are any of our 'friends', over,'

'Okay, let's wait to see what happens,' came my reply.

The wait was endless. Eventually it was dark when Jena came back on the radio saying he had enough and was getting out of the drum, and could we meet him on the road leading to the farm. I picked him up. He told me that he'd had great difficulty moving around in the drum and hadn't been able to see much. At one stage, some guys had rested up next to his drum and had even leaned against it, whilst he'd huddled breathlessly inside. The fact he could well have been within spitting distance of any potential terrorist whilst stuck inside a hot drum, took some damn gumption, I can tell you. This was no social interlude; being discovered could have had deadly consequences for him.

The end of the soccer group:

About three weeks later, some strange spoor was discovered. These tracks were found by one of our local informers on a farm overlooking the Zambezi Valley and not too far from where Jena had done his drum-hiding trick. We always had one unit on standby for events such as this. A Police Anti-Terrorist Unit (PATU) team was always on standby and prepared to follow up any such reports. A PATU stick was usually made up of four or five local farmers, who were also Police Reservists reporting to Centenary Police Station. The men were deployed and were quickly onto the spoor, but the tracks showed that the group was big, upwards of thirty terrorists, so they called for a Fire Force backup. This backup would come from Mount Darwin and would have been made up of three to four helicopters carrying four soldiers each. They would be available once the terrorists had been spotted and not before. The country just didn't have enough resources to have this valuable part of the defence flying around all the time. There also would have been a 'push-me-pull-me' fixed-wing aircraft, with an engine and propeller at the front and the same at the rear of the plane. The push-me- pull-me was a spotter aircraft that would fly high above any battle scene, controlling the movement of soldiers. It was armed with two Napalm bombs and had machine guns mounted on its wings. Fire Force was a Rhodesian invention and was instrumental in the annihilation of countless terrorists ... a highly-efficient killing-machine. Generally, the main helicopter commander would be in an Alouette 3, mounted with a 20mm cannon, and was always called '6.'

Sam, the tracker, came with the PATU unit. The spoor led all the way from the farm, down into the depths of the mountainous escarpment and possibly beyond toward the Zambezi River and then north, onwards towards Zambia. Sam indicated that these tracks were carelessly left and that these terrorists were on a mission to get the hell out of Rhodesia as fast as they could and into the relative safety of Zambia. It was decided to place an ambush group up ahead on the river at the base of the escarpment, where the river disgorged itself onto the open plains of the Valley. The ambush team of five men had been driven in by Land Rover. Their first undertaking was to do a quick recce of the river and its surrounds. They found no tracks, so it was clear that the terrorists were still on their hurried way down the steep gorge made by the river. We all hoped that they had not seen the deployment of the ambush team. The gooks were being followed by the PATU team, and additional men were being hastily rounded up to bolster their numbers. Fire Force, with its helicopter-borne troops and gunships, was on standby in neighbouring Mount Darwin, not twenty minutes' flight away from any potential contacts with the enemy. In addition, the Fire Force team would await definite feedback, as they could also have been pulled off this standby situation and onto another in minutes.

The PATU stick, which by now had been joined by another four PATU men, eventually caught the gooks in a steep ravine and all hell broke loose. Ferocious fire raged in every direction. At the end of the battle 36 gooks lay dead; none escaped. The PATU guys suffered no losses. This represented the biggest number of terrorists killed in one battle in the Centenary area to date, and was the end of 'The Soccer group' as they had become known to us. The lift to our forces was palpable; this was the kind of unmitigated success that galvanised and united our small numbers.

A year later, I walked down this treacherous river line with Matt Taylor. The area was scorching hot. As we descended, it was patently clear, from the steep hills on both sides of the river, that escape would have been impossible for the terrs. In these inhospitable surrounds, we found four skeletal remains. Two of the skulls exhibited half-inch blue marks below each eye socket, as well as marks on the forehead. This told me they had been from the Karanga tribe. The Karanga had a custom where they would cut two small slits into their skin and then rub ash from a particular tree into the wounds. The cuts healed, but left scars. These resulting scars would swell up, similar to a person who had Keloid disorder. It was this ash that would discolour the skulls, leaving distinctive marks.

As the river broke through the vast mountain range of the escarpment, it fell, in cold veils, over rocks and splashed into a sparkling clear pool 35 feet below. Sowe Falls was named after the river. In my time in the area, I was fortunate enough to get back to see the falls three more times. It was well worth the tough four-hour walk through the thick bush. Sowe Falls was magnificent. It had a peace and tranquillity that bore no correlation to the fierce battle that had once raged here. It offered a little bit of heaven, a chance to take stock, to let the world pass and to forget mankind's politics.

My team and I spent many months in information-gathering and ground-coverage operations, and long hours were spent in collating details and following up on leads, feeding back information and keeping close to all the activities in the region. Routine formed no part of our day; every day was different. In time, some of the intensity had eased off in the Centenary area and so, after serving its purpose, Whistlefield camp was closed down. I was tasked to move to the Zambezi Valley to open up a new police camp in the Gutsa area. A shortfall of men was again a problem. This move was a formidable one. The area we were going to was as remote as you could find. Aside from the environmental challenges, the chances of full back-up and immediate support in a contact were zero! Zut! Aziko!

6

The Zambezi River Camp (Gutsa)

To reach the Great Zambezi Valley you would travel north from Centenary, through the farming areas and, in time, descend down the escarpment to the valley below. In those years, entry into the valley consisted of a single, rough, dirt track, which wound this way and that, round thick bush and large boulders and across river cuttings. In many places, nature's natural obstacles like erosion, broken trees or wildlife formed the greatest hazards. Sections of the road had extremely steep angles. Care had to be taken not to slip off the side of the track and plummet headfirst down into the gorge below. In those parts of the road that had been washed away by the rains, the only way to continue was to repair the road damages. I found out that by positioning a person and sufficient kit in the right spot, on the opposite side of the vehicle, that I could balance a Land Rover on three wheels sufficiently enough to change a punctured tyre. Without a glut of options at our disposal, we forged on. On that journey, my six-week driving course was looking decidedly tame, compared to the gamut that this 'road' was putting in my path.

The Zambezi Valley is massive, with a basin of more than 1,330,000 square kilometres. It is a wide, flat area, bordered by mountain ranges on both sides. The Zambezi River itself starts its journey in the North-West of Zambia and undulates, twists and turns through an incredible 2,574 kilometre passage, before flowing into the Indian Ocean at a point north of Beira in Mozambique. The river and its myriad of tributaries, like the Luangua, Kafue, Mazoe and Shire, supports large populations of humans and animal life in over seven countries. It is also home to species like cichlids, tiger fish and cat fish. It is life-blood to millions. One of this rivers' most noted features are the spectacular Victoria Falls, truly one of Nature's most breath-taking splendours. The water plunges down as a spectacular torrent, roaring mightily over thousands of rocks, to fall hundreds of metres below, sending up vast plumes of spray. The Vic Falls mark the natural boundary between the upper and middle sections of the Zambezi River.

One of the Zambezi Valley's legendary characteristics is its severe temperatures, which often soar to over 45 degrees Celsius during October and get no lower than seventeen degrees in winter. We jokingly called October 'suicide month', but the truth was that it was so searingly hot at times that it was no wonder that mortal expiry would have been preferred as a welcome relief. Hotter than hell, it was. It was impossible to move between 11h00 in the morning to 14h30 in the afternoon. Rhodies shortened the name to simply 'The Valley' and any troopies who ever served in the area will attest to its unsympathetic nature. Remote, hostile and, for the most part, still very wild. Here malaria was a constant scourge, tsetse flies reigned, lions and elephants were plentiful and there were a vast range of Africa's most deadly beasties that could shorten your life, if fate decreed. Being so isolated, this region offered decidedly little in the way of mankind's comforts within its vast expanse. If I did not keep my wits about me, I could considerably increase the unwelcome expectancy of a bumpy trip back into town in a body box.

Three of us, Shoko, an old black police reservist and I moved to Gutsa in the Valley. We were later joined by a National Serviceman called Kavenar. Gutsa was located about 20 kilometres towards the Zambezi River, from the base of the escarpment. As our bush-beaten Land Rover approached, we could make out our new HQ up ahead. It was cunningly disguised as an old house. Not quite a palace because that was just what it was: an old house. It also lacked the few basics, like electricity and inside running water. We quickly found out that water was only obtainable from an outside tap. It came from an old diesel borehole just in front of the house that supplied not only the new 'Police Station', but also Chief Gutsa's kraal and a few taps along the road used by other kraals. The borehole was sunk next to the small, often dried-up river that we overlooked from the verandah of the house. The building was an old District Commissioner's 'travel' house. In prior days, the area had been administered by the Ministry of Internal affairs and, as such, the District Commissioner, or any of his deputies, would have used the house during their trips to the valley to assist

Stores like One Stop were a gathering point for local folks

in administration of the rural folks. With the bush war escalating the house was no longer used, so it became assigned to our section. The white paint was fading away in many patches and the neglected corrugated iron roof was showing signs of dilapidation. A 6-foot, diamond-mesh fence surrounded the entire property, a property that boasted one 'luxury' ... a swimming-pool. But before the image of an extravagant lifestyle springs to mind, the only real relationship it bore to 'luxury' was its luxuriant green colour from all the algae. Going forward, the swimming-pool actually became our fridge, mainly because there was nothing else in which to keep things at a cooler temperature – even if it was tepid, it was preferable to boiling.

On the one side of the entrance driveway were three, 5000-litre, steel, diesel drums. This would have been a boon to any unit that was utilising diesel-powered vehicles, but held little value to us as we were driving a petrol Land Rover. Our petrol supply had to be brought in, using 44-gallon drums. The diesel was therefore used only for heavy Army or Internal Affairs trucks if they ever came past, and our little borehole for the water. Leading up to the house, along the dusty road, were huts and various kraals where people lived. Chief Gutsa lived next door to the Police Station, in his sprawling kraal. He was in charge of the local people who lived in this area, and his authority stemmed from the old days, long before any outside visitors arrived. The area had some huge trees and their shade offered a modicum of welcome relief from the blistering heat, even if limited. The kraals nearby were neat, with two or three conical, thatch-roofed huts. They were made in the age-old way with sticks, grass and polished earth floors. Each kraal was surrounded by a rough perimeter made from cut logs. The people grew maize in any spare patch they could find. The fields were not large and were more higgledy-piggledy than arranged. There was also the usual small section where cattle and goats would be kept overnight, surrounded again by prerequisite logs designed to try and keep lions out. Chickens and ducks would wander around the kraals, scratching for food and, at night, they would roost under a small hut, built on stilts for protection. By far, the majority of people owned virtually no material wealth at all and survived mainly on subsistence-farming from the land.

There was a single convenience store to serve the entire area, called 'One Stop.' The owner sold glass-bottled Coca-Cola, maize meal, tinned beans, batteries for radios, a few odd bits of clothing, matches, paraffin for lamps and cooking purposes, and soap. The store had the usual corrugated iron roof, and had been painted with lime wash many years ago, but now had worn and dirty patches where people had been leaning up against the walls. One Stop was the focal point of people wanting to socialise and have a chat. One would often see the younger folks idling or milling around, talking. The larger-than-life owner of the store was one of the only wealthy people in the area and swelled his income by selling quantities of bottled beer on weekends. The noise and racket from some of the people who indulged and partied could be plainly heard from the police station. Most of them had precious little money for alcohol, but drank nonetheless. The shop owner also sold a homemade, distilled drink called 'One Days.' The name originated from the fact that this ninety-per-cent-proof alcohol was distilled from maize in one day. The stuff was ruddy lethal. Many of the folks who drank at One Stop were older men who would get absolutely paralytic from half a bottle of One Days. They would often become argumentative and, on occasion, would try to beat up their wives when they eventually found their way home.

I cannot tell you how many times we were called across to break up domestic disputes. There were even times where a husband would have been pulverised by his wife and we would have to separate the warring couple and attend to the cuts and bruises, or worse. Women were not allowed to drink at One Stop store - a cultural rule. Actually, One Days was an illegal drink and one could get jailed for selling, or even drinking it. In general, our police policy was to uphold the Law, but trying to stop its usage would have been like trying to stem a river with a toothpick, and no doubt would have started a veritable riot. The local women also made One Days from corn that they grew around their huts. In addition, they brewed up a 'healthy' local beer that was made from sorghum. It was a heavy beer and all the ingredients stayed inside it, so it had all sorts of 'heavy mush' at the bottom. The beer was most often served from dry calabashes, which were grown around the kraals. Drinking this beer was an acquired taste for someone who did not grow up with it; however, I never acquired a taste for either of these brews.

There were neither telephones nor electricity in the whole area, so communication with the outside world was non-existent. When the roads were sufficiently improved, a bus would periodically pass through, stopping at some of the kraals and at the store to drop off any post and pick up passengers intent on shopping in Centenary, some 100 kilometres away. The highlight of the day would be when the bus chugged in, amid clouds of dust, and disgorged its contents of people, including their suitcases and chickens. All luggage was stored on the roof of the bus and, on arrival, the driver, plus his assistant, would clamber up onto the roof of the bus and hurl suitcases and bundles down to the waiting passengers below. It took some skill to catch a fully-laden, flying suitcase and not get flattened. Nobody owned a car and anybody with a bicycle was considered upwardly-mobile and rich. The few assets that people did own would be treasured and taken care of. One would typically see a husband walking next to his bicycle to save the tyres, whilst he draped his shoes around his neck to stop them from getting dirty. Just before he got to his destination, he would put on his clean shoes and ride his bicycle, thus arriving in style and looking his best. The local women did not ride bicycles – another cultural rule. If a family was off to visit friends for a few days, the family column would be led firstly by the husband, walking next to his bicycle followed, at about 4 metres behind, by his wife (or wives), who would be carrying all their luggage and babies, with the older children clinging to their skirts or walking, carrying bundles of their own. Such was their strength that many wives would have a baby on her back, bundles to carry, small children walking alongside her, and still be able to balance a heavy object on her head. Having more than one wife was regarded as a good thing for a man. He would have more work done for him, and any daughters that the wives produced could be sold to future husbands in exchange for cattle, via an age-old custom known as '*Lobola*.' In fact, one only got a wife by adhering to the practice of *Lobola*. The prospective husband was first vetted by the bride-to-be's father and, if he was considered suitable and had sufficient money or cattle, the transaction would be agreed upon. With Shona culture, if the husband died, his brother would then 'marry' his sister in law. In this way, there were no older, single women and it was an effective means whereby the community could look after its own.

Women tilled the lands, cooked the food, did the washing, kept house, looked after the kids and, in general, attended to all the needs of the husband. They were considered to be subservient to the men and would have to serve their husbands and male guests when their husbands had friends over for a party. They also swept the area around their huts, and within the small kraal area, every morning. As I travelled along any dirt road in the early morning on my rounds, I would see all the womenfolk cleaning the sandy patch around the kraals. The custom behind this was that any bad things from the past would be swept away in preparation for a new day. Sons, on the other hand, were regarded as an asset for later on in life, when the boys would be expected to look after their father during his retirement period.

Shoko and I needed to fully acquaint ourselves with the area that we were sanctioned to oversee in our role as policemen. As was our custom, we strove to learn every detail to the 'nth degree, but it was a big task. We took the Land Rover out to the furthest parts. The going was often tough, with the roads sometimes barely visible or, in places, simply no longer there. We would have to carve our way through riverbeds that had not seen a vehicle in years. Thick vines, fallen trees and long thatching-grass, made travelling down the road a venture that held no assurance of a successful arrival at the end point. We often had to stop and cut through fallen trees. Thickets of thorny Jess bush had begun to encroach across the roads in some places and driving through that would guarantee four flat tyres, so we had to be very careful how we went. Nobody lived in these far-off parts, but we still made it our business to understand the terrain. The areas were as wild as David Livingstone would have found in his travels more than 200 years earlier, when he explored the interior of Africa to find the source of the Nile. We regularly encountered wild animals such as elephants, buffalo, baboons, lions and snakes, and were careful to never hinder their natural routes or behaviour. In my later game-ranging days, I continued to observe this practice.

In our journeys, we came across some beautiful spots. Some of these could be found along the Mzingedzi River. The Mzingedzi was the largest river running through the area. It eventually joined the great Zambezi River. If time ever allowed, we would stop. At times like this, I would sit on the banks of the river listening to the sounds of the bush and its many inhabitants, from the small winged ones to its much larger residents. It would take me back to when I was on the farm as a young boy and to the endless hours that I spent ensconced with Nature, immersed in my own world. Mother Africa can be a formidable parent, but also a great healer. The day's light would tell us when it was time to continue the journey. It was better to leave the distant sections well before the sun disappeared and caught us out late. The Zambezi Valley was a route through which terrorists would infiltrate from Zambia and Mozambique and we had to be mindful of that.

We sometimes needed to travel to a place called Hoya. Hoya was desolate and had only a group of coloured soldiers to protect it. These soldiers fell under The Rhodesian Defence Regiment. In the Southern African region, children that resulted from black and white relationships were commonly called coloureds. The village was located deep within the Valley and was situated on top of a small hill, more like a rise as opposed to a hill, as the area was almost as flat as a billiard table. It lay to the North East of Gutsa and we would have to travel for 3 hours on rough roads to get to it. The coloured soldiers were a rough bunch of characters. There were twelve of them and they protected the local Internal Affairs men who were stationed there as well. Suspicions were always rife that they were not averse to indulging in some pot-smoking, but one thing was certain - they had the best sense of humour. Their accents were very different and we would be highly entertained by their stories and jokes the whole time we were together. They had a very relaxed style and their uniforms were never worn as the regulations demanded. I had no jurisdiction over them, though, as they were army men. The three Internal Affairs men at Hoya were as young as I was. Their job was to ensure the development of the local people in agriculture, education and other matters relating to normal village life. I was responsible for Law and Order in the area, but I must say we never had problems from Hoya.

Experience taught me to respect the land and its ways as much as it taught me how to best implement Law and Order to ensure a stable flow in everyday life in the region. I was always a great believer in good communications and strove to keep in touch with as many people as I could throughout the Valley. Keeping things in order, maintaining statistics, administering to the local population, applying first aid when needed and monitoring movements in and out of this vast area, kept our small police camp very busy .... and lean. We carried no extra weight, either physically or in our requirements; the bare basics were our norm. Nights were often disrupted with call outs and we never knew what to expect. Invariably, gut instinct was our best tool. Socialising was as rare as the prospect of meeting Harold Wilson, or having lobster for supper. Police work was our day and night, and the simple life was our way of existence, no frills, no fat.

Mzarabani:

Six months later, I was called to a meeting in Centenary with Cassidy.

'A new camp is going to be built at Mzarabani,' I was informed. In the beginning, the choice of location was not unanimous. The powers that be insisted it be placed at the foot of the hills, believing that from there we could vet the movement of vehicles coming and going from the valley. To my way of thinking, however, there were two problems with this position. Firstly, the camp was far too close to the hills and any attack from unfriendlies would be to their advantage, as they would have the high ground. Secondly, there would be no radio communication with our base station, Centenary, if we were to use the normal radio we had. Unfortunately, these observations did not find a supportive ear and, despite my concerns, the camp went up at the foot of the hills.

Without any further ado, the first truckload of tools, cement and wood arrived the following month, together with a live-wire character called Bruno. Bruno was Italian and hailed from Sicily. His broad accent when cussing the workers was as comical as his attire. He wore long shorts and a summer shirt, with a broad-brimmed hat and packed a 44-magnum revolver on his right hip. The long shorts, wide hat and long-barrelled revolver attached to a short, stocky man called Bruno, brandishing a hot temper, was wonderful, humorous relief from the hardships of the area. Bruno actually couldn't wait to 'get the hell out of here' and his workers were passionately slave-driven as a result. We would hear him bellowing at his staff early in the morning – even before our morning tea. His stories of life back in Sicily were always filled with wild hand gestures and load-heavy phrases in Italian. The new camp was up in record time and it was a sad day when we had to say goodbye to Bruno and his team. We missed the fun and his unique company.

In our previous camp, a little over 800 metres from the base of the mountains, we could contact Centenary easily with the radio we had in the Land Rovers, so it was frustrating to be in the shadow of the mountain now, with no communications at all. Following a very solitary month, our communication problems were solved later with the installation of the highest radio mast I had ever seen. The camp itself was made up of prefabricated buildings constructed entirely of wooden slats, with an asbestos roof. It had the mandatory diamond fence surrounding it. The refrigerators were run on paraffin and therefore had no freezer capacity and would occasionally stop working altogether. At best, the contents of the fridge would get only moderately cool. We would then have to wait for a chap to come all the way from Salisbury to fix them. The stations' radios ran off batteries, which were charged by a small generator.

Take the fridge on a game drive:

On one memorable occasion, one of our two chest refrigerators had given up the ghost and we waited and waited for a technician from Salisbury. It wasn't long before our meagre supplies started to rot. It was hot, events had been demanding and my tolerance levels failed. I got really mad with the system. I loaded the faulty unit onto the Land Rover, intending to exchange it for a working one in Centenary. After driving all the way up the rocky road, wending way my through the escarpment, I reached town and explained the problem to Cassidy. Unfortunately, my powers of persuasion must have evaporated along with my sense of humour, as Cassidy promptly told me to return to our camp and await the arrival of the technician in a week's time. So, there it was ... back went the refrigerator down the rocky road. When I eventually got back to camp, and probably from pure exasperation, I started it up again and, to my utter amazement, it worked. From that day on, if we ever had a refrigerator on the blink, we took it for a ride on the rocky roads, for an outing you could say. It was a peculiar technique, but we couldn't care less; it worked and, more importantly, so did the fridge.

New folks arrive

Not a month had passed after we had moved into our new Police Station, when a whole entourage of civilians arrived at the Police Station. They told me they needed to start to map out the area of bush just to our North and East. A vast agricultural development was to take place, by a company called Tilcor, for the planting of cotton to help the local black population with employment and development. A vast tract of land was bulldozed in a couple of weeks and all the tools for farming arrived, including tractors. A couple of the huge Baobab trees were blasted out of the way, with explosives. Many of the local population got work with Tilcor, primarily as labour for weeding the fields, or picking the cotton. Some were lucky enough to get jobs as tractor drivers. Along with the fields, the bulldozers ran up an airstrip for us. We didn't have any aircraft as yet, but we knew that one day it may well be necessary to medivac somebody out of the valley, or fly in a special service.

All this development brought a whole new vibe to the valley. New stores started to crop up, selling a greater variety of products, and people actually had some money of their own. The local black population comprised an essentially peace-loving lot, who just wanted to get on with life. One of our Parliamentarians, Allan Savory, had once been scorned when he warned that 'The guerrillas only need the mass of the population to be actively passive for us to lose this war.' If only the local population had become active in the defence of their lifestyle, the terrorist problem would by and large have dissipated. The trouble was that the terrorists had been abducting local people, including children, and forcing them to support their cause. Fear stepped in and many who had previously been passive, acquiesced. In an effort to counteract this tactic, the Government employed a 'carrot and stick' approach to increase cooperation with the locals. Funds were made available to be issued to the local people, and Gutsa was no different. This is what had happened in Vietnam. Local tribe's people were offered large sums of money to point out the location of terrorists. Then there was the stick with arrests for collaborations. The plan worked for a while, until the prospect of certain death at the hands of the terrorists (as retribution for working with the Government) overshadowed the rewards offered.

Back at the new camp it was clear, from a defensive point of view, that it was in a bad position. I could have thrown a rock from the camp to the foot of the great range of hills which made up the escarpment. Any attacking party would have had a huge advantage by taking this high ground. Thumping us at night with mortars would have been child's play. Frankly put, we had no defences at all, therefore I embarked on a mission to surround the camp with a rock wall to at least prevent a walk-in; a shelter was also to be included against rocket and mortar attack. Granite rocks in the surrounding area, many of which were roughly the size of footballs, were ideal for the job and, with the help of the local cotton-growers next door, I was able to scrounge the cement we needed. Labour was easy to find and, together with all the staff at the camp, we built a magnificent six-foot wall all the way around the camp. It featured gun-ports and, on each corner, a substantial bunker commanded the area. These were, however, strictly for show as we didn't have any heavy weapons, just our personal FN rifles. Full retaliation against cannons or mortars was therefore impossible and the best we could hope for was to buy time. One thing on our side was that the gooks couldn't shoot straight, on most occasions. If they were positioned high up on the hill, trying their luck with pot shots, they would almost surely have fired too high and we would be fine. The problem was mortars, as they came down randomly and vertically, so we had to watch out for that possibility.

A generator was used to charge the 12-volt battery needed for our radio system. It also provided for a limited supply of power requirements, mainly for the charge office. However, at night we generally moved about using paraffin lamps. The generator also supplied power to the borehole pump, which pumped water into two, big, steel-water tanks. We had to balance our power requirements though, so we established a shift system and only powered up when necessary.

Shoko The Hunter:

Rats were a problem and we just couldn't get rid of the buggers. Nothing worked. The resident rodent population was proliferating daily. One day, I gave Shoko my pump action .22 rifle and told him to shoot any that he found. In the beginning, he had reasonable success; however, several days later a shot was fired, followed by an indignant howl. Nobody could figure out where the howl had come from. On tracking it down, we discovered that it came from one of the prisoners. Shoko had been walking along the top of our fancy, new perimeter wall, on the high end of the property, when he had spotted one of his targets scuttling along near the roof slates. In his haste to annihilate the rat, he had fired rapidly. Unfortunately he missed – totally - the bullet went clear through a small gap in the roof and, due to its angle, entered the prison-cell section and embedded itself in the luckless prisoner's foot. This brought Shoko's short lived 'big hunter' role to a grinding halt and nursing duties were implemented, instead.

The Escarpment Road:

Every now and then, the coloured soldiers from Hoya army camp were relieved of their duties for some R&R. They would head straight for Mount Darwin by travelling down the only road leading out of the valley and, in doing so, they would pass our camp. One day, our day's responsibilities had come to an end and we were gathered on the grass in the early evening, discussing various events. In the distance, and far up the hill, one could just make out the sound of a heavy vehicle grinding gears, as well as other decidedly peculiar sounds. We stood up to listen more intently. The clamour was increasing. Suddenly, a troop-carrying truck became visible, bearing the coloured soldiers in the back, who looked to be shouting their heads off.

'Can you hear what they are saying?' I asked rhetorically, as we cupped our ears to hear better. We strained to hear, but the army truck drowned out their voices as it ground down the steep, narrow, tar road. What was alarming was that the truck was travelling at full tilt. Bloody hell! The driver was madly trying to get the engine down to the lowest gear and the engine was whining loudly in high revs. As they drew closer, we could make out the call from the frantic soldiers.

'Get the boom opeeen.... get the boom opeeen!' they shrieked. Jeez, they've got no brakes. We rushed to the boom at the road and speedily unlocked it, just in time to get a strong whoosh of wind as the vehicle came screaming past us. They eventually scudded to a halt in a cloud of red dust by driving into the middle of Tilcor's ploughed lands. Shakily, they disembarked from their racing truck and took the shortest route to the camp's little pub - which had never seen so many clientele at one time before. The camp's coffers made a pot of money that night, as those lads happily celebrated their continued existence by cleaning out all of the liquor in stock. In the morning, I took a walk down to the vehicle - it was a total mess. I could see how the driver had been trying to scrape the vehicle against the rock cliffs to slow it down. To put it euphemistically, it must have been a nerve-wracking experience. However, when their shock levels came back down to earth, the soldiers saw the funny side of it, and so did we.

Farmer Murdered:

One of the local farmers in the Northern Centenary area had been murdered early that morning. A group of eight, heavily-armed terrs had struck. With the odds so greatly stacked against him, the farmer stood no chance. Peter Beck, a friend of mine who had trained with me at Morris Depot, was first on the scene. Peter was now stationed at Centenary. He found the crumpled body of the farmer next to a desk, where he had been paying the workers' wages. An RPG anti-tank rocket had been fired close to him and he had died, right in front of his terrified labourers, from the resultant shrapnel wounds. Peter looked around and a few metres away from the scene, was another large pool of blood - but no body. A separate blood trail left the verandah and headed off into the thick maize field. Some 300 metres into the field, they found a badly-wounded gook. His lower legs had been shattered by the same blast that had killed the farmer, and he had lost a considerable amount of blood.

I was in Centenary at the time so, having picked up Peter and his team, together with the wounded gook, we rushed him to the distant Mt Darwin hospital, about an hour and a half away. Peter worked feverishly in the back of the open Land Rover to get a drip in, but struggled. The veins had all gone - collapsed. There was not much time, and this man had a story to tell! He was the leader of the 8-man terrorist 'stick' and had been standing close to the farmer when the shooting had commenced. The conundrum was why he was shot, too, and by his own guys?

One thing the Rhodesian Forces learnt early on in the bush war was that gooks planned ahead for a worst-case scenario. They would always agree to a rendezvous point so that, if they ever got into a contact situation, they would know where to regroup. In this way, they could bombshell in different directions and meet up safely again, later. This terrorist knew he was dying, but it was apparent that he was angry. He had been double-crossed and left to die. From what Peter understood, it was a leadership issue. Despite his wounds, the gook spat out the group's rendezvous point, where the rest of the terrorists would be that evening. Peter immediately radioed this back to Centenary and a PATU stick of local farmers assembled and set off for the meeting place. Using one of the trackers, they were able to pick up spoor and proceeded to attack the now remaining 7-man group. The group was caught completely by surprise and three of the seven were killed in the contact. The other four escaped, but were now 'lost', as they had not had the chance to set a new meeting place. The area was now on the lookout for the remaining killers.

Got Ya:

The next day, Peter and I were travelling back from Centenary to the Zambezi valley and, just before we started our descent down the escarpment, we were waved down by a local black fellow. We stopped the Land Rover and he pointed urgently back down the road.

'There is a terrorist hiding back there in the bush a bit further on,' he exclaimed in urgent tones and then took off into the hills.

The first thought that went through our minds was that this was a possible ambush and that we were being set up for a hiding. However, with the knowledge that there were four terrs that were on the run, we wanted to check it out. We had to come up with a plan – fast. We had seen a large, yellow, Roads Department truck a few kilometres back. The road was being repaired. We decided that the truck would be the perfect Trojan horse. We quickly drove back down the road to find the truck driver. With his ready agreement, we grabbed our weapons and climbed into the back of the truck. The truck continued its way down the road and we psyched ourselves for an encounter, trusting that surprise would give us an advantage. As we neared the spot, the driver slowed down and Peter and I leapt from the truck whilst it was still travelling. This entailed some risk because the drop to the road was about two metres and, with our heavy kit, the possibility of injury could not be ruled out. By good fortune, we landed safely on the verge and immediately stormed into the bush, weapons at the ready, fully intent on capturing our targets. Not five metres into the long grass, we came across the gook. He was lying flat on the ground and was completely naked. He had the typical, overly woolly hair of someone who had lived for extended periods in the bush and he bore scars across his shoulders from carrying heavy packs from Mozambique. His weapon and kit were, however, nowhere in sight. He surrendered without resistance and he told us that his clothes and weapon were hidden in the mealie field. We were tense and deeply aware that this could be a trap. We had no handcuffs or anything like that, so Peter improvised and used some twine he found in the back of the truck to bind the terrorist's hands behind his back. The gook was told in no uncertain terms that, if we are walking into an ambush, 'You'll be the first to go.' To keep this threat from back-firing, we needed to make sure that he stayed close by. As we needed both hands to hold our weapons at the ready, the only plan we could devise was to put a noose around the prisoner's neck and tie this to Peter's webbing. We proceeded this way into the maize field. We found his Chinese, rice flecked camouflage kit and weapon and then knew exactly why he had abandoned his kit. He was indeed one of the missing four. With this capture, it was good to hear that later two more were seized.

In a few months, the three were brought to trial in High Court for the murder of the farmer. The defence attorney tried to make a big deal out of the use of the noose and made an accusation of torture. Peter was flaming mad about the charge. Torture? Was the man delusional? With effort, Peter remained calm throughout the court case ... which was presided over by Justice Beck, of all people, a relative of Peter's, and a stickler for the law. This journalistic morsel made it to the second page of the next day's Herald newspaper. Still, the wheels of justice had to turn and run their course. After a battery of questioning, and in light of indisputable evidence and hard facts, the prisoners were convicted of the murder of the farmer. We never heard anything more about the remaining gook and wondered if he'd just dumped his weapons and gone back to civilian life, or had died.

We went back to work. Police matters continued, but seemed discernibly quieter than before. At the time, I was not immediately aware that the terrorists were embroiled in their own internal civil war. Many of the groups which habitually passed through my area were being shot up, or were being jailed by the Zambian Police. Considering the number of groups that had passed through our area, Shoko and I were damn fortunate that, in our years of traversing many dusty roads, we never hit a land mine. Our vehicle was not well-protected so, had we encountered a direct hit, this would most certainly have sent us straight to the proverbial "happy hunting grounds".

Big Kill:

An old man stormed his way into our camp and angrily expressed his rage over a group of men who had invaded his kraal and who were demanding food. His story held no particular distinction, until he got to the part where he started to talk about the weapons that they were carrying, at which stage Shoko and I were glued to his every word.

'They have a banana shape at the bottom,' he frowned, using his hands to try and describe the gun he had seen.

'AK47s' came my hushed undertone to Shoko. With some careful questioning, we drew all we could from the old man, who was only too happy to have willing listeners to his story. The group's arrogance had upset him and had left him feeling helpless and unable to defend his family from this blatant intrusion. He also did not know how to rid his home of them. When we were finished, we gave him some tinned meat to take home. He turned to go, his demeanour showing noticeably less outrage than had been evident on his arrival, but worry still crossed his face. I reached for the radio. Centenary answered immediately and the conversation was short. A mobilisation was quickly arranged and, within hours, two Land Rovers full of PATU men arrived. These were all farmers from the area and I knew them well. We spent time that evening pouring over possible strategies. A couple of cold beers helped to alleviate the monotony of the hours. We needed to avoid the group dispersing in all directions, as that would have vastly reduced any chance of success.

In the end, we elected to nest one unit of four soldiers alongside the main bridge that crossed the Mzingedzi River. The other four soldiers would head for the old man's kraal, where they would create a disturbance. The idea was to flush the terrorists away from the old man's kraal and, through strategic positioning, force them into using the only means of crossing the river, which was via the bridge. The teams prepared themselves to be deployed.

At three o'clock in the morning the sound of distant gunfire came pounding across to us, and we knew that the teams had made contact. I crackled the radio into action to check in with the bridge-ambush crew. 'We are all good,' they confirmed. They had fired for all their worth at the terrorists crossing the bridge, but the darkness prohibited good visuals and they would need to wait until first light before a full assessment could be made. In situations like this, it was not impossible that the terrs would come up with some retaliatory manoeuvre. Planting a land mine that kills indiscriminately (and did), was a favoured option. At first light, we drove cautiously to the bridge, peering onto the road ahead to look for tell-tale signs of land mines. We met up with the PATU men at the bridge, who greeted us wearily, as it had been a very long night. They stretched their legs and we started to sweep the area, looking for tracks.

Mzingedzi River with the bridge crossing where the ambush happened
(Google Earth)

'How many did you see?' I asked.

'Damn hard to see anything,' said the team leader frankly 'but we did see some shapes against the whiteness of the bridge – I don't know for sure ... hey, boys – what do you think?' he asked turning to his men.

No-one had a chance to answer; our attention was suddenly drawn to Shoko. He was standing at the end of the bridge, with his hand up and finger pointing downwards towards the tracks he had found. We moved quickly across the bridge in single file. The terrorists could have easily picked us off, one by one, from the thick jungle, but we moved anyway. When we reached the other side, the signs were there. 'Shit!' Darkness had obviously given them some cover. The tracks were many and showed that the terrorists had high-tailed it across the bridge and headed North-East into the jungle, but not without injury.

The PATU guys began a sweep of the area as I turned to go and pick up the other stick.

'See you back here,' I called, as I made off rapidly toward the Landy. Shoko simultaneously swirled round and followed my steps. The PATU stick disappeared into the thick trees and we disappeared in a cloud of dust. As I picked up speed, I gave the other stick a call.

'On my way, pick you up east of the kraal,' I told them. In no time, I was there. As I screeched up to a halt, the guys leapt into the back of the Land Rover quickly settling in sitting back to back, weapons pointing outward. I turned tightly and sped back to the bridge. As we approached, we could see much activity on the other side. I slowed to try and read what was happening.

'They've got a captive,' I bellowed, realising that the other PATU boys had somebody down on the ground between them. I pulled up next to them and was stunned to see a terrorist with a tangled protrusion of organs palpitating in a bloodied mass from his midsection. 'Jeeez!' I had seen many serious injuries before, including gun shots, panga mutilations, knife wounds, broken-bottle cuts and everything in between, but this was rough. A line of bullets from the night shooting had ripped into him, causing a gaping hole in his stomach and he was in extreme pain. I jumped from the Landy. The PATU guys had checked his shirt and had found a notebook full of information.

'Bloody hell, a Detachment Commander,' exclaimed one of the stick.

The PATU boys had found him hiding in the long grass just off the road. The grass where he had been lying was flattened and bloody. He must have been thrashing around all night in agony. I had spoken once to a Fire Force Doctor and he said that a stomach wound was the most painful of all. With the core stomach muscles shredded, it is virtually impossible to stand with an injury like that. Any pulling of muscles in that area would have caused excruciating pain. Infection was a hazard and, along with it, a high possibility of death.

As is traditional in any war, we needed to get information as quickly as possible on the rest of the enemy. Shoko came past me and bent down to speak to the now quiet man but, even before Shoko could open his mouth, the terrorist started pouring out everything he knew. He told us about an arms cache in the jungle and the names of all his comrades; he spoke, too, of the history of his training. During this outpouring, I pulled back and went to the radio on the Land Rover to call for medical assistance. If this man was a Commander and had such valuable information, we needed to keep him alive. With urgency in my voice, I tried to summon help. The answer I got back from the medics in Mount Darwin was not what I wanted to hear. After a brief exchange, the medic ended with 'Get what you can from him, that's it.' From the tone, I knew that the status quo was not negotiable. I slowly lowered the radio mike, staring at the dash board, my mind registering the situation. I grappled with my thoughts. Why did this even matter, the man was the enemy for God's sake but, despite everything, I could not shake off a sudden sadness. I tried to fathom the moment, but had no answers. Maybe we are just not programmed to see life ebb from the young, or to witness suffering of such magnitude. The medic had said he wouldn't make it for very much longer, a few hours at most. The fact was that the Air Force and the medics were on standby for

Fire Force duties and could not spare the men to come all the way to us there in the remote Zambezi Valley. I went across to Shoko and together we carried the wounded man into the shade of the Land Rover to get him out of the increasing heat of the sun. Shoko moved off. Despite every reason to do so, I could not just leave. So, there we were - two young soldiers from opposite sides, far from home, in a bloody war. He looked me straight in the eyes. I knew he was going, but there was nothing I could do; only be there. He died right there in my arms; a last breath of air left his lungs, his head dropped over my right arm and he was gone. Death claimed him and wrought confusion in me. I stood up slowly. After covering up the body as best as possible for the interim, I turned to refocus on the job at hand. I sent Shoko and one of the PATU guys back to collect the heavy vehicle that we had at base - a four-kilometre drive. We knew which kraals the dead commander had been talking about, where they had been getting food and roughly knew the place he was describing to find the arms' cache.

A Change of Subject:

As we waited for the heavy vehicle, I chatted with the PATU guys and the subject soon turned to farming. The unusually good rains had given bumper crops that year. The guys were all tobacco farmers and shared a concern about the prices they might get at auction, especially as it was global demand that dictated the ultimate prices. If the Chinese were not buying, or if there was too much stock, the prices would be down. Most of the Rhodesian farmer's tobacco was exported around the world, through an intricate chain of sanctions-busting companies, and the tobacco was sought-after due to its good quality. Rhodesia, at that time, had full sanctions placed on it by the world community, but the ever-innovative spirit of its people found ways to circumvent this bothersome impediment. In those days, Salisbury housed a vibrant and efficient tobacco auction warehouse. It was also a place to meet up with old farming friends and to make new acquaintances. As we spoke, the discussions took my mind back to the days when, as children, my sisters and I had run up and down the long avenues of tobacco bales that stood awaiting sale. The auctioneer would make his way steadily through the warehouse, with a posse of buyers in tow. He would stop at the bales, lifting up the pressed, yellow leaves and calling out prices in auctioneering-gibberish. The smells and sounds of the tobacco auctions still lingered. At that moment, our short discussion was disrupted by the arrival of Shoko in the Land Rover and the PATU lad in the heavy vehicle. We would pick up the dead terrorist later – there were more urgent things at hand.

The Big Find:

We drove off along the main dust road and turned at a sign some six miles further down. The sign consisted of a set of old cow horns stuck onto a bush; this signified we were going to a kraal. We bumped along a very rough road for an hour and came upon the settlement in a clearing. Everyone jumped out and quickly surrounded the kraal. We believed that this was from where the gooks used to get their food and that the arms cache would not be far from here. We had leap-frogged ahead of the terrorists, having surmised that they could be heading this way. I was determined to capture the arms and ammunition stock – especially the lethal land mines. I knew that we had to follow the dry little river-bed downstream and, when we came to a large Baobab tree, turn left into the jungle and start looking about eighty metres in. Two of the PATU men were left at the kraal as a nice surprise-package for any visiting terrs, whilst the rest of us made our way down the little riverbed. It was tough going and the intense mid-morning sun started to beat down upon our sweat-soaked camouflage. Our hats were pulled down low, to cut out the sharp light and break some of our facial outlines. We had spread out to minimise the impact of ambush, and toiled our way through thick bush.

Eventually we arrived at the baobab tree, where the bush cleared a little. At this point, the balance of the group remained behind and one PATU chap and I moved on. Working with concentrated purpose, we began the systematic task of finding a safe route through to the armoury. With senses on heightened alert, I was watchful for the inevitable booby traps, especially the deadly trip-wires, the type so typical of the Vietnam War. Anything out of the ordinary would be a giveaway; anything not arranged as Nature would have done, would be a warning. At the outset, I had selected a long, firm piece of grass and held it lightly with my left hand so it dangled just above ground level, simultaneously keeping my FN rifle at the ready. The grass served as an early alert to the presence of wiring. Just the right softness of touch was needed; something like fishing, I guess, where the practiced finger could register even the slightest tug. This simple tool allowed me to extend the visual search for other signs of ambush. It took measured time. A swarm of tsetse flies seemed instinctively to understand that our focus was placed elsewhere and took full advantage to launch a dogged attack. Knowing that any relapse in concentration could cost us dearly, there was no time to offer a defence, so the little bastards moved with us. As we closed in on the site, we could see that the ground had been dug up in a twenty-metre circle. What lay below that was anybody's guess but, whatever it was, looked hugely substantial. Evidence of other mounds showed that there had also been burials between the tough roots of nearby trees. The thick, dank undergrowth was heavy with jungle feeling and an eerie silence reigned. The long, twining vines clawed their way through wet, dark, green leaves to grasp small shards of sky above the large tree canopy. Its very

isolation made this an ideal place to position such a cache. I moved in a circle to sweep the surround for possible explosive devices or fresh tracks and, when all was clear, guided the rest of the guys forward. Working together, along one side of the site, we started to dig the earth with our hands and bayonets. It did not take long to realise that what we had here was a sizeable stash. In fact, by looks of it, it could easily have been the main armoury for the entire Northern sector. We uncovered anti-tank rocket launchers, both anti-armour and anti-personal rockets, AK sub-machine guns, SKS rifles, RPD machine guns, boxes and boxes of ammunition, grenades, first aid equipment, land mines and more. For the full length of the day we worked tirelessly, dragging back tonnes of weapons. In the end, three heavily-laden truckloads made their careful way back to our little police station. As we wrestled to remove the last batches, the heavens opened and a huge rain storm bucketed down on us, drenching everything in its path. Whilst this lashing offered some respite from the days' heat, it effectively destroyed all evidence of tracks and brought to a grinding halt our plans to follow them to see where they led. Undaunted by the thunderous clouds and with our euphoria undiminished by aching muscles, the party at camp that night was long and loud.

Terror Tactics:

Of all the cases that I investigated over the years, consisting of every conceivable type, some of the most troubling were the cases of torture. Torture, of the most heinous and brutal kind, was inflicted on the local folk, predominantly the rural people, and most especially upon those who dared to put up any resistance to terrorist demands. Some of the mutilations were monstrous in the extreme. Mercilessly sawing or hacking off great chunks of flesh with bayonets or pangas were ways of meting out punishment to anyone who did not co-operate. Lips, ears, breasts, genitals or fingers were severed. Rape and beatings, often to a senseless pulp, took place with impunity. Not surprisingly, we harboured deep-seated abhorrence for this inhumane behaviour. Babies chopped from their mother's wombs and smashed to death in front of them, transcended every code of behaviour known to man. The simple folks whom I had come to know in the Zambezi Valley were being systematically terrified into supporting the terrorist cause, regardless of whether they wanted to offer their support, or not. Whilst there were sympathisers amongst them, the majority were everyday folk, who just wanted to get on with cultivating their fields, tending their animals and living life as they had been doing for years. Gruesome pictures appeared in the newspapers that were deeply shocking and of such staggering callousness that it repulsed the nation. Inexplicably though, these images only received a diluted response from the global community. Rhodesia's isolation continued - unabated.

To treat mutilations or wounds, I could only use what medicines I had. The limited medical supplies I was issued didn't stretch far, but there was no clinic in the Zambezi Valley in those days. People turned up for help, or I went to them. Those that were too seriously injured or ill were carefully placed in the Land Rover and I would make my way as quickly, as the roads would permit, to either Centenary Hospital or to the Catholic nuns at St. Albert's Mission at the top of the escarpment. The nuns were exceptional and so good to everyone. They even had a school for the children and fortunately kept a well-stocked clinic. They were often harassed by the terrorists and many in the vulnerable missions suffered rape, beatings or massacre. The nuns were adamant, though, that the Lord's work transcended evil and, at great risk to themselves, they continued to administer to everyone who needed help. Their kind and compassionate dedication made it impossible to believe that anyone could kill or harm such gentle, holy servants, but cold facts proved otherwise. Many nuns paid the ultimate price for their calling. My God, I thought, what name could you call humans who murdered like this, and who even stooped to the merciless and coldblooded killing of children? I could not find anything that fitted; no word carried enough revulsion, disgust, abhorrence, nausea or incredulity. No word!

These tea estate workers were tied up by terrorists who mowed them down with automatic weapons.

A pamphlet produced by the Government showing terrorist atrocities.

No Escape For Them:

In front of our camp stretched a large airstrip, primarily for military purposes. One of our unenviable tasks was to clear the strip of any animals, such as warthogs or elephants, before any aircraft could land. The incoming pilot would radio us in advance and we had to rush out and onto the grass-and-dirt strip, searching for animals. At the same time, the other more abhorred chore was looking for land mines. I guess the country could afford to lose a mine-protected Land Rover in preference to a precious military aircraft. That was rather less comforting for those of us who were the drivers of the Land Rover.

Another group of terrorists was tracked from the Zambezi River, heading south towards the escarpment. An Army call-sign was hot on their tracks and called us for support. Les Jellicoe and his Cessna plane were actually at our base camp at the time, so we commandeered him and his plane to act as a spotter for the Army chaps. At the same time, a young Army private was trying to catch a lift from our camp, over the escarpment, through to Mount Darwin Army base. For whatever reason he also jumped into the aircraft, most likely hoping that the plane would take him to his destination. He must have been desperate to get out of the area, because he actually had no idea what our destination was. We agreed to his presence, as he could help with spotting from the air. We were too absorbed in our mission to engage in social chit-chat and were hastily preparing for the flight. Within minutes, the aircraft took off and radio contact was made with the army guys on the ground. Quickly, we were in the area where we understood the terrorists might be.

'Roger AF, this is 390J. Tell me when I am over the position,' was Jellicoe's call to the Army, as he attempted to try and pinpoint their location.

'Roger, we see you. Come straight, left wing down a bit, come straight, left wing down a bit ... roger **now**,' came the response.

We flew over the top of some very large trees and now knew exactly where the army call-sign was.

'Keith, I'm going to swing around and come in low, to see if we can spot these guys under those big trees,' shouted Jellicoe over the noise of the engine. We made a tight turn to the right, at which stage the G-forces kicked in and my stomach departed my body to the left. The Army chap in the back was sliding about all over the place. Jellicoe reduced altitude and we came in at tree-

top level. The thick foliage made it difficult to pinpoint any human presence. With no sighting on the first attempt, we readied to repeat the exercise and swooped in again for another observation. As we pulled up from the trees to gain a bit of height, the radio crackled.

'Ah 390J, this is AF, your engine appears to be having problems, you copy?' Jellicoe and I exchanged surprised looks. Engine problems? As their message sank in, it dawned on us then that each time we had been running the tree line the terrorists had been opening up fire upon us with everything they had. The sound of their combined gunfire must have sounded like an engine in distress but, for us, the aircraft engine had drowned out any sound of the shooting. Kismet was favourable that day. Truth was we were damn lucky not to collect a bullet ... or ten. Les said that the only time you really knew you were being fired at was when rounds went through the aircraft and you would hear a distinctive click as the bullets tore through the aluminium frame. With the position of the terrs now more apparent, the army guys managed to make contact with the small group of terrorists and to knock off one. The others turned and hot-tailed it as fast as they could back across the Zambezi River and into Zambia. The Army chap in the back of the plane landed back at base with us, looking very ashen-faced and shaken. In the end he never did get a lift with Jellicoe; instead, he caught the first truck going out of town. Bet he had a story to tell his mates.

Cordon Sanitaire:

A young, local chap came running into the station and, in a torrent of words and animated hand movements, he nervously blurted out that a herd of elephants was destroying their crops. We dropped everything. Elephants can cause havoc. Shoko and I jumped into the Land Rover, with the young chap between us, and we headed straight for his kraal. Fortunately it was not too far away, by Valley standards that is. As we sped toward his home, we could see a number of thatch huts dotted within the shade of some large Albizia trees. To one side was a large, fenced field and, sure enough, there in the middle of the field was a breeding herd of elephants. A breeding herd consists of a matriarch and many youngsters. Male elephants normally leave the herd when they reach puberty, at about 13 years old, but the females invariably stay with their mothers, aunts, sisters and grandmothers. The matriarch presides over the herd, and she would normally be the oldest, largest and wisest. I parked next to the nearest large hut. After first greeting the chief, Shoko and I took a walk down towards the herd. The local family of people looked on cautiously from behind some large trees. Normally elephants would traverse through fields of maize at night, easily stomping down a few strands of fencing, which made it unusual that this group looked intent on staying where it was. As we approached, the elephants' trunks went up, as they sought to identify us. With nothing else at our disposal, I decided to see if they would move off of their own accord with a bit of persuasion.

'I'm going to fire off a few rounds and see if that gets them to go,' I told Shoko. I fired five quick rounds into the air from my rifle. Instead of moving off as they would normally have done, this only made them more jittery and edgy. It was now clear that something was radically amiss. Watching their body language, it was suddenly clear to me what the problem was.

'Shoko, that matriarch is in distress. She has seen something before that has made her frightened of fences.' Elephant are incredibly sensitive and the females will always fiercely protect their young from any threat. Sometime before, Rhodesia had laid a barrier of land mines and fences along its borders with Zambia and Mozambique. We weren't too far from this deadly fence. The fence had been installed to try and reduce the infiltration of terrorists from those respective countries. The munitions used within the fenced area were a lethal cocktail of anti-personnel mines, plough shears (a Rhodesian-made circular, concave disk, filled with pellets) and a whole bunch of other nasty things. It was called the 'Cordon Sanitaire.'

'I believe that this group has seen an explosion by the Cordon Sanitaire fence-line and it is very possible that one of their group was killed there. That's why they don't want to go through or near this fence,' I told Shoko. Often elephants would be severely wounded by these munitions and still be able to hobble around, until infection knocked them down.

We retreated back to the village, where I spoke with the chief. I explained what we needed to do. I had intended for just a few people to help, but the entire kraal warily made their way around to the other side of the fence, furthest from the huts. We started dropping the fence and moving it out of the way, making a gap in it of about 100 metres. All the while, the elephants were standing still in the middle of the field, heads up and trunks sniffing the air. When the job was done, the people made their way, the long way round, back to their kraal. Contending with a herd of nervous elephant is not something you wish to do while on foot. The elephants remained where they were. To reduce the animals' distress, I asked the chief to try and keep everybody out of sight of the elephants. At night they were to light fires in the kraal and, with luck, the elephant group would make its way through the gap in the fence. It worked and when Shoko and I returned early the next morning, the elephants were gone. The damage to the fields of cotton and maize, though, was a heavy burden on the people, but they had already started to sort their fields and the fence was up again. These were tough and resilient people. The chief came across and offered Shoko and me a drink of local beer as a mark of thanks.

'Thank you,' I said, as I accepted the bowl with two hands as a sign of respect. To decline would have been considered impolite. I took a small sip and passed it to the eager hands of Shoko. I still didn't like the taste of the local beer and was definitely not accustomed to having a sip so early in the day. I watched Shoko raise the bowl for a second sip, when my brow furrowed.

'What the hell is that?' I said, pulling the bowl back again. To my great astonishment, I realised that the bowl was made from an old Russian landmine base. Someone had obviously emptied the mine of its contents and cleverly bent the metal into a round-shaped bowl. Hell, now there was something you don't see every day. After surveying this innovative piece of 'kitchenware', I passed the bowl back to Shoko, who didn't really care what the beer was presented in anyway.

After acknowledging the chief's hospitality, Shoko and I took a walk down to the river to look for the tracks of the herd. As we walked, a Tamarind tree came into view. Its vast, majestic branches stretched way across the nearby river and cast shade upon much of the bank. The sweet smell of fruit filled our lungs. A family of baboons were leaping boisterously from the tree's branches to another as they gorged themselves. What a wonderful place this  was. Shoko and I spontaneously sat down on one of the massive sprawling roots. We sat in silence, taking in the scenery, gazing out upon its untouched beauty. The soft sound of spilling water soothed the spirit and Africa's many colours merged in a landscape of supreme splendour. It was at times like this that the price of war seemed impossibly high.

The fruit of the Tamarind was used to make a type of curry. Actually, the locals produced an incredible range of products and it never ceased to amaze me how self-sufficient these people were. They grew maize for their staple diet of Sadza, a stiff porridge. Ground nuts were soaked in brine for twenty-four hours and then roasted over an open fire. This tasty snack served as a convenient and sustaining 'fast food.' Ground nuts were also crushed and milled on a large, smooth stone, featuring a shallow indentation in the middle. Using a rounded granite rock, the woman made a nutritious peanut butter. It was so fresh that it was difficult not to get sick eating too much. The uninitiated soon learnt not to chew down hard when eating maize or ground nuts, as fine rock-grit is not palatable and wears down the teeth. On occasion, if I encountered a small stone when chewing, I would get a shiver all the way down my back and the hair on my arms would stand straight up. It was a strange effect and not particularly enjoyable, and the art of chewing became more of a conscious practice than a mindless repetition.

Fresh fruit of many kinds were grown. In December, the mangoes came out. Large buckets of them could be found for sale along the side of the roads near most kraals. Teetering stacks of carefully-balanced mangoes advertised the roadside markets and the juicy, yellow flesh was a much sought-after food. Sugarcane, cassava roots, sweet potatoes, tomatoes and spinach made up the vegetable range. These simple people existed with very little money for commercial purchases; however, they were incredibly happy with what they had. Their days and lives were full and wholesome. Cultural events formed an important part of their lives, with gatherings of family and friends often held around an open fire in the middle of the kraal. These get-togethers were held with much laughter, kids running here and there and food being prepared by the women. If a stranger happened to arrive, they would immediately be offered food and a bed, with the only recompense desired being the sharing of a good story or two.

Culture in Local Society:

Respect for elders was a revered rule. As you approached a kraal entrance, you would be required to stop at its upright log fence and greet the elder of the village. You called out and, as you did so, you would clap your hands together, keeping your head bowed. The head of the kraal would welcome you by clapping in response. Any women entering the kraal had to do so after the menfolk and, at all times, her head had to be kept lower than the kraal elder's head as a mark of respect. A visit to any kraal was never quick. After the initial introductions were made the men would sit, generally in a circle, and the conversation would turn to how the weather was, the state of the crops and cattle, stories of the journey taken to get to the kraal and so on. Only after all these subjects had been thoroughly covered could you begin to discuss  the reason for the visit, or to state your business. By that stage, a plate of snacks or food would be presented to the men and you would all eat together. Before eating, a bowl of water would be passed around to enable the washing of hands. The food would be placed on a grass mat on the ground and the men would help themselves to the food with their hands. Only the right hand was used for eating. It was acceptable to roll some sadza into a ball, press it in the middle using the thumb, and to use that as a sort of spoon to scoop up a mixture of chicken and spinach that was served in a bland sauce. The food was always very simple. It was a tough life for these people, but I look back and realise how well they lived. They lacked for little in the important things of life and I guess the thing I learnt was that no matter how poor they were, their generosity was abundant.

Religion was interesting. The locals believed in a single God called Mwari, but their day-to-day lives were controlled entirely by their ancestors. If you were sick, you would consult with the local 'Nyanga' or healer. These were herbalists or medicine men/ women, who would commune with the ancestors to find the best relief for a patient's ailment. The treatment often included a variety of herbs, often foul-tasting. The belief in the *Nyangas* was extremely high and the guidance of the ancestors was not to be taken lightly. Consultations included physical healing, or solutions for emotional or relationship problems. Superstitions were also huge within daily life. If an owl landed on your roof, or if a python was seen near your home, then these would all have significance. You would need to consult a nyanga to get clarity on this event and you possibly would have to be 'cleansed.' A bad spell could also be placed on someone with whom you had a quarrel.

Tragically Kenneth's younger brother died at the age of 24, following revelation that a bad spell had been placed upon him. So great was his belief in the spell's power over him that the results were lethal. He actually died in the rear of my Land Rover on the way to hospital. He had faded away so much that, by the time we got to him, it was already too late. The mental pressure on him was enough to kill him - in two short weeks! It was surreal. The fearful effect of the occult on minds and body was patently clear. It was also surprising how much evidence of this type of activity was around. It could be as obvious as a small, black cloth hanging in a tree near a hut, or as subtle as broken egg shells, or a smearing of fats in strategic places. If you unearthed a tick in a bottle, this was often the work of a spell-maker looking to cause the demise of a chosen victim. Cattle horns placed on the roof of a small, unused hut may easily miss one's attention. Black beads around the belly of the young boy, running naked by the chickens, may have been wrongly viewed as a simple piece of jewellery; however, they were there to protect him from evil spirits. Complex as all these things seem to us, they were clear to the simple folks who lived in the valley.

The people in the valley were essentially primitive; however, their depth of culture ran deep within each family. I had been to many kraals and spent a great deal of time with some really amazing people. At one particular kraal, we met up with a very inventive chap. On entering the kraal, I could see a bunch of nifty devices that he had made to make his family's life easier. One

such invention was a homemade trailer. It was made entirely by hand, with few tools and almost 100% local materials. The two wheels were cut pieces of a tree and they, in turn, supported a pole axil. A 'Y' shaped branch had been secured across the axle with inner bark from the Mopane trees. The trailer's only foreign part was a metal hitching-ring on the disselboom to which two oxen would be tethered. I guess it was a simple method of removing a pin through the axil to replace a wheel.

The Big Roundup:

In 1976, radical change came. With directives from the government, the rural population was to be shepherded into 'Keeps' or Protected Villages. A military light aircraft dropped pamphlets from the sky onto the numerous kraals dotted around the valley, informing them of the impeding change. The local Internal Affairs guys were delegated to go around and explain the new system. They were also made responsible for loading the villagers onto trucks and taking them to a protected village or keep, which consisted of a cleared area where the people would have to build their huts and live. The keep was surrounded by a six-foot high, diamond-mesh fence and members of the Ministry of Internal Affairs manned the gates to monitor people coming and going. The keep in the valley was not large compared to others in the country; about 2,000 people were housed within the secured area. In the entire country six foot high diamond mesh more than 240,000 people were herded into PVs or keeps. The idea was to stop the terrorists from getting help from the locals in the way of food and shelter. All old kraals outside the keeps were to be burnt to the ground. Most of the folks lived along the Mzingedzi River and the move took about two weeks to complete. The police were not involved six foot high diamond mesh so we continued our normal duties. All the little kraals were deserted. The chickens, goats and cattle had gone and an uneasy quiet reigned. In time, Nature would have its way with the huts and grass; the strangling vines and tenacious trees would engulf evidence of man's presence. The locals were in disarray over these new arrangements. Some didn't mind because there was water on tap, plus a clinic and school would be provided. Others were actively rebellious. It was an offense to leave the keep and stay out during the night. A curfew was enforced, whereby inhabitants had to be back in the keep by 6h00 in the evening and could only go out to their fields at 6h00 in the morning.

The keep system changed relationships within the entire valley population. The locals either hated us, or lived off hand-outs of cash for information about terrorists. It was never the same again and the area became ripe for the terrorists to infiltrate. The keep system worked in reducing food access for the terrorists, but it did huge damage to the hearts and minds of the locals. Information all but dried-up and our meeting with the heads of kraals became more of a business meeting than a friendly visit. It seemed to me that the terrorists had won the 'hearts and minds' game and that we had scored an own goal.

Vietnam Wayne:

I was called to Centenary Police Station one day for various things and was also introduced to a tall, blonde fellow with an American accent. We drove to the country club and had a few beers together. All the locals were there and the session lasted a while. I learnt that he had been in Vietnam for four years and was in the country to fight communists. He didn't talk much about the war in Vietnam, but one could see in his eyes that he had been through a great deal. He was a big man, who held a good conversation, attached to which was a great sense of humour. Everybody liked Wayne, long, blonde hair and all. I spent a few days in Centenary catching up with some administration and I was delighted when Wayne asked to come back to the valley with me. He had attested as a police reservist, so I was able to take him with me. We spent a number of days scooting around the valley. He had so much to talk about and I listened with bated breath to some of his stories. Wayne's company was a welcome relief. He gave me a pair of American Para boots with a metal plate inlay, and explained that the plate was to stop the pungi sticks from going into their feet when they parachuted into contacts.

By this stage, I had served an eventful two-year stint in the Zambezi Valley. We had seen the changes, including the establishments of the Keeps, the building of the new Police Station, the development of a vast cotton farm for the locals, the upgrading of the main road leading from Centenary to the valley and the laying out of the airfield. The terrorist infiltration through the valley continued to increase and the Government spent more and more money running around trying to find the elusive enemy, without the benefit of good information from the locals.

The Biltong Tree:

Near the end of my time in the valley, things began to hot up. One night, a couple of badly-trained gooks tried to lay a landmine on the road near the end of the airstrip, just down the road from our base. They wanted to give us a short, sharp flight. We heard an awful explosion during the night and, in the morning upon investigation, we came across a huge hole in the road. The trees and grass all around were covered in white dust and here and there were strips of what looked like dried meat. We took a good look around to see if there were any further devices, but that appeared to be it. A tree right next to the road attracted my attention. It was covered with bits of meat and bone and the flies were going half crazy. We found two weapons nearby and worked it out. The terrorists had detonated the landmine whilst trying to lay it and had themselves ended up all over the place, but especially in the tree. From then on, the tree was known as the 'biltong tree.' Biltong is a Southern African name for dried meat.

I was eventually shipped off to Bindura to resume my normal police duties, having served my stint in the valley long enough – I think. We later heard that the Police guys in the valley were ambushed by 60 terrorists and the entire crew was killed. One young black lad, who had been hired by me as a police reservist called Never, ended up being dragged to the roof of the heavy troop carrier vehicle, where his throat was cut with a bayonet. Wayne stayed on in the valley. I later heard that he had been driving along one of the bad roads deep in the valley, with one of the police sergeants, and had been ambushed by a large group of terrorists. He got through the ambush area unscathed and, upon realising that he hadn't fired his rifle, he promptly turned the Land Rover around and sped back through the ambush killing area, blazing away. He wasn't so lucky this time, as he got a Czechoslovakian anti-personal rifle grenade straight through his left leg. The grenade didn't explode and he made it through – what a tough guy. The terrorists had, in the meantime, taken tail and disappeared into the thick bush. I guess they got quite a fright when they saw this lunatic come back for more. I never heard about Wayne again.

Things began to get worse and more men started to get posted to the valley to help with the security situation. I was joined in the valley, for a short period, by Peter Beck as he was going to take over from me. We ended up being involved in a number of altercations with terrorists, including the capture of five terrorists in separate incidents over one week.

The Beautiful Animals:

Looking back, it must be said that the valley was an incredibly special place. The vast expanse of untouched, natural bush, teaming with wildlife, was Africa at her untouched best. Beautiful and balanced. The rivers were unpolluted and teamed with fish, amphibians, reptiles, birds and all sorts of creatures. You could drink from any of the rivers and the sweet, clear water was always cool and refreshing. I would often rest up, overlooking herds of buffalo, or elephants as they moved together in their daily search for food. I would switch off the engine to wait for their safe passage across the road, watching in wonder at the complex interactions between the individuals. On occasion, they would hesitate in the middle of the road and look at this strange metal box, which smelt bad. Their trunks would first test the ground area for scent and then you could see them testing the air higher up in an attempt to establish what we were. Occasionally, one of the young males would voice his opinion of our intrusion by trumpeting loudly and give us a mock charge with dust pluming from his fat feet, as he tried to show us his strength. Then they would amble off the road and melt into the thick jungle of vines and heavy-wooded trees. Lone bulls, with their huge flapping ears, would ignore us as they stood and devoured a branch, and the sound of munching could be heard a way off. They knew they were the lords of the jungle and had nothing to fear. If we came across a lone bull standing on the road, we would generally wait until he walked off - in his own time, of course. If you tried to chase him off the road, your next emotion would be one of regret. He would often swing round and give you full view of what extreme anger looks like when it has wild flapping ears, huge tusks and stomping feet. Reversing the car at break-neck speed, was the only answer to this kind of attack. The roads had been hacked through the thick jungle and thorny Jess Bush, by bulldozer. There was very little chance we could turn to get away fast, so we had to be very careful with big bulls, as they could give us a serious hammering.

The only time we really got close to big bulls was when we walked through the bush. One of them may have been in a ravine just below us, and we would be able to get up close enough to see the wrinkles in his thick skin, with the short thick hairs sticking straight up. If he did get to hear or smell us, we would be quite safe because elephants can't jump. A big log, two feet high, would stop an elephant and this was one way we could escape from him if he chased our tails. They could run faster than us, but we had to use our brains to outsmart him if we were being chased. I remember a time when we were fishing in one of the rivers and a huge bull came down one of the gullies to drink water. He was now in between us as we sat on the banks of the river, not ten feet from where we were. He knew we were there, but drank his fill anyway. Then, taking a last look at us, he turned back up the gully, while we carried on fishing for another half hour. When we packed up to leave, we used the same gully he had, to get up from the river and, just as we poked our heads up above the bank of the river, we got such a fright, as he had been standing right there all along. We had two choices: either run back to the river and swim upstream, or go down stream a bit and make our way around him, by making a wide arc through the jungle. We ended up doing the latter, as he was dead keen on giving us a hiding, and swimming upstream would have been tantamount to asking for a crocodile attack. We could hear him crashing through the undergrowth, following us, as he caught our scent every now and then. We ended up walking a further five kilometres through the bush to get away from him, but eventually made it back to the Land Rover, exhausted and scratched all over from thorns. We asked the local

Game Department Head Ranger why some of the elephants were more hot-headed and keen to flatten us than others.

'Two reasons,' he said. 'Bullets from AK47 rifles and also the males could be in musth.'

The absolutely pure state of the bush in the Zambezi Valley was breath-taking. Early morning was the best time to see and feel the beauty of the land, with the sun filtering through the large trees by the river. The birds would be up and about and the orchestra of sounds echoed in constant songs through the thick undergrowth. Man had not made his contaminated mark on this part of the planet. Everything was as God had intended it to be. This was a place where the elements could give full expression to their creative forces, where the sun kissed the golden grasses of Africa in ritual blessing every day, and where the soul could find solace.

The years had been long, and lonely. It was time for me to go back to the mainstream of human life, to restore contact with friends, to refine my social skills with the feminine species, and to leave the Valley behind.

A Short Break

On the 21ˢᵗ May 1978, I decided I'd had enough. I had been transferred to Uniform Branch in Bindura and couldn't handle the daily chores of being a normal Policeman, especially in a town. I had finished my three years contract with the Police.

I resigned and got a manager's job on a large farm in Norton. This didn't last long, either, and I found myself sitting in Monamatapa Hotel drowning my sorrows with my good friends. I had reapplied to re-join the Police Force and my interview was set for 14h00 that day at Police Headquarters, twenty minutes from where we were. As we sat drinking and talking about nothing in particular, The News broadcast told us one of my mates had been killed in the operational area. Well that was it; we ordered another two rounds of drinks to celebrate his life. By the time I arrived for my interview with the Assistant Commissioner at Police Headquarters, I was walking obviously intoxicated! I apologised to the Officer for my state and explained the circumstances. To his credit, he understood and I signed up for another three years just a couple of months after having left.

I was stationed at the Police Radio Repairs Section in Salisbury for a few months, where I learnt how to repair radios under the guidance of some very innovative technical men. I enjoyed the technical side of things and learnt about the art of installing aerials and circuits. Kenneth was with me as always, but I was getting itchy feet and wanted to go operational again. During my time at the Radio Section, I also installed radios into new Police vehicles and, on one particular day, three differently-coloured Land Rovers rolled into our yard for new radios. They were not the usual green colour chosen by the Police, but each sported a different colour of dark brown, blue and sandy-coloured livery. What I didn't know then was that I would soon be driving with these vehicles within a Special Forces Unit.

Back to Bindura I went, but this time it was to be different. No more arresting drunks and stopping cars to check licences.

7 & 8 Squads of 1974 passing out parade, Morris Depot - Salisbury 1975

Keith's' family at my passing out parade, note the marksman badge on the sleeve

Keith in new camou-flage. The FN rifle is also painted.

Honda 250cc Police motorbike.

Passing out Parade dressed in our Number 1s

Whistlefield farm house showing anti-rocket poles across the
main office.

Land Rover at Whistlefield
farm with mine protected
driver and passenger sections

PO Harry Edwards

Centenary Air Force Control Tower

Bunker at Whistlefield farm

Kenneth

*Matt Taylor and Field Reservist Never scramble into our truck
Mzarabani Zambezi Valley. Never was captured by a group of
60 terrorists and had his throat slit.*

On the road from Hoya to Gutsa with a prisoner.

A typical kraal in the Zambezi Valley before the
Protected Village scheme came about. Note the
Baobab tree in the center.

The set of horns marked the entrance to a kraal close to where we
found a huge cache of weapons.

*Ground Coverage team in one of the kraals whilst sitting on a
homemade trailer with wooden wheels. This would have been
drawn by two oxen or donkeys.*

*Keith on patrol with Shoko in the Zambezi Valley. The escarp-
ment can be seen in the back ground.*

Callsign Alpha Charlie in the courtyard of the Bindura Special Branch. Note I have a telescopic sight for sniping on my heavy barreled FN

Musa with Keith outside the Shamva Police armoury, ready for deployment into Mfurudzi Wildlife Reserve. Notice how untidy Musa had his backpack.

Rob Parker at training in Mazoe.

Callsign Alpha Charlie in Chiweshe Tribal Trust Lands.

An Alouette 111 taking off from Centenary Air Force base 1975.

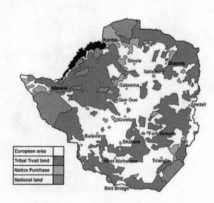

Land distribution in Rhodesia. The blue areas were Tribal Trust Lands.

Pachedu "A" Desk Projects Section Special Forces 1978

Back row – Charles (Mozambique Resistance Movement, RENAMO), Instructor, Instructor, DPO Keith Chisnall, FR Theuns Elloff, DSO Ben Pretorius (2 I/C), DI Ken Stewart (MIC), FR Brian Lawrence, PO Noel Erasmus, Unknown, Unknown SB Man, Keith Meadows

Seated – DPO Gova, DPO Danger, Moses (cook), FR Dennis Thompson, FR Frank Stobbard, FR Pat Walsh, FR Noland Payne, FR Cedric Jonker, FR Ross Robertson

Kneeling – All Unknown On top of the bar at Retreat Farm Bindura

Pachedu team in Borrowdale safe house Salisbury

The badge Keith wore when working with ZANLA men to uplift gooks during the ceasefire

The distinctive Pachedu Emblem

Service medals for Rhodesia on the right and Zimbabwe on the left

BSA Police marksman badge issued to the author at training.

The 'T' shirt issued to Auxillary recruits during training

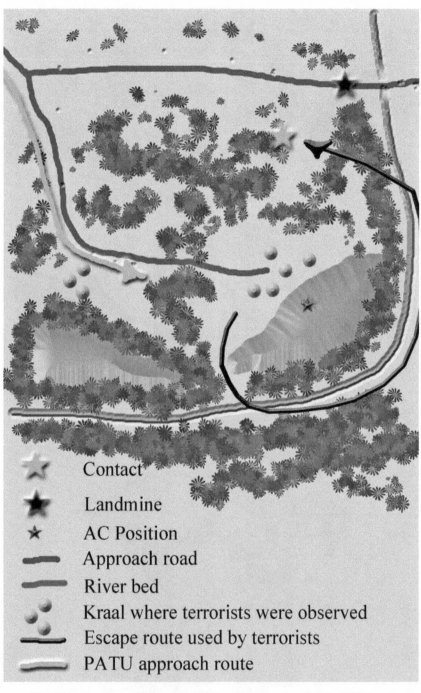

Map showing the actions when S.I.S. Call Sign AC called in PATU and Motorbike section onto a terrorist base camp.

Pachedu Land Rover after a Land Mine exploded beneath it on
Ceasefire Day 21st December 1979

Keith at Retreat Farm with our 75mm Chinese Recoilless Rifle,
note Theuns's bunker on the right.

The scene of the land mine; Keith carrying Ian's sawn off RPD machine gun, Neville Henley (Pachedu) and daughter of the farm owner look on. Two men search for bits of equipment beyond

The Chinese land mine made a large hole; Engineers look for evidence.

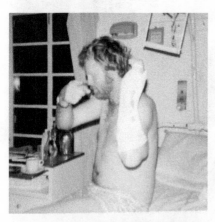

Billy Grant recovering in Hospital after being seriously injured in a land mine incident on ceasefire day.

Webster getting ready for deployment two days before he was injured in a land mine incident.

*Pete Lawrence, Billy Grant, Ian Suttil and Jake Harper Ronald the day before
they were injured in the land mine*

Jake

*Ian and Jerry kitting up
for deployment*

Keith arresting Zambian poachers on the Zambezi River. They were in a dugout canoe made from a single tree

Keith on the Police jet boat on the Zambezi River

The water tank at Police Chirundu kept getting shot full of holes by the Zambians. It was clearly visible from the Zambian side.

Blowing up old ordinance in Chirundu – this was a phosphorous grenade.

Chirundu Bridge across the Zambezi River. Zambia is on the other side.

7

Special Investigations Section

It was July 1977.

I was sitting having a beer with some friends when I came up with the bright idea of making my own 'night' sight for my rifle. The sight derived from the idea that if you look down a small pipe, a quarter the size of a pencil, then the smaller and longer the pipe, the more carefully one has to 'aim' to look through it. I cut a small copper pipe (about the size of a drinking straw) about 8 inches long and lined it up with my barrel, ensuring they both visually met at around 100 metres. The sight and barrel were true to each other. I used an epoxy cement to mount the sight to the fore-grip of the rifle. I sprayed the pipe, both inside and outside, with a fine coating of matt, black paint. The little pipe ran down the left side of the front hand-grip of my FN 7.62mm rifle and I left the normal sights alone so that I could still use them if I needed to. I filed down a red LED (light-emitting diode) and, once it was small enough, stuck it in the front end of the pipe. I connected one wire of the LED to the rifle to act as the earth wire, and sent the other in a snaking fashion through the rifles parts to the pistol grip. In the hollow pistol grip, I inserted a battery holder (1.5 volt torch battery) and attached a small switch and rheostat. I could turn the LED on and adjust the brightness of the LED with the knob on the rheostat with my little finger of my right hand, so I didn't have to remove my hand from the weapon at all. In the early evening the LED would be brighter but, as night fell, I would have to dim the LED to stop the light blinding me. I used the 'night' sight successfully and the beauty was that I could use both eyes. The concept of using both eyes to aim with, was how we were taught to shoot during the war. The right eye was used to line the LED onto the target and the left eye was used to focus on the target, as well. I was so pleased with my little invention. With this simple device, I could now shoot more accurately at night.

Special Investigations Section - Call Sign 'Alpha Charlie':

I was walking across the lawn courtyard at the Special Branch offices in search of Phil Hartleberry's office. The offices were made up of a series of buildings with corrugated iron roofs, surrounding a well-trimmed, grassed rectangle. Superintendent 'Mac' Maginnus appeared at one of the office doors and beckoned me to come into Phil's office. Phil had sent me a message that I should report to the hallowed offices of Special Branch. Although the offices were constructed from sheet metal, they were cooler inside than it was outside in the hot sun. A large table stood on the left of the office, with two dove-grey steel cabinets opposite the door. The room was cluttered with an assortment of papers and war materials and I could see this was no normal office. There was a pile of odds and bits stuffed into the corner next to the cabinet to the right, including an East German camouflage jacket draped over an FN rifle, and a crumpled FRELIMO (Front for the Liberation of Mozambique) jacket was jammed into a metal ammunition box. I would have given a week's wages for the FRELIMO jacket.

The opposition to FRELIMO was a small rebel group called RENAMO and they had been created with the help of the Rhodesians in 1975. FRELIMO now ran Mozambique, after they succeeded in taking it over when the Portuguese opted out of Colonialism in 1975. RENAMO started as a small band, but grew in strength with our Special Forces help. They had huge successes against FRELIMO, with the help from our SAS. The more we disrupted the FRELIMO Government the less likely, we thought, they would help the ZANLA terrorists we were fighting. Little did I know that I would later work with some of these RENAMO soldiers.

A Chinese army cap lay on the floor, next to a bundle of maps. A large hornet's nest hung from the ceiling near the far side window, with hornets lying in ambush with their painful stings. You didn't want to disturb these guys on a hot summer's day. There was a map of the Northern operations section of Rhodesia on the wall to the right, as you entered. This was made up of nine 1:50 000 scale maps, stapled to a pin board. It showed the entire area that fell under the control of Special Branch Bindura. There were various coloured pins dotted around on the map, with a row of spare ones down the one side. The different colours represented different points of interest, such as last sightings of terrorists, last terrorist contact points, landmine explosions and other information which would be important with regard to decision-making for future operations. Terrorist groups responsible for these acts were operating throughout the whole of Operation Hurricane area and I was standing in the nerve centre of the most powerful Intelligence buildings for the Government counter-terrorist operations in the Hurricane area. Rhodesia had been broken down into various operational zones; code named for use in military and intelligence work by Government forces. We were part of Operation Hurricane.

Predicting future occurrences, like ambushes, farm raids and the positioning of landmines, could be lifesaving. The names, rank, descriptions and various bits of information, including what weapons each member of a terrorist group used, was needed and Phil, with his team of staff and informers, were past masters at getting this information. Special Branch was the Intelligence Section within the British South Africa Police force.

Phil, together with two white officers (Tony Granger and Colin Evans) and 5 black detectives, was responsible for running the Bindura Special Branch offices. The team had to oversee a vast tract of land, stretching from the borders with Salisbury to the South, Shamva's eastern borders, Umvukwe's Eastern border and with Centenary and Mount Darwin on its northern borders. The area was made up of various types of inhabitation, including white farm land, black farm land and a number of sizeable Tribal Trust lands. The team also had the Mfurudzi wildlife reserve to contend with.

Phil was leaning back in his maroon-coloured, swivel chair, with his hands clutched behind his head. He had longish, brown hair down to his shoulders, which had waves as opposed to curls. Special Branch personnel were allowed to dress in civilian clothes, and don beards and have long hair if they wanted to.

'Come in, Keith,' he welcomed, as he stretched, anticipating the beginning of the briefing. He had an English accent, betraying the fact that he had immigrated to Rhodesia as a boy.

Mac, as he was affectionately called, was a big man, with a cropped, greying beard. He stood gazing at the maps on the wall, with crossed arms, deep in thought. He had an aura about him that made those in junior ranks jump. Mac was the Special Branch Liaison man within the Selous Scouts. His 'offices' were in the huge Fort within Bindura Police Station. All sorts of things went on within the Fort, and no unauthorised folks were allowed either within the Fort, or within close proximity to it. The Fort was made from huge sheets of galvanised, corrugated iron and took up a sizable spot next to the football field.

The SB men had obviously been talking about various security issues within the Op Hurricane area.

'There's going to be a new S.I.S. Operations Team and I want you to be a part of it,' said Phil, without turning to me, whilst studying a tight group of coloured pins around the Shamva North area. Standing nervously at the door entrance, I stepped rigidly into the room and looked directly at Colin for some support in understanding what was going on.

'On Monday morning, you are to report to Mazoe and link up with other chaps from Mtoko to start training,' continued Mac, without looking up. He continued to examine the map behind him and peered at the Mazoe area South East of Bindura, where I was to undergo training.

'The plan is to get an additional two teams of Special Branch chaps to work in the field as an Intelligence structure, to act on the information we get from Special Branch. You'll get to hear more about it when you get there. Are you game?' He enquired, turning his head to look at me for the first time.

Mac was a Superintendent but, to us juniors, he seemed to be higher-ranked than that. He was often in Phil's office and, on many occasions, I had seen him walking between various offices. He attended the Joint Operational Command meetings with all the military and Police Heads of Departments. Phil bent forward on his frayed chair and moved some papers from his cluttered desk into a wire mesh 'In' tray. He had obviously been involved in the discussions about this operational team. The S.I.S. programme was already working in other areas.

I couldn't say much, but blurted out an 'Affirmative, Sir.' That was it - that was essentially the end of the meeting!

'Uh....... how do I get there?' I enquired.

'You can catch a lift with me, Monday morning. I'm off to Salisbury. I'll meet you outside the comms room at 07:30 hours,' was Phil's response. I stood to attention and backed out of the room, heading in the direction of Peter Beck's office to tell him the news. *Who are the guys who are going to be with me and what have I let myself in for?* There was no period attached to this adventure - it could be for the next 17 years!' I began mulling over the implications.

With this move to Special Branch, I was promoted to Detective Patrol Officer. Peter was one of my best friends. We had been through much together, as Policemen and friends.

'Are you crazy?' Peter said when I told him the news.

'Well, what the hell could I do' I responded.

'You're going to miss Maggie's birthday bash at her flat.'

'I know, but I'll make up for it some other time,' I said.

Peter was just one month behind me in attesting into the Police Force, which made him a junior to me in service, but not in rank. We were both Patrol Officers. We had worked together in Centenary and the steaming hot Zambezi Valley. Between the two of us, we'd had many a drunken party and some nerve-wracking fights with terrorists to boot.

The weekend went along without much to do, except the usual trip to the pub to join Peter and his girlfriend, Maggie, for a beer. The Police pub was near the charge office. It had a straight, wooden bar counter, behind which stood Never, the barman, within easy reach of beers in the fridges below the counter and hard tack bottles on the shelves behind him. The pub was small enough to make it quite cosy. Beer was cheap at 6 cents a bottle. There wasn't much choice in beers as you either had Castle, Lion or Black Label laagers, served cold in brown bottles. On our salaries of R$400, we could get well plastered every weekend. Next to the junior ranks pub, but in the same building, was the senior ranks pub where we dared not enter, except on invitation. Section Officers and above could use this pub.

'So, what's this new project all about?' enquired Peter, as he leaned across the bar to grab three beers for the three of us.

'Mac is starting up a new Intelligence Section, you know, just like those other S.I.S. guys who sleep in the lounge.' The S.I.S. teams were not issued rooms and slept where they could. 'I don't know much about it, other than we have to get to Mazoe on Monday.' Peter turned to give his Maggie a tighter grip around her waist.

'Intelligence, my ass! What do you know about that sort of thing? I mean, you've been a policeman here. Okay, I grant you worked as Ground Coverage in Centenary and Mzarabani, but what has Mac got to do with it? Are you going to be working with the Scouts?' and so Peter carried on with questions that I couldn't answer.

'Ah, to hell with it let's have a party. Never, where's another beer for PO Chisnall?' he called to the barman, as he swung Maggie from her bar stool and started a slow-shuffled dance with her.

Packing a couple of short trousers, T-shirts and odds and ends was all I had to do to be ready to move into a new adventure. I also needed what little military clothing and equipment I had. I already had two sets of full camouflage and an assortment of webbing articles, into which I would be able to store my ammunition magazines, water bottles and other items. I withdrew my FN from the armoury, with two magazines and 40 rounds of ammunition.

S.I.S. Training:

Mazoe was a citrus estate that produced vast quantities of oranges. The bowling green on the farm, used by the local farmers and members of the Mazoe Country Club, had been built by my grandfather before the First World War. An old farmhouse, set well into the bush, was the main building used for the training. Ten-man green canvas tents, with no flooring, made up the accommodation for the trainees. A variety of metal tables, chairs and piles of odd boxes full of kitchen stuff was waiting on the dusty driveway, to be unpacked and sorted out. I dumped my kit bag on a stretcher in one of the tents at the back of the house and joined the other recruits at the front to await instructions. All the guys on the course were experienced, as we had all been in the Police Force for years. Rob Parker, a friend of mine, was there (ex Mtoko Police Station), together with a bunch of other white Patrol Officers and four black Policemen. I introduced myself to the other chaps and settled down on a tin trunk, with a cup of tea, to await the arrival of someone who knew what was to happen next.

A Section Officer, two Police Reservists and an Inspector emerged from the old farmhouse building and stood in front of the men. The taller of them, the Inspector, read out the list of names to which 'Sir' was the required answer from men present. Everybody on the list was here, a total of nineteen men.

'We will spend a couple of weeks together and I want you guys to split up into three groups and these are the sections...' carried on the Inspector.

'You are to carry your firearms at all times and there will be a guard section posted at night, so make sure you sort this out between you all.' He carried on giving us a summary of the course and what the objectives of the teams were. He told us about the type of operations we were expected to do, once we went back to our stations. He introduced the other instructors and handed the parade over to a Section Officer.

We were introduced to the men who were going to be either deployed to Bindura or Mtoko. This is when I met my friend Musa. I shook his hand and we looked each other in the eye. The handshake seemed to last a little longer than normal. Musa was a sergeant, as indicated by the three 'V' shapes on his shoulder badge. You know when you get that good feeling when you meet someone; well, I had that with this man. His dark eyes showed he was assessing me.

'Hello Musa, nice to meet you' I said, releasing my hand grip. We turned to face the instructors as we stood shoulder to shoulder. Musa was a tall man.

'Okay, boys, pack all this stuff away, grab some chow at the main building behind me and meet me back here at 14h00 hours,' commanded the Section Officer.

Thank heavens we weren't going to be doing the cooking as well. There were three cooks in attendance to do that. The training given didn't include anything more than what most of the recruits knew already. It was assumed that it was really to get the various 'sticks' to get to know one another. None of the men had ever had serious bush warfare training and any knowledge they had, had come from training they received when they'd first started and what they had learnt along the way during their normal police duties. Rob Parker was to prove to be a remarkable man, with many successes obtained during his stint with SIS. I was later told that, for his troubles, he had ended up with a steel plate in his forehead - the repairs necessary for a bullet that had just scraped his skull. My team of five black policemen arrived the next day, from Bindura. The team comprised Sergeant Musa, Constables Pedsesayi, Hombore, Dube, Nyati and me. My entire team was black, excluding me, but that didn't matter – we were all there for the same reasons.

I had trouble with my rifle in that it would jam and be impossible to reload. The round would stick in the chamber and nothing I did with the gas-return system helped to eject the round. I had sent it to Morris Depot Armoury, where they had completely revamped the barrel and it never again caused any trouble. I never did find out what had caused all the problems with my rifle, but after that it sported camouflage colours so that the matt black would not show up against the green of the bush. My choice of colours may have been questionable, but the colour selection of paint I had was not vast, and my lethal weapon now looked like a washed-out field of sweet peas in full bloom as, in amongst the greens, were some pale pinks. The effect was still good and, after a short time, some of the paint started to peel off anyway. The painting of rifles to reduce their visibility in the bush, was now common throughout the Armed Services. Sorting out kit was of importance, too. Rifles had to be in excellent condition. It was rumoured that soaking your boots in gun oil was the answer to keeping them dry in the rainy season. I soon found out that this was some urban rumour, as I used a pint of oil on my boots and they stank of oil for the whole training course. My feet suffered with wet blisters from the moisture retention. They had been great boots, with straps up the ankle giving me support when walking over rocky terrain, but as soon as the training was over I had to give them away. We were not issued boots for warfare, so tended to search for the best there was from the local shoe manufacturer called Bata. They must have made a great deal from chaps just like me. I would later change my footwear, as I preferred to wear Veldskoens, which would soon dry and were a lot more comfortable anyway. The word 'Veldskoen' comes from the Afrikaans words 'bush shoe' and was a basic shoe made from the inner shaving from cow hide, with a flexible plastic sole. In fact, this shoe became rather popular and Rhodesians could be seen within any crowd as they walked around with their Veldskoens and no socks. Two sets of camouflage trousers and shirts were issued to each recruit. It was expected that most operational men would buy their own rucksacks and other necessary items for their operation in the bush. Government military webbing was available, but didn't always suit us so we preferred to buy our own gear. A wide variety of 'civilian' bits of attire were seen. I had bought my rucksack from a shop in Salisbury and it sported an aluminium frame, and had nice, thick, shoulder-straps. My sleeping-bag folded neatly underneath and there was enough space in the four pockets to take all necessities for a two-week bush trip. The shoulder straps to the rucksack had been replaced with heavily padded ones. Magazine-webbing was issued and consisted of four extra magazines, with two, double-magazine pouches, that slipped easily into my green canvas belt. Two green, plastic water bottles, nestled in aluminium mess tins, completed the issued kit.

My complete kit consisted of the following:-

- Small backpack on frame
- FN 7.62mm rifle (camouflaged with paint)
- 6 x 20 round magazines with one on the rifle
- 1 x Z40 Anti personal rifle grenade
- 1 x mils 36 grenade (WW11 issue)
- 1 x large knife (made from a plough shear with an aluminium handle bought for $5)
- Medic's Pack, including bandages, plasters, saline drip and giving set (which consisted of the tubes and needles), 1 x ampoule Sosagen (Morphine substitute), burn pack, aspirins, halogen water-purifying tablets, etc.
- 2 x green, plastic water bottles
- metal cooking pots
- Sleeping-bag
- Rifle-cleaning kit
- Camouflage face cream ('black is beautiful')
- Small gas burner (which I later dumped in preference for dry food)

No spare clothes were packed. My camouflage floppy hat had a 'dayglo' orange patch stitched onto the inside, which was used to identify friendly forces to aircraft whilst in a firefight. I would turn the cap inside out and hopefully the heavily-armed aircraft above would be able to identify me as a 'friendly'. I used a wide-brimmed hat, instead of a peaked cap, for a number of reasons. Firstly, the peak cap had a defined round top, which was an unusual shape in the bush and if you wanted a bullet in the head, then show it off. Secondly, the hat gave more shade and sound would bounce off the brim and help in hearing better than the peak cap. I also had a 'bunny' jacket, which was a shortened, camouflage-issue jacket. The jacket was only really used to keep out the cold and was never used to hold anything in the pockets. I had cut and sewn it shorter, in an attempt to look 'the part.' How naive I was then.

After hauling around the bush for a few weeks, we had been pumped up to believe we were invincible. We had courses on combat medicine techniques, map reading, weapons handling, aircraft control from the ground, communications, camouflage techniques, tracking, etc. The training was nowhere near what we needed to be sent into the bush and complete the tasks we were to perform, but it did begin to knit the sticks together.

There was one funny episode during training, where camouflage techniques were being taught. One stick was asked to camouflage themselves into a nearby set of bushes, as though they were on an ambush. The other stick was to stand off about 25 metres and see if they could spot the ambushers. Well, not one could be seen so the point of good camouflage was proven, but then the instructor asked each man in the ambush group to move a finger or something so they could be seen. Eventually, all except one had been spotted but, for the love of beer, we couldn't find the last chap. He suddenly jumped up out of a grass patch no less than 5 feet from us. Two of the black chaps nearly passed out with fright.

Essentially, the main object of the training was to get the sticks to work as a team. Everything was done as a team. I started to cement my understanding of my men and them of me.

Contact with my arch rival:

Only one serious incident is worth mentioning whilst training was underway. During the last week of training, the recruits were to spend two nights out in the field. Two teams were made up and each was given a coloured ammunition box. The object of the exercise was to capture the opposition's box without them knowing. The rules were simple in that only two members of any team were allowed around the box, as a defensive position. The rest had to be out and about stealing coloured boxes. My stick of men were to be on the slope of a hill, bordering the tribal trust land. The teams were no more than 3 kilometres away from one another. After quite a trek, we arrived at our campsite just before last light.

'Ishe, if we get in amongst all those thick bushes, there is no way that the 'enemy' will get even close to us without making a noise,' suggested Musa.

'Okay, get the box right in the middle of those bushes and put Pedsesayi and Hombore in amongst the rocks,' I instructed, pointing out the various sites.

Each recruit had been issued with 20 blank rounds of ammunition and all live rounds had been carefully withdrawn. The instructor was just about to leave my camp when I saw Musa staring out into the distant valley. He called me over and pointed to a number of figures walking in file next to a path. The light was getting bad but, using binoculars, we could see well.

'Ishe, those people are gooks,' he said, without moving his

pointing finger. I immediately recognised this as a terrorist group; there was no way local people walked next to a footpath and in single file. The group must have been at least a kilometre from us, but were walking away. They were carrying backpacks, which were clearly visible, but it was difficult to see any weapons. It turned out that this group was none other than Mudzimo Nderinge (a Detachment Commander and in charge of the entire area – well in charge of his gooks anyway) and 6 of his senior staff. The names of the men in the terrorist group were all different to the each person's original name, in an attempt to protect their families back in their homelands from being questioned by Special Branch. Gooks such as 'Stompy Machateen' (literally meaning 'short bush') and 'Piston Number Seven' were part of this group. What weird names! All of them were senior gooks for the entire Op Hurricane area and were an extremely vital part of the terrorist operations in its Northern sector. They were the main 'management' team of the whole area, although we didn't know it at the time. Frantic radio calls went out to the base camp about 5 kms away, calling for live ammunition and spare radio batteries to be sent up, with haste, to my men. By the time the supplies arrived, it was dark and no move was made to start after the gooks. Plans were made to call in the RLI (Rhodesian Light Infantry – a highly-trained, motivated and professional section of the Army) for a morning pursuit. The other S.I.S. teams were pulled out of the area and my little section had a restless night thinking about the possibilities likely to develop in the morning.

At first light next morning, the RLI arrived in style with 3 helicopters and a Cessna 337 Lynx 'pushme-pullme' aircraft. We used the training we had learnt for aircraft communications and, together with our map of the area, were able to call the Fire Force teams in on the location where the terrorists had last been seen. Mudzimo was sighted 3 times that day, but not a shot was fired. I just wished that we'd had him plugged that day, because many lives would have been saved in the future if we had. He got away to fight another day and caused all sorts of trouble for us in our stint in S.I.S. This was one sly opponent. We didn't know it, and he sure didn't, but that terrorist squad, with Mudzimo in charge, was to be annihilated within the year in Operation Enterprise. The S.I.S. were not involved in any of the operations that took place that day. Anyway, the 'stealing boxes' campaign was cut short and, for that, we had to hike back to camp but via a triangular route that took us the whole day to complete. What would have happened if we had been given the green light to engage Mudzimo? We would probably have been hammered. The training was over, and we travelled back in Land Rovers to our respective destinations of Mtoko and Bindura.

Musa and I began our long friendship on this trip. He seemed to be a very gentle chap, but had the heart of a lion. He never complained about the weight we had to carry and was always first up the hill. His gentle side was evident when he would pause at the top of the hill, turn back, and see if the other chaps in the section were okay.

Back at Bindura Police Station, I quickly found out that my room in the Patrol Officer's Mess had been taken over by another Patrol Officer. My kit had been placed in one corner of the lounge. Rooms were for normal Police Officers, not the 'funnies.' A stretcher would have to do and I tried to squeeze all my kit and possessions into a corner of the lounge. My black colleagues moved down to the junior Policemen's quarters. The team had been given a weekend to have a bit of rest and were to report to SB offices on the following Monday.

SIS Goes Operational:

That Monday, the team met promptly at promptly at 08:00 hours and then stood aimlessly in their civilian clothes in the courtyard of the SB buildings. None of the black chaps wore shorts - in fact it was extremely rare to see any black male with shorts on. It was not the fashion and jeans were the dominant attire. The white SB chaps invariably wore shorts. Colin Evans greeted the team, as he made his way across the courtyard to link up with Tony Granger at the briefing-room.

'Hi guys, are you ready for this?' he said, as he slapped Musa on the shoulder in a friendly manner. Colin was a Section Officer and regular Policeman and had been in Special Branch for more than 3 years. His blonde hair was fading away and his bald front dome shone in the morning sun. He turned to Tony Granger, who was thumbing through some Monty Python records that lay on the corner of the wooden desk. Tony was a tall Patrol Officer, who was doing his military call-up time with SB. He had but a year to serve. He had an LLB in Law, was considered a master in espionage and had been nabbed by SB top brass. Phil followed, with a whole pile of sitreps (situation reports) clutched in his hand and a briefcase in the other. I waited outside whilst the normal morning briefing took place between the three Special Branch men.

Radio Communications:

Rebro or rebroadcasting stations were a vital link in the communications network of the Op Hurricane area. Essentially, the communications system was such that an outlying station may have struggled to communicate directly with headquarters in Bindura. The message would be sent to the Rebro station and then transmitted onwards to its final destination. The signals could not cover the great distances in which we were working for various reasons, including bad weather and the weakness of the sets being used. There were a number of Rebro stations situated around the area and they were manned by very dedicated people. Invariably, the Rebro stations were pitched high up on a hill and included a wide variety of Government-issued radios that covered all channels used by the Army, Air Force and Police services. The one we most often used was run by an extremely dedicated gentleman called

John. He had his little station atop a hill on the North-East border of Chiweshe Tribal Trust Land, not too far from Umvukwes. John was well-known in the Armed Forces as always being there for the lads. If you couldn't pick up your station on the radio, then all you needed to do was change to a channel on the UHF radio and John's voice would be there for you... what a guy!

At eight o'clock every day, one of the Patrol officers in each police station around the country would sit down, typewriter ready and type out all reports received within their areas. We had to be rather quick at our typing to keep pace with the reports. The reports would be handed to the station commanders for their information and possible instruction. All sitreps from each police station that were related to terrorist activity, had to be typed out by officers in their respective areas and then sent, via code, to Bindura on the telex machines. The sitreps were read by all relevant Members in Charge of the various Police Stations and were also subjected to overview in the Joint Operations Command in Bindura. Joint Operations Command or JOC was a meeting and operations office manned by heads of the Army, Air force and Police. Most major operations by the Armed Forces were coordinated at JOC and the tactics and manoeuvres were created by the members of JOC. Operation Hurricane's JOC was in Bindura. Coordination of troop movements and their deployments came from this office and would happen as a result of the accumulated information received by the SB, police and other sources. Local issues were handled by each respective station.

Frozen Areas:

'Frozen Areas' were demarcated from here as well. 'Frozen Areas' were marked-out areas on the map in which Special Forces were operating. It normally meant that the Special Forces involved in those areas were pseudo operations, where the troops were dressed and operated as 'terrorists', wearing terrorist clothing and carrying Eastern Block weapons. Nobody was allowed to operate in Frozen Areas. The Police performing their normal Police work needed special permission to enter these areas. We, as the local police, and performing pseudo operations, often had the areas designated as Frozen Areas. We knew that we would not be bothered by soldiers shooting up our tails. We just had to be aware that if we saw 'terrorists', they could in fact be the 'funnies.' The Selous Scouts, and then later the S.I.S and Special branch units, were termed 'funnies' as they operated in unconventional ways.

Chiweshe Tribal Trust Land Operations:

Phil beckoned the team into the briefing room, where he was half-way through a briefing with Tony and Colin.

'Those PATU guys have not come up with anything yet,' he carried on, to nobody in particular. There were three PATU sections out in the Madziwa TTL, all of which were after a group of 34 terrorists in that area. We listened intently as he described the situation in Madziwa. The Police Anti-Terrorist Unit, or PATU, essentially comprised police reservists, who formed sticks of 5 or 6 men and went tear-arsing around the bush after terrorists. They were predominantly farmers from the area. They fell under the command of the Member in Charge Bindura Police Station, but they liaised with SB all the times. Most of the farmers in the area were Police Reservists and, on occasion, local folks from the towns were also incorporated in sticks. The terrorists had a name for the PATU men: 'the old men who can shoot straight.' They were tough, hard chaps, who fought with all they had, as they were essentially fighting in their own backyards to protect their families and livelihoods.

The S.I.S stood around a metal table, in the centre of the room, trying to take in as much information as possible. Maps covered every inch of the walls. Each map reflected different bits of information. Coloured pins stuck into the map indicated positions of friendly forces and reported terrorist sightings. The pins were similar to the ones found on Phil's maps but lacked sensitive information, which was considered secret and for the eyes of the three SB men only. The maps in the briefing room were more for a general-viewer meeting. Phil shuffled through the papers and then pinned a red marker in the middle of the Chiweshe TTL area.

He turned to us. 'Twelve gooks were reported to have collected food from outside the Keep last night. Keith, take your guys and set up an OP (observation post) on this gomo (hill) to the East of the Keep,' Phil continued, as he twisted the red pin in the map as if stabbing the terrorists with his action, too. Phil turned to Colin for his support.

'The Gooks have just arrived in the area, so we reckon they are not that clued up on the terrain,' Colin interjected.

'Take a week's rations and I'll drop you off on this farm just outside the T.T.L and you can walk to the position. Keith, get down to Barbara at comms and set up a call sign for yourself. What would you want to be known as on the radio?' After a quick thought, 'AC' or Alpha Charlie was chosen. The word Charlie indicting Chisnall's team.

'There will be no other sticks in your area, so anybody carrying a weapon is pure game.' Colin continued. 'Don't forget that we have Fire Force backup in Mount Darwin, if you need them.'

'By the way, you will notice that Constable Nyati is not with us. He has dropped out of the programme, but you will have the services of Constable Sona from my office just for this trip,' Colin said.

That was it, our first adventure together as an S.I.S. team. We had packed and were ready to go at 17h00 hours. I went through everything in my kit to make sure I had enough for the stint. I also went through each of the other chaps' gear to make sure that spare batteries, spare ammunition, medics pack, radio, etc. had been packed. Each chap had to jump up and down with his full kit on to make sure he did not make any noise, with loose bits of webbing or let magazines of ammunition fall out of his pouches.

'Hombore, why is it that there is always something loose on your kit?' I said, tightening one of his buckles on his backpack. He looked at me sheepishly, without giving an answer. Hombore was the comedian of the group, since he had a lighter attitude to life than most. I also checked that the radio was operational by calling Barbara up for a test call, using the Alpha Charlie call sign for the first time.

'Aaah 204 (pronounced two zero four), this is Alpha Charlie. How do you copy?' I enquired.

'Alpha Charlie, this is 204. I read you strength, fives over,' replied Barbara.

'Roger, I'll give you a call at 07:00 hours (pronounced oh seven hundred) tomorrow, over,' I followed.

'Roger,' came Barbara's response. She knew I would go off air until that time to save batteries and also to maintain radio silence, unless there was an emergency. During the night, one of the Patrol Officers from the station would take over radio watch in the comms room and be relieved when Barbara came on duty in the morning. Barbara was one of those ladies who knew everything there was to know about running her operation. She controlled the three telex machines and the range of radios that lined up on her counter by the window. She was one very efficient girl - with a body to match.

Everything seemed fine.

'Any questions, guys?' I asked. Everybody in the stick seemed eager and ready to get out onto the operation.

'How many water bottles have you got, Pedsesayi?'

'Two, Ishe,' came his reply.

We climbed up onto the back of the canvas-covered Land Rover and headed out to the farm for drop-off. Colin was driving, accompanied by one of his sergeants in the front, acting as shotgun. Alpha Charlie sat in the back of the Land Rover. If we hit a landmine, none of us would survive. Drop-off was scheduled for 20h00 hours (eight o'clock at night) and Colin slowed to about 15 kilometres per hour when he got close to the spot. AC readied themselves and then came a knock on the window from the Sergeant in front, indicating that we should de-bus. We gingerly clambered out and leapt to the road, whilst the Land Rover continued travelling. This was not an easy task when you have a rifle, all your kit, and are travelling at 10 - 15 kms per hour, so very often we would end up head-over-heels in the dirt. Hombore lost his hat and came to a dusty landing, as his feet couldn't find their required balance. Everybody else made it fine after the debussing. This slowing down and not stopping allowed the team to be dropped off at any point, without anybody knowing where the exact drop-off was, or if anybody had been dropped off at all. Colin would slow down at other points to confuse anybody listening, as to exactly where anybody was dropped off. The only vehicles travelling on the roads at that time would have to be the Government Security Forces, as there was a dusk-to-dawn curfew in the farming areas. If you were caught wandering around during curfew, it was likely that you would get shot. I had instructed my men to keep their eyes shut for the last 20 minutes of the journey so that they would not be night-blind when they deployed. The lights from the Land Rover were not good on the eyes so, by keeping our eyes closed, we found we would be ready for action the minute we hit the dirt. I had a great fear of being night-blind and walking into an ambush. It was amazing how the light affected our night vision. Colin was gone and we could no longer hear the vehicle, even before we had made it to the side of the road.

'Musa,' I whispered 'let's just wait a bit and settle in, before we move off.' He agreed and instructed the others to move to the left-hand side of the road and take up a position about 5 metres into the bush. Muffled giggles were still heard from the guys, laughing at Hombore's antics with the debussing. Any tracks would alert the Gooks to our presence, so we doubled back in the direction we had come from for about 300 metres, until we came to a rocky area and then headed more inland to escape the road. We swung west towards the Chiweshe T.T.L and our long walk through the bush. The walk was about 30 kilometres, but it turned out to be a cinch because the moon was waxing at half-strength and we could see quite well. The problem was that the land between the farm and the hill we were heading for, was riddled with old gold mine shafts and there was no map showing their position. Even with a map of the shafts, we still had to be very cautious. The mine shafts were not protected with fences and it would be easy for the first two members of the stick to disappear down one of them before anybody could react. We came upon two of the shafts and gingerly walked around them during the march. After arriving at the foot of the hill, we were tired and breathless, with sore shoulders from carrying our full kits. It was 03:45 hours in the morning and we climbed the hill directly. It was not so difficult; however, we were aware that the local population was sleeping just over the other side, so we had to keep any noise down to a minimum.

I found a spot near the top of the hill, which looked a likely position to have our base.

'Musa, I think we can have a quick sleep before the sun gets up,' I whispered into the next guy's ear. 'Hombore, can take an hour's guard duty and he can rest when he wakes us up.' I positioned the men in their sleeping arrangements. We made a rudimentary circle, each facing outward from the centre. Our heads were two or three feet apart. The idea behind this was that, with our rifles lying next to us and facing outward, too, it would require only a small lift of the rifle to open fire on anybody approaching our make-shift base. Forming a ring of protection, with rifles pointing outward, was a good defensive position for any action, in any direction. If the stick was come upon by terrorists in the night, we felt confident that we would be able to protect ourselves with honour. With heads close together, it was also possible to whisper from ear to ear, in order to wake everybody up in relative silence. The hill was not well-covered with trees and was about 200 feet high. Small bushes and rocks were the only cover we had. We would have to keep our heads down on this one.

The Tribal Trust Lands, or T.T.Ls, were where black folks had been given land by the Government and most of the families stayed in these areas. They were controlled by the local Chiefs, who held fair sway in law-making, in conjunction with the Department of Internal Affairs, headed by a District Commissioner. Wood was the main source of fuel for cooking, making houses and cattle paddocks and the T.T.Ls were therefore reduced to having almost no large trees left at all. This didn't help us in our quest for hiding places, but it was also not so easy for the terrorists, either.

All our sleeping-bags were made from materials that did not make a noise when crumpled. I was very proud of mine, as I was able to roll it up into a sausage of about 300mm long and 150mm in diameter. Musa always seemed to have a very untidily rolled-up sleeping-bag, which was forever flowing out of its straps. He never did find the right way to roll it up and, every now and then, I would stop him in his tracks when we were doing a route march, to stuff it back into the pack. He eventually learnt not to roll it up, but to fold it, instead. Zips on the sleeping-bags had been rubbed with candle wax to reduce noise. Boots were removed and placed near our heads when we were sleeping. I used to turn my Veldskoens toe to toe and use them as a pillow. That also kept any creepy crawlies from making them their home. Nothing like putting your foot into a boot, which had a spider or scorpion in it - now *that* would wake you up! Hombore took first guard- watch for an hour, while the rest of us got a quick hour's sleep. He woke everybody at 05h00 hours and immediately turned in to catch up some sleep himself. He was one guy who could sleep anywhere and at any time; whether it was amongst rocks or a thorny bush, he would just turn over and that was it.

At 05:30 hours, the sun started to show its first glows in the East. The cockerels from the nearby village had started to crow, announcing the coming day. The sounds of the locals emerging out of their mud-and- daub-grass, thatched huts and going about their daily routine, started to pick up. A dog barked at its neighbour. Musa was up and about, with binoculars in hand when I looked for him. He was perched on a small rock, behind a scraggly bush, as the sun peaked over the horizon. Everybody left their sleeping-bags as they were, because we would be based here for a week whilst we observed the immediate area, using binoculars. Musa's routine search of the landscape, from right to left, was interjected with a shuffle of his feet to ease the cramps in his legs. Pedsesayi was bending over a small gas stove, trying to get some tea on the boil. A small line of Matabele ants crossed in front of Musa's boots, intent on searching out termites for their breakfast. I drew a line across their central column with my finger, effectively erasing the pheromone trails of the leaders. All the ants left behind started to chant and squeak in search of their original trail. It took them five seconds to find their mates and then they were back in line and on their way again. Musa didn't stop his endless search for the enemy.

Mujibas:

We sat for a while, enjoying the early morning sunrise. Musa lowered his binoculars and looked back at me. He beckoned with his eyes for me to come forward to his position. I slid onto the rock next to him and leaned towards his ear.

'What's up?'

Following his pointed finger down to a clump of small trees, I could make out two young boys walking in the bush towards the hill. We never pointed with our arms out straight; the movement was too much and a bent finger, from wherever the hand happened to be, was enough to indicate the direction. Musa's pointed finger directed my search to the boys as they were making their way towards the hill, following our spoor. I twisted around and motioned the other chaps to spread out, facing the oncoming duo. Pedsesayi had to stop his tea-making, whilst he shook Hombore. Hombore slipped out of his bag and joined Pedsesayi and Sona to the right of Musa and me. I pointed out the two boys and they knew immediately what we were watching. The boys picked their way up the hill in our direction.

'Mujibas,' whispered Musa.

We lost sight of them as they started to climb the gomo but, after about twenty minutes, the heads of the boys appeared over a little rise in the front of the S.I.S men. They were scantily clad, wearing shorts and ragged T-shirts. It was obvious, with their loose genitalia swaying from side to side as they walked, that they had no underpants on. Each carried a stick that he would use to push thorns out the way. I looked straight into the eyes of the leading one. The boy froze, with fright in his eyes, when he saw armed soldiers. They had obviously been told to do a scout of the area by their adult mentors. I motioned for him to move towards us. As the two boys came up, Musa grabbed them and pulled them down to the ground.

'What the hell are they doing here?' I whispered to nobody in particular.

Musa started to ask them questions about their movements. He didn't go through the customary greeting, but got straight to the point.

'What are you doing on this hill?'

'Where are the terrorists?'

'Are you a Mujiba?' etc.

The boys, with lowered heads, explained that they were looking for a missing goat that had not come back to the kraal the night before. They were about 12 years old. Musa didn't believe this, as the boys had been seen following our spoor. A quick discussion followed between Musa and myself.

'We have to move. If we keep these two with us, they will be missed at the kraal and the whole village will come out searching,' I told my second in command.

'If we let them go, we had better get picked up, otherwise the gooks could catch us,' replied Musa. That seemed the best way out, as the gooks would know within the hour about our presence. I got onto the radio and called Barbara to let her know that we had been compromised. Colin would have to drive all the way out again, but it would be a good idea to meet at the kraal so that AC could interview the residents of the village. That was it - compromised on our first patrol. I was sick with disappointment.

Nothing came from the talk with the people in the kraal. This was to be expected since, if there were any gooks in the area, anybody who showed even some form of cooperation with the Security Forces would readily be dealt with by the terrorists. It was important that they didn't know who the informer was that Colin had bribed for information. He lived in the village below. Perhaps there were no terrorists in the area anyway! Informers often told stories when they were a bit short of cash, invariably from gambling debts. The stick was pulled out and sent back to Bindura. However, we had learnt some valuable lessons on that first patrol. With the sandy soils, lack of trees and relatively high population in the TTLs, it would always be a problem keeping our tracks and ourselves hidden. Our tactics would have to change drastically in the future, in order for us to survive.

Mujiba Tactics:

Mujibas were informers and errand boys for the terrorists. They were invariably young boys, whose normal job was to look after the village's cattle and goats. The Mujibas were a vital part of the terrorist information network. They would report any signs of Security Force presence and tell their masters, and heroes, of any suspected informers within the community. They were often fanatical. I guess the terrorists and their weapons must have made a huge impression on these young boys. If the terrorists suspected that a person from a village was an informer for the Government Security Forces, he would be killed in the most gruesome way, in front of the village people. He may even have his whole family wiped out. The informers would be executed, often with barbaric methods such as the use of bayonets, fire, bullets, or purely being beaten to death with sticks. Cutting off lips, noses and other parts of the hapless victim was also a form of punishment that the terrorists would dish out to so-called traitors of the revolution. AC was to have many altercations with Mujibas.

Shamva - The Main Operational Area for SIS
Call sign Alpha Charlie

Our team was sent to Shamva, with instructions to take enough kit for a month. Shamva was 60 kms east of Bindura and was a small gold-mining town. It also supported the local farmers with a couple of shops. I met up with the local Police chaps at Shamva, including a stout young Patrol Officer called Mike White. Mike was to become one of my best friends and many a party, with booze and girls, would transpire in the future as a result of this friendship. Shamva was a small farming town, with very little in it save a Post Office, Police Station, a couple of shops and the mandatory fuel station. The Police Station was set amongst Jacaranda trees that had been planted years before, but which shed their tiny leaves all over the ground every winter. The leaves were forever getting into everything and effectively stopped any grass growth below. Jacarandas are beautiful in October, when they bloom all over with a mass of light purple flowers. The spectacle presented with Jacarandas lining the streets was truly magnificent. The unkempt garden was an arid area where somebody, years back, had tried to plant flowers and lawn but, due to lack of water and attention, it had struggled to survive through the years. The lawn and 'flower' beds were neat, but dry, with a covering of dust which had been blown up from the passage of vehicles on the dirt road leading to the station. Rocks neatly lined the circular drive leading to the Charge Office, with the whitewash paint on them fading into browns caused by the dust. On entering the station, I noticed a cable lying rolled up next to one of the Jacaranda trees. Mike later told me that the Duty Constable had the task of lifting the cable and stringing it between the two big Jacarandas on opposite sides of the road. There was a fear that the terrorists would commandeer a civilian vehicle and drive down the station road, shooting up everything in sight. The cable would put a stop to that and, hopefully, decapitate the attackers.

I settled the men into their barracks, a tented section next to the black policemen's section, and ran an equipment check. The stick was short of ammunition and could do with a couple of extra goodies, such as hand grenades and rifle grenades. One hundred rounds per man was not nearly enough. If we were ever in a firefight with a large group of terrorists, we would struggle to get enough backup to us in time and we would have to rely on our own supplies to survive such an event. I remembered being caught out before with no ammunition and I was not going to let that happen again, no way. I met up with Mike and scrummaged through the Police Station armoury's meagre stock pile. Two Mils36 grenades, two Z42 rifles grenades and 150 rounds of 7.62mm ammunition was all that Mike could spare, but even that small donation was eagerly grabbed. The two Mils36 grenades had come from stock left over from WW11 and, on checking the fuses at the bottom, they appeared to be 'okay.' We had to trust that the grenades would work, because there was no way of testing them. 'Stealing' from the local Police station was not on, since they had their own problems in getting armaments. They had to issue equipment to their PATU sticks, but my needs were for now and that's what counted most. My stock was not enough and Mike was a real gentleman in releasing some of his own.

The station's 'rat pack' store was the next on the list, as I had to draw our rations for the team from Mike's reserves. Ration packs were not as difficult to get as ammunition and Mike opened his stores to us saying that whatever we took needed to be written down, so that he could restock. The ration packs were numbered A through to K, as each one had different goodies inside to give troops a variety. They were presented in small cardboard boxes, with the designated single letter stencilled on the lid. 'F'-rated ration packs were the ones most sought after, as they contained a really nice selection of food items. We received no cigarettes in the packs. The rat packs had everything needed for a full day's rations, including a tin of meatballs in tomato sauce, so called dog biscuits (hard as wood but, when soaked in a cup of tea, gave you a good, small meal), salt tablets to stave off heat exhaustion, a small tube of butter, tea, sugar and small items such as sweets. The black chaps on the stick always chose to use the rat packs, as their meagre salaries didn't give them the option of buying anything extra. I couldn't stand anything in the packs and always made up my own mix. I would dish my rations out to the other chaps in the stick. I made up a mix of milk powder and sugar, which I would eat from my hand. I also liked to buy what was called 'cut finger' from the local stores. I liked cut finger, as it was chopped ham in a tin and tasted great. It was called cut finger because, invariably, everybody was hungry all the time and when it was decided to have some grub, we would more often than not cut our fingers on the sharp tin when it was opened with the little key that was attached to the tin's lid. Cut finger was loved by all the members of AC and I found tins being bought by the other members of the stick later on. Often, when I did an equipment check before an operation, I would always laugh when the chaps would run down their food list and include 'two cut fingers' in their list.

The briefing that I had been given by Colin Evans was to infiltrate the Madziwa T.T.L and 'clear the area of any terrorists.' There had been no real time-limit given to the operation, but it turned out that Shamva would be the base for AC for a good while. Colin knew that the resident terrorist group habitually spent time around the South East of the T.T.L around Keep 3. A full look at the Protective Villages (or Keeps) was done to ascertain the strength of Guard Force personnel, as well as the position of each Village to nearby hills and the defences each had, or didn't have. The overview of the Protective Villages was to prove vital in a number of actions to come. The TTL had 4 Keeps within it. Farm land surrounded the Madziwa TTL to the South, West and North and the Mfurudzi Wildlife area bordered it to the East. It was known that a group of around 21 gooks were operating in the area. The area was also considered an important corridor for gooks travelling from the Northern areas, bordering Mozambique, through to Salisbury, the capital of Rhodesia.

Getting to know the area was very important and a two Land Rover recce tour of the area was arranged. Mike and a Constable from Shamva police station travelled in one vehicle, whilst Musa and I followed in another. We didn't use the heavy vehicle because of its hunger for diesel fuel.

'Mike, we had better just go straight to Keep 3 to see the layout of the land and pretend we have business with the guys there,' I said, as we were about to jump into the Land Rovers.

'I'll follow you at about 500 metres and we'll work off channel eight on the radio.'

Pseudo Operations

The S.I.S. team was very active, but we found we needed to do something a little "extra" in order to perform our duties. It wasn't long before we changed our tactics, as well as our weapons and clothes. We were now going to dress up and act as local terrorists. I 'borrowed' my Grandmother's fur coat and cut off the sleeves to make a 'jungle jacket'; she never used it, anyway! To dress up as a terrorist was not that difficult; you just had to wear darker civilian clothes and carry some Chinese weaponry. We were each issued with AK47s and Chinese webbing. We also used badly-fitting backpacks and the rest of the gear was up to us to sort out. I must say we looked the part and we spent many hours going over our modus operandi to infiltrate the kraals, pretending to be the boys from the bush. Hombore really looked like a gook. We hoped to gain information of the location of the real terrorists and also find out who was supporting them in the communities. I was also issued with a small black box and a little sister box. The little box was the transmitter and the larger one was a receiver. The idea was to talk with local people and then leave the transmitter in the thatch roof. After moving a short distance away, we would then listen in on the conversation to see what information we could glean. Perhaps they would talk about the need to tell the terrorists that we were in the area and we could also begin to understand the mechanisms that the local people had in place to communicate with the terrorists. If someone said they were going to the terrorists, we would try and follow them and pounce on our enemy. The difficulty was getting the transmitter covertly installed into the hut and we ended up not using it that much.

My problem was my blonde hair and blue eyes. If we met the locals during the day, it would be Musa and Hombore who would do all the talking and I would hang back in the distance with Pedsesayi. I wore a dirty bandage around my neck in the pretence that I had an injury and couldn't talk. I also used a hair-net, with a large, wide brimmed hat, to help cover my hair. 'Black is Beautiful' camouflage cream was used to darken my skin colour but, no matter how I applied this awful stuff, I always looked lighter in complexion to the other lads. Thankfully, most of the meetings we had with the locals happened at night, so it was not difficult to disguise myself.

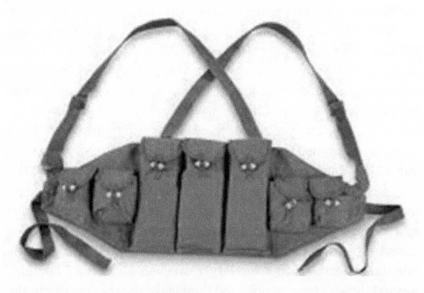

At one such meeting, we were all sitting around the small fire in the hut and Musa was sitting next to me on the floor. He was merrily chatting away with the local chief and I found my eyes drooping as I began to fall asleep. The meeting seemed to go on for hours. Musa had finished his speech and promised that we would be back in the morning to get some food from the kraal. I understood everything they were saying, but I mentally switched off as I was so tired. Musa ended up nudging me with his elbow to usher me up and out of the hut. His explanation to the chief was that I was still very sick from the injury to my neck. Naturally I said nothing, with my wound being a good excuse. Anyway, we eventually made our way out of the kraal and based up not fifty metres from it to sleep. Very early in the morning, we were up again and watching to see if one of the men left to go and call the terrorists. This was typically one of our strategies and we managed to get a great deal of information this way.

At one stage, we tried our luck with the locals and told them that we were 32 men in total and that they were to bring food up to the hill. We must have caused quite a stir, because a line of 15 young girls and boys brought the food up on enamel plates. I actually felt sorry for them because they had to kill about eight chickens for us. Well, Hombore was happy but we had to dispose of a lot of the food. We operated as Pseudo Terrorists for most of our time in S.I.S. and I must say it did give us a great deal of insight into how our enemy worked. The lessons I learnt in this little group helped me a great deal in later operations.

How to Drive:

Distances between road turn-offs and the keeps, between hills and rivers, kraals and shops etc., were important to know. Landmarks, such as hills, for use by us in route marching were noted. Water points and access roads where looked for and notes made on maps to indicate possible ambush sites. Knowledge of our operational area was vital. The drop-off and pick-up points had to be remembered well, since these actions were normally carried out at night and every aspect of security had to be taken into account. An easy way to check the distances would be to zero the mileage indicator on the vehicle every time a special spot was recognised, and the distance between it and the previous one would be jotted down on the 1:50 000 map, which we carried for this purpose. At night-time, it would be just a matter of reading the mileage to the point we had to be dropped off – simple. It was also vital that these events did not arouse the suspicions of the local population. Invariably, the drop-offs were made at points where the road dropped down to a river, or as it wove its way between two small hills, to minimise the possibility of people hearing the change in gears or lower-engine noise. Trying to keep the noise down was also vitally important. Sound travels great distances in the quiet and cool African nights. The areas were well-known to us and the drop-offs were always done to within 100 metres of the chosen place. Pre-planning would make for an easier deployment and get the group as close to their final destination as possible, without giving any indication of where they would be going. Another factor to consider was tracks left by us as we jumped off the vehicle. The roads were generally dusty and it didn't take too much of a trained eye to spot such an event. Anti-tracking would have to take place. We would walk backwards off the road, walk parallel to it and then cross again backwards and so on, until we had found a suitable site where we could head off in the desired direction. Once the group was securely positioned, and before we headed off across country, we would stop and listen for about ten minutes. This would give our ears time to accustom to the night sounds in that area. Any night birds and frogs calling were listened for. All this preparation would get us separated from the domestic world and into a very different, clandestine world of warfare. Our very survival depended on small things like that.

Travelling at night in a vehicle was difficult enough, but travelling with the lights out was more so. By switching off the lights at irregular intervals, it would often be difficult for people some distance away to establish exactly where the vehicle was. Often the only way to drive without lights was if you knew the road intimately, or there was help from a full moon. We didn't have night-vision equipment for night-driving at that stage. No revving of the vehicle was allowed, as the sound would arouse the attention of people who may not necessarily have heard it in the first place. Dummy stops and lights on and off would confuse any would-be listener as to where the drop-off, if any, was to take place.

The System of Walking:

The small team was now working well together. Every man knew exactly where he should be when walking on a road, path or through the bush. Typically, on a path through the bush, it would be Musa first then me at about four metres behind him, followed by Hombore and Pedsesayi at equal distances. The team would stay closer together at night, so as to not lose touch. It all depended on the light from the moon, or from the hazards encountered in the bush. Walking along a path with a full moon meant the chaps spread out more, whilst on dark nights and with thick bush, we walked within almost touching distance. Musa, up in the lead position, had no idea how the last man in the line was doing and it was up to the man in front of the last man, Pedsesayi, to watch that he didn't fall back. If he did fall back, Pedsesayi was to warn me and so on up the line.

Warnings were normally done in discreet sounds such as bird calls or, if it was an emergency, then the men would make a faint 'stssss' sound. When walking with all senses trimmed and sharp, it would be relatively easy to hear if somebody in the stick was falling back. Every man made a different sound when walking and the absence of any of these sounds would stop the stick in their tracks, so that the problem could be evaluated. We trained constantly to have all our senses actively at 100% - all of the time. Each man would look forward, then into the bush on either side, whilst almost consciously listening with one ear to the rear and one to the front. Pedsesayi was left-handed and this really aided the readiness of the walking men. His rifle pointed to the right, whilst the other chaps' rifles faced left.

Rifles At The Ready:

Rifles were always held across the front and at the ready, with safety catches on and each man's index finger on the trigger and thumb on the safety-catch. It was an automatic action that if the weapon was trained onto a target or area for any reason, the thumb would ease off the safety-catch and onto single-shot mode. This action was so quick that it was done in one natural movement. If a dove flew up in front of us, we would find Musa had it in his sights before it had flown two metres. The safety-catches were always kept well-oiled, to allow easy and silent movement. One 'click' down from safe mode is single-shot mode and a second 'click' was to automatic mode. That was one of the differences we found when we used AK47s. We would not have the silent action that the FN had in changing the safety-catch from safe to fire. With the AK47, the sound is very audible and distinctively tinny. There was nothing we could do to reduce the sound of this action and, in our game of bush warfare, that specific click was a dead giveaway. The AK47 has a real problem in that to change the safety-catch position, one had to reach over the weapon with the left hand or take one's right hand off the trigger. In our kind of war, that small delay in getting the safety-catch onto fire could cost you your life. With the FN, that changing took place instantly - it entailed a simple flick of the lever with the thumb of the right hand, without removing your finger from the trigger, or losing your aim. You therefore could do this action whilst raising the rifle to your shoulder, in one smooth movement. AC members never ever used automatic mode in any of our contacts. During training, 'double tapping' was the method used to get accurate fire onto a position. Accuracy was more important than volume of fire and the team just didn't carry enough ammunition to go blasting up the neighbourhood. It was found that firing two shots in quick succession was a lot more accurate than firing a burst on automatic. Invariably, the second shot was the one that would find its mark. Using both eyes to look at the target was also a better system. After a great deal of practice, eventually I was able to look at a target, bring the rifle to my shoulder with the butt of it directly under my chin and let off two rounds in under 0.4 of a second, with the second round normally hitting the target. The sights were never really used in close-quarter contacts. It came down to a feeling one had with the rifle and making it as an extension of one's body. I had trained with my men by squeezing a piece of grass into the round, rear aperture of the sights, effectively closing the sighting mechanism, so that they got used to firing without trying to peer down the sights.

I found that the more comfortable the rifle was to handle, the more accuracy gained. I said that it was better to use a .22 calibre rifle and get the shot home, than to use a stronger but uncomfortable rifle and miss. By constant practise, we were generally able to overcome the instinct to shoot high and, carrying the rifle all the time and getting very familiar with it, meant that it became second nature to use it and we would never be frightened of it. If a soldier was 'happy' with his weapon, he would be a lot more efficient when using it.

The length of the rifles' butt needed to be longer for a taller person. To get two accurate shots off in 0.4 seconds could never be done if the weapon was not held with both hands and across the body in the 'ready' position. Carrying a weapon over the shoulder, on a sling, was not allowed in my stick. A carrying sling was never seen on any of the weapons used; even the heavy MAG machine gun had to be carried at the 'ready', all the time. If we got tired, it was better to rest in a defensive position than carry the weapon on our shoulders. Constant training and firing thousands of rounds of ammunition stopped the so called 'gun shy' syndrome. Men would blink with every shot, if they weren't used to firing the weapon. We called it being gun shy. They would also flinch and not squeeze the trigger. If you flinched, it normally meant that the shot would miss the target and hit somewhere to the bottom right of the target. The sighting mechanism on the 7.62mm FN rifle was not the easiest to use, if one had to be really accurate. At 100 metres, the front sight bar would be the same width as a man's shoulders. One needed to aim for the groin area of a man, the thought being that this was about halfway up the body. Any hit on a man by a 7.62mm x 52mm round would be enough, generally, to make him think twice about shooting back, or running away. The round was powerful enough to stop him in his tracks at distances up to 450 metres, if he was hit in the right place.

If the man was lying down, and the shot was taken, it would be better to aim at the ground just in front of him. A low shot would pick up rocks and debris on impacting the ground, and the rocks and sticks from the ground, together with the round itself, would smash into him. Higher shots would propel him straight to a meeting with the good Lord above, provided they weren't too high. If you aimed at him, instead of the ground just in front, any high shots would miss, for sure. It was therefore, from a probability point of view, better to aim lower into the dirt just in front of him, so as to have a 50% better strike rate. The FN bullet was strong enough to go right through smaller trees, so anybody thinking he would be safe by hiding behind one or more of those, would be in for a surprise.

Know The Man Next To You:

Marching at night was a most demanding exercise. So many things had to be taken into account, at all times. The silhouette of each soldier was well-known to all the others and, just by glancing at another man within the stick, we would know who it was. I remember a story where my friend Peter Beck had been walking with a stick of 8 men in the dead of night. They had stopped for a rest next to the road and not far from a kraal. When they got up to move again, Peter was the last man, so he counted his men, but kept on counting 9. To his utter disbelief, a Gook had joined the stick thinking that those were his men. Peter had to work out who this chap was, but once he realised, he shot him on the spot. Later on in my career, when I joined a Special Forces team under the name of Pachedu, this carelessness could cost one or more of my men their lives. I guess the attention to every detail, all of the time, was what pulled me and my men through until the end of the war.

Walking was an art of its own. When walking through the bush or on a road, it was very important not to scuff our feet on the gravel or brush. This noise is almost peculiar to humans. Animals don't do this so, if one heard this type of noise, one could bet it would be from a human, so beware. The way we overcame this was to walk more on our toes than on our heels. When taking a step, we would reduce the length of the stride and try to place our foot flat from the toes first. Our balance would be more on the front of the foot and not on the heel. It is very difficult to shift your foot quickly, if you place your foot down with a long stride and on your heel. Being able to adjust our feet by being 'light-footed' meant that if a twig or bunch of dry leaves was encountered, we would be able to avoid it instantly. The foot would only take all our weight when it was almost directly below our bodies and, at that point, we would lift the heel slightly. This seems an ungainly and tiring way of walking, but it sure did reduce the noise considerably. What was also important was that we were able to stop instantly to listen, or jump off to the left or right. By walking in this manner, we were able to walk right up to kraals at night, without fear of being heard. It would also allow us to hear better and to have an advantage of some 5 or so metres on anybody approaching us on the same path. If I walked normally, a sort of jolting sound was created where my kit would 'thump'. My brain also seemed to 'thump' in its cavity. By walking in a gliding movement, I could reduce all of this noise. The sooner we were able to hear or see the enemy, before they saw us, the better chance we had of gain-ing the upper hand, and this would give us the winning ticket, every time. Half-a-second's advantage would be enough for us to win the day. That was how tight it was. We were never caught by surprise due to making too much noise. This method of walking was difficult to maintain, especially when walking the distances we did at night. Invariably, a route march would be upward of 20 kms and sometimes reached as many as 30 kms in a night. That's a long way to walk looking like a duck! Frequent rests were pre-ferred and I would stop the team for a rest every 2 or 3 kms, even if it was just to stand still. Soft-soled boots were preferred to hard soles. Thin soles were also great, as we could better 'feel' obstruc-tions. These were also better for anti-tracking methods. We even shaved the sharp edges off the sides of the soles of our shoes to reduce the sharp indentations left behind in the sand. Walking on our 'toes' also reduced the depth of footprints, as our weight would spread evenly across the entire footprint and not leave a heavily-indented heel mark.

To Hear The Enemy First:

A strange, but useful, method of listening was also used. In gen-eral, I would hold my mouth open, with the tip of my tongue pushed down on my lower jaw, and my head tilted slightly down. Just this small action would increase my hearing ability. On the march we would do the above but, when we looked into the bush on either side, we would consciously direct our hearing to either the right or left ear, depending on in which direction we wanted to hear better. By consciously listening through one ear, we would be able to find direction and identify any sound ever so much bet-ter. Often a sound made would not be repeated and we only had one chance to hear where it came from, how far away it was made and what sound it was. Wearing a floppy hat was better than a cap, since any sound would be more easily heard with the brim of the hat collecting the sound. When we were not walking, it was better to cup our hands around our ears to increase the collection of sound. The direction of the sound could also be better judged. The tongue position is similar to that when one makes a preschool sound of the letter 'G', almost making the sound 'ga' but not really doing it. There was no second chance for beginners in this game.

So-called jungle warfare was very different to conventional warfare in that stealth was our main strength and advantage. Disregard this law at your peril in the thick bush of Southern Africa.

Some general tricks to survival:

- The shape of one's backpack was important. No object was to stick out, as it could snag on a bush or thorn. Getting snagged in a bush would make a loud noise and, because the object would be caught behind you, it would be impossible to stop it from happening and even more difficult to remove.

- A half-full bottle of water could be a noise problem. The water would slosh around in the bottle at every step. However, the use of plastic bottles reduced this noise, compared to aluminium ones. Keeping the bottle more to the rear of the body, as opposed to the sides, would reduce the movement of the water. The sound would also be reduced by being nearer the back, as the body would deaden some of the noise received from the front.

- The front rifle-sling-catch on the rifle had to be removed, so that it wouldn't swing and make a clicking sound at each step.

- Any loose items in one's webbing or backpack had to be sorted out.

- If eating from a metal container, like the one issued with the water bottles, it would be better to craft a spoon from wood to eat with. Never use metal against metal, as the sound is so distinct against natural sounds.

- Never talk in the bush, as the peaks and troughs of speech travel a great distance compared to a whisper. When whispering, reduce the 'sss' sound one tends to use on certain words and reduce the pitch.

- Never snore, cough or cry out for any reason. To stop snoring, pick your nose; don't blow it to clean it out. Train yourself to sleep with your mouth open, but not breathe through it, by raising the back part of your tongue to the roof of the mouth, just the same as listening better. Breathe through the nose. This was a tricky one, which could take some months to perfect. One tends to sleep well, but not in a deep sleep, giving you some advantages namely, a quicker waking-up time if you have to react to a compromising of the camp, and zero snoring.

- Never cook with potent-smelling foods, like onions etc. Better still, is not to cook at all but to use alternative foods, like raw roots and fruits found in the bush, or biscuits. This is not always possible, and one can increase morale with a warm meal or cup of tea, but be sensible.

- Never, but never smoke, in the bush. A burning cigarette can be smelt on the other side of a hill! We were able to smell people who smoked from a great distance. I think the furthest we smelt cigarettes was on the other side of a hill – a good 600 metres away! Unbelievable, but true.

- Never use deodorant or soap, as they are not natural bush smells and can be smelt from a long way off. Wash with plain water. Washing your pot with sand is just as good as using dishwashing liquid.

- Make sure you clean your body at every opportunity. Not only will this reduce fungal growth, but it improves morale.

- When camping in a base, always remove all your refuse when you leave. This is in case the enemy comes across the camp and will realise that this is where you would most likely camp if you were here again. What follows from this is that you should NEVER camp in the same place twice. Always lift up the grass from the place where you've slept, so that the enemy cannot count how many people have slept there. Use different routes in and out of the base to reduce wear on the grass. After you have used a base, place dead branches and dead leaves across paths to hide the fact that anyone has walked there at all. In other words, don't leave a 'human footprint' anywhere.

- Look at all your equipment and remove or paint over any shiny items, or items which are not coloured the same as the bush. The small, blue gas camping burners can be seen a mile away, so get the base painted green or brown.

- Whilst in the base, reduce the amount of movement to an absolute minimum; even crawling around is better than showing movement. Reduce your silhouette at all times. If you look up at a hill, it is normal to trace the horizon in your scan. Anyone poking his head over the top will be spotted easily.

- If you are trying to look at an area for a terrorist, you can slightly blur your eyes to increase your field of vision. By not looking at anything in particular, and by keeping your eyes still, you will cover a much wider area in your quest to search for movement. Movement is a big giveaway, so stay still. Be aware that the enemy could be 3 metres from you, so start your scan near you and work outwards.

- The age of uniforms is very important. Uniforms that have been washed repeatedly tend to have very fine, bleached white fibres sticking out of the main fabric. Many of these fibres will be paler in colour and on a moonlit night would cause you to shine like a glow-worm. Uniforms that are too new would appear too dark on moonlit nights. In both situations, it's better to wait for the moon to settle over the horizon before moving out.

- Anti-Tracking and tracking were vital tools to use in jungle warfare. This is an art and only through rigorous training can it be perfected. Wearing different boots or shoes during a long march can confuse the enemy. Taking off one's boots and walking the way the locals walk can help a great deal.

There are so many things one needs to know to try and stay alive in the bush. These are just a few of them. It takes at least six months to a year of constant bush work to get just a little bit tuned into the bush.

Back to Keep 3:

Travelling to Keep 3 in a convoy of two vehicles, was not uncommon in this area. We drove relatively slowly so that we could take in all the information we could. We arrived at the Keep, swept through the outside security-gate and meandered around the numerous huts until we passed through the steeply-banked soil surrounds to the centre of the keep, where the Internal Affairs chaps were based. We linked up with the chap in charge, had a general chat, some tea of course, and then headed back out. There must have been 2000 people living in the Keep.

'So what do your reckon?' I asked Musa, as we left the keep behind us.

'Ishe, the gooks probably come up to the fence at night to get food and girls. Those Intaf (short for Internal Affairs) guys are always asleep and I bet they're too scared to check the fence for breakages anyway,' he wisely responded. Musa was a quiet chap, but had a very common-sense attitude to many things.

'So, if we camp out in that hill during the day, it will be far away enough to be out the way and we can move in next to the Keep at night?' I questioned, looked to the North where a hill about 200 metres high overlooked the Keep.

'Roger,' Musa agreed.

'So, we will drop off from the tar road and walk to the hill,' I summarised. We bounced our way back along the dirt road, the way we had come in, and struck north to search for a suitable drop-off point on the tar road. We hadn't gone 3 kms when we snaked through two hills, where the road made an 'S' bend.

'Here, Ishe,' Musa indicated.

It was a perfect spot. No tracks would be seen leaving the road when we debussed and there was nobody in close proximity to hear or see the drop-off vehicle. We carried on for about 10 kms and I radioed Mike to tell him that we were happy. We then did an about-turn and headed back to Shamva Police Station.

Observation Post (OP):

The drop-off at 20h00 hours went fine. We got to the hill at around midnight and climbed onto its western side, where we found a great place to set our base halfway up the hill. The guys were tired.

'Okay, tonight we will split up and have a good rest. See you back here at 05h00,' I instructed. The chaps were happy. No guard duty tonight and we could sleep well. By splitting the team up, each man would be responsible for his own sleeping position. In doing this, we would be apart but the chance of anybody walking into us was very small, especially at midnight. If anybody had trouble they were not to open fire, but were to stay hidden. We would follow the spoor in the morning and catch the gooks that way. It is almost impossible to see a trained soldier when he is snugly asleep in a little bush, at night. We used this technique on most of our patrols when the guys were tired. The chaps would normally walk off about 100 metres in each direction, so that we all would be about 200 metres from one another. Our mental alarm-clocks would wake us up every time. I would normally keep the radio with me. If one of us overslept we would not worry, but would just waited for him at the arranged base and he would come in later, giving his familiar call to let us know it was him. Each chap had his own choice of call and everybody knew these calls. When he called, one of us would respond in our own calls and we could safely link up. On a link-up like this, we often used the call of the Red-Chested Cuckoo, as it was a common bird throughout Rhodesia and was an easy call to mimic.

We used to say that the bird was saying 'half-past five', with the first two notes the same and the last a higher pitch in the form of a whistled note, with the breath drawn in. It was part of a little joke between us. Sometimes the guys got too good at the call and we would think it was just a bird. The incoming soldier would have to call again until one of us responded, before he could approach the base.

Everybody was at the base at 05h00 and Musa and I did our normal thing by searching for a good observation point where we could look out over the surrounding countryside and the Keep. The sun was still just below the horizon and its warm glow hovered in the distance. Hombore and Pedsesayi stayed back at the base, but were instructed to keep an eye out on the route we used climbing the hill, in case some bright spark decided to follow our tracks up.

I had to reapply my 'black is beautiful' camouflage cream, because most of it kept smearing off in the sweat of getting to the hill, and whilst I slept. The cream was definitely not created by a dermatologist, since it stank to high heaven and filled up all the pores of my skin. It was impossible to get it out of my pores and I always had skin problems, or acne, because of it. Back in Salisbury I would try and scrub it off with a brush, but I never was never able to fully remove it all. I always decanted the cream into a small, green, Russian AK47 rifle-cleaning oil bottle, which was small enough to pack into my backpack. I didn't have a mirror to use, as it was too shiny and not allowed in the bush.

'So, did I miss anywhere?' I asked Musa, showing him my face at all angles.

'Aikona (no), Ishe,' he responded, looking at my face, neck and arms with a smile.

'One day I'm going to get a white cream for you buggers!' I joked, as I packed the bottle away in my trouser pocket. The black guys didn't have to worry about camouflage cream and I experienced what it was like for a woman having to put on her make-up every morning.

The day was going to be a bright, sunny 25° C, with patches of cloud. Musa and I shifted a little to get deeper into a bush, so that our silhouettes would not be visible from down below.

'Where do your parents live?' I asked, whilst I panned the bush to the right with my binoculars.

'My mother lives near Salisbury in the Tribal Trust area, Ishe. She is now madala (old),' he said, as he lowered his binoculars to take a rest, and ... possibly thinking of home.

I looked at Musa's hands. The long, slender fingers showed signs that he had worked hard all his life. The calluses on his palms showed that he had lived a life of toil. I saw the veins on the back of his hands standing up, showing that he was fit. I liked Musa. He had a good soul and was respectful. I wondered what his mother was like – did she make his special meal that he liked when he got home? I thought of my mother and the warm tenderness she had for us as kids. I didn't ask Musa anything more as I sensed that he missed home. We were the same in many ways, although we had been brought up in such different circumstances. I understood his way of life from all the friends and families I had learnt from on the farm, but somehow he had a mysterious manner. I could sense he was more of a man than I had first thought.

Both of us were sitting on our haunches. Our knees formed a great platform on which to rest our elbows when using the binoculars. It kept the binoculars from moving around too much, especially important if we were looking at bush area around a kilometre away. Not many people can do that for hours on end, as the blood circulation to your legs below the knee stops after a while, and you get pins and needles. The black guys, however, could sit like that for extended periods, but I guess it was because they generally didn't have well-developed calf muscles. I was also able to sit like that for long periods, so there the two of us sat, without saying a word, until Pedsesayi came creeping up to us with two cups of very sweet tea. The sun was now well up and I thanked Pedsesayi for the tea and told him that he could take over from Musa, as it was now 07h00 hours and I would go back to get Hombore to replace me. This was often the routine. Musa and I would go back to the base and get some grub ready for the other two and then take a rest in the shade of a tree, but still looking back to where our tracks came from up the hill. The tea was hot and I had to find my little piece of tin foil, which I folded over the edge of the rim, to stop the hot metal cup from burning my lips. The day was uneventful, with routine shift changes at the 'front.' We didn't see anything unusual. Many of the local population would leave the Keep early in the morning, at around 06h00 hours, and walk to work in their maize and pumpkin fields. The Intaf guards at the Keep would search any people leaving or returning to the Keep for weapons. More often than not, they would spend far too much time chatting up the local girls, instead of performing their duty properly. I suppose it was difficult living with and, at the same time, also having to search the locals. There was a tendency to be friendly and not regimented; however that kind of attitude could have led to their own and others' deaths one day, if the gooks had arrived unexpectedly or infiltrated the Keep, because of their inept behaviour. The bush was still quite green for the middle of April. The savannah had been almost denuded for about 3 kms around the Keep and maize fields filled that space, instead. A small river ran about 100 metres from the northern side of the Keep. It was more like a brook than a river and was heavily overgrown with bushes and long elephant grass. The bush surrounding the maize and pumpkin fields was relatively thick, with Msasa dominating the trees. Later in the afternoon, Musa and I worked out a route to use to get down the hill and onto the Keep's fence-line.

'Look at that section of bush near the river, where it gets close to the fence,' I indicated to Musa. 'Is that not a good place for the gooks to come to the fence, or what? I bet if we walk upstream to about 50m before that bush, and stop by that bigger bush, we will have a good view of the fence-line. We will be able to look straight down the fence next to the river.' So, our plan was set. The moon was due to come up at around 19h00 hours, so that would help us get into position.

We neatened the camp and left our backpacks stuffed under some bushes. There wasn't going to be any rain, so we didn't cover them with anything like our rain coats. We filed down the back of the hill just as the sun was setting. The walk to the ambush site was easy, as we had all day to work out the route. The decision to walk upstream was a good one, as we could look up at the horizon and anybody looking downstream would have difficulty in seeing us, as we would not be silhouetted. We arrived at the bush in good time, picking our way through the long grass. We tried to stay off the paths so that we would not leave tracks and arouse the suspicions of people when they came out to work the next day. We settled down in an extended line, facing the bush, which was close to the fence line. We had a good view. The Keep lights came on but, funnily enough, two of these bright lights by the corner fence-pole didn't work. The last faint glimmer of light from the sun was fading, but it silhouetted the viewing area perfectly. The crickets were singing madly in the soggy soil and two dogs, within the Keep, barked at nothing. The folks were busy cooking or settling in for the evening. A continuous hum of talking and activity emanated from around the huts.

'Stsss,' came a faint alarm-call from Musa, as he pointed to the corner fence-pole. Everybody strained their eyes to see what he could see. Just visible was the top of somebody's head, as they stood next to the corner fence-pole. What the hell were they doing there? We tensed, as we anticipated the developments. Nothing happened for about two minutes. The head kept quite still and so did the soldiers. Every one of our senses was strained to identify what was happening. All of a sudden, the frogs stopped their high- pitched chorus. Somebody was down there! We could see nothing. Just then a pair of arms reached up to the top of the fence, extending what looked like a pot towards the outside of the Keep. One of the local people must be passing food over the fence to somebody on the outside! Then it was over, as quickly as that. We saw nothing else. We couldn't open fire, as we hadn't caught sight of any terrorists. The frogs started their chorus again. Whoever had received the food was gone.

'Gooks have just got their supper,' I whispered to Musa. 'We'll move out back to the hill just now and see what happens tomorrow.'

The return trip to the hill was uneventful and we discussed the evening's events when we got back to the camp. We'll keep an extra eye open tomorrow for any suspicious movement. We split up and got some rest. I couldn't sleep. *Where could the terrorist camp be, how many were there, where was the best spot to ambush them?* Counting terrorists could not replace counting sheep in order to get to sleep. Around midnight, I felt the few drops of rain splat onto my sleeping-bag... Aaaaah! Then it came down; torrents of rain. I curled up in the sleeping-bag and tried to keep the cold water from getting to me, but the inevitable happened as a trickle of water snaked its way down my arm and made its way right down to my feet ... and then the trickle turned into a small river. Shit! I eventually drifted off to sleep, cold and wet, but was awoken early by Musa, as he crept past me on his way to set up his morning observation of the area below. I slid out of my sleeping-bag, grabbed my rifle and webbing, and joined him in our little bush, just as the first rays of light started to open the day. I wish I had brought my jacket down with me; it was flipping cold. We didn't move or speak as we scanned the Keep and surrounding bush for any signs that would give us an idea of where the terrorists were camping.

'Musa, keep your eyes on the Keep gate and see if we can spot any Mujibas,' I whispered. It was at about 06h30 that we saw two young boys walk past the gate-guards and head off into the riverbed. We tried to anticipate where they would reappear from the river. About 500 metres upstream they popped out, heading for a small, rocky outcrop. They stopped short of the hill and stood there.

Pedsesayi joined us with his cus-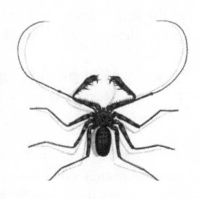
tomary cups of sweet tea. He real-
ised that we were looking at something interesting, as we didn't
even pause to reach for the tea
cups. He balanced them on a small
rock and slid down next to us. We
watched as the two boys took off
their shirts and then headed into
the cluster of granite rocks.

'I bet they're in there,' I whispered, as Musa followed the same scene.

'Why do you think they took off their shirts?' I asked Musa.

'They are telling the gooks, with a sign, that they have not seen any Security Forces and they think they have not been followed,' he responded.

'Well, they are in for a surprise,' I commented.

Hombore, feeling lonely back up the hill, joined us and shifted a rock to make himself more comfortable. He nearly flew into my arms with fright as he uncovered a whip-tailed scorpion.

'Holy Shit,' I said, as he fell across me. This scorpion has to be the ugliest critter in the bush, totally harmless to us, but it can sure make a person jump. It has long 'grabbing' pincers that have hooks sticking out menacingly. It had to happen to Hombore of all people. Pedsesayi realised that he didn't have his rifle with him and slunk up the hill to arm himself, leaving the three of us to continue a longer observation session than usual whilst we finished off our tea.

We kept the bunch of rocks under constant surveillance the whole day, but saw nothing that would help us in our quest to find Gooks. The two boys had spent hours in the rocks, had re-appeared and had then headed back to the Keep in a long-way round fashion, circumventing the maize fields.

'They are going to get food again tonight,' I whispered to Musa.

At sunset, our little team repeated the trip we had made the previous night. We positioned ourselves in exactly the same place as before and waited. Sure enough, at the same time the same head appeared at the same fence-pole.

'Okay, boys, wait until I open fire and aim to the right of the pole. Keep your aim down,' I whispered to the huddle of men as we prepared to initiate combat. I could sense the lads settling down to the now routine process of getting into battle. A shuffle here or there to reposition ammunitions pouches, a faint deep breath as Musa prepared mentally for the physical and emotional overload to follow shortly.

'Just watch my tracer and you will know where the gooks are,' I said, under a heavy breath.

As the arms reached up with the pot of food I opened fire, closely followed by the others. The noise of battle was deafening. I didn't see much as I emptied my magazine of 20 rounds and reloaded.

'Cease fire!' I screamed above the roar. The noise from the SIS men stopped, but gunfire could be heard from our left from within the Keep. The rounds were clipping overhead and I could sense that the guards from the Keep had been rudely woken up and had let rip at anything towards the noise of our small battle. Eventually, the shooting stopped altogether. I could hear my men frantically reloading magazines, as the smell of cordite filled the air. With the muzzle flashes from the rifles, I found I was now night blind and could not see a thing.

'Everybody okay?' I asked in a lowered voice, so as not to alert any wounded terrorists as to where we were.

'Yes, Ishe,' came the response from the guys.

'How many do you think we got?' I enquired from Musa.

'27, Ishe,' smiled Musa.

'Okay let's withdraw 100 metres,' I told Musa and he indicated to the guys to retreat from the ambush site. To withdraw was necessary, in case any wounded terrorists could hear us and throw grenades onto our position. There was no way we would enter the 'killing zone' at night for the very same reason. We would find out what happened in the morning. Another restless night, as we strained to hear any moaning or the like from the killing zone. It was dead still the rest of the night, except for a short but sharp downfall of rain at 04h00 hours, which soaked us through as we didn't have any of our kit with us except our rifles and webbing. As I lay flat on the ground, a little river of cold water snaked its way down past my cheek and made its way, seeping, into my camouflage shirt and eventually my trousers. Aaaaah... not again! But there was nothing that I could do about that.

At first light, we got up and walked through our position of the previous night and continued slowly towards the corner pole, where we expected to see Musa's 27 dead terrorists. We strained our necks to peer through the grass and into the bush next to the pole, but couldn't see a thing. We levelled off, after having passed over the spot where the gooks had been, and looked across at each other enquiringly. There was nothing - not even a cap or blood spoor. It was as though the event of the night before had never taken place. This was very frustrating and we scratched our heads for answers.

Nothing:

'We hit nothing, guys,' I announced. We walked back with a more focused eye to the ground, searching for anything, anything that would prove we had actually fired on the enemy, but there was nothing.

'I reckon we shot too high,' I said, as we finished the second sweep of the area. We found a track, deep in the mud, leading down to the river so tried to follow that, but ended up losing it in the thick reeds near the soggy riverbed.

'Musa, we had better go and see those guys from the Keep before they open up on us, thinking we are the terrorists,' I said, worrying that the trigger-happy guards would unknowingly fire on us. We had a chat with the senior man at the Keep and told him the story. He said he would see if he could follow up on the possibility of locating the supplier of the food from the Keep. We made our way out of the Keep and carefully through the river, long grass and up to the granite rocks where their camp could be. As we rounded the little collection of rocks, we came across the terrorist's camp. It was well-concealed in amongst the trees and would have been impossible to see from our observation post. We counted a possible 8 positions where we thought the gooks had slept. There was nothing in the camp, as they had taken everything with them, and no tracks either, as the rain had effectively washed the soil clean.

We called up Mike on the radio and asked him to pick us up at the Keep. I gave the radio to Pedsesayi and asked him and Hombore to get back up the hill to pick up our kit, whilst Musa and I went to the Keep to see if we could get more information there. The rain had washed away any spoor inside the Keep area as well, so we were none the wiser as to what happened.

'You had better keep an eye on your fence-line at night and also check those two lights by the corner,' I told the senior Internal Affairs chap.

'There are supposed to be patrols at night' he responded, trying to defend his guards.

'Well, maybe they start too late,' I said.

'Maybe,' he answered, his head lowered.

Colin gave me a call and I sent him a telex, giving him the basic details of the contact. The next day he sent two of his SB men into the Keep to see if they could get some more information. They learnt that the group of eight terrorists were in transit through to Salisbury and we would probably not hear from them again in this area. What was more important was that we would need to keep watching this area, as it was obvious that some of the locals were communicating with the terrorists and that this could be a food-resupply spot for them whilst they were in transit.

To shoot straight:

That was it - a contact with the enemy, but no bodies or any-thing to celebrate about. I was shocked that we had not hit a thing. How could our shooting be so bad? We had pumped 80 rounds of rifle fire into a concentrated area and yet, had it been a barn door, we still would not have been able to hit it. I took the guys down to the shooting range two days later. It was late in the afternoon when we arrived. Mike came with us, accompanied by two of his Constables. I lined up the S.I.S team, standing with rifles at the ready, but unloaded.

'We are now going to learn how to shoot at night,' I said, as I ushered Mike's team to move across our firing front in the long grass. He led his two men to a distance of 30 metres and stopped. He placed three 'half man', or figure 12, targets in the long grass and walked away to our left and out of the firing line. The sun had now disappeared behind the hills and dusk had set in.

'Okay, you have seen the targets walking and you know exactly where they are, so I want you each to fire ten shots into them,' I said. I asked Mike to repeat the placing of the targets. Mike walked back, picked up his targets and repeated the exercise, placing them in slightly different positions and moved off again. The team was now ready and indicated that they definitely knew exactly where to shoot.

'Fire,' I commanded.

After the firing, we walked forward to have a look at the 'shredded' targets. Not one had a bullet hole in it! Mike chuckled.

'We are going to do this again and again until we get it right,' I said, and we did. The lads began to learn about shooting low and we were getting more and more hits as we repeated the training. We even had small rocks from the bullets striking the ground and flying through the targets. Eventually we left, but promised to repeat the exercise again and again as needed. Over a beer at the Shamva Police Station later, I thanked Mike for his help.

Which rifle was better?

We were always arguing about the strengths and weaknesses of the different weapons we used in the conflict. Some interesting facts about the main weapons used, respectively, by the Rhodesian Government Forces and the terrorists came up. One of the things that made us choose the weapons we did was the impact effects. Just by looking at the different amounts of damage each weapon could cause was enough to help us make up our minds. There was absolutely no doubt that the NATO cartridge 7.62mm x 51, with a velocity of 838 metres per second, was our favourite. Our ammunition came from three manufacturers in

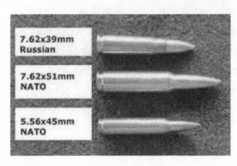

South Africa, and we were lucky enough to get Israeli ammunition, too, on occasion. The Russian's typical AK ammunition was 7.62mm x 39, with a velocity of 710 metres per second, was further down the list. I guess the difference was in the mass and velocity, which essentially provided more 'stopping' power in the NATO round. The Russian cartridge had 2970 joules of energy, whilst the NATO came in at 3265 joules. The old saying of 'stopping power' came true when you had to drop your target with one shot. I saw many instances where the energy from the NATO round had obliterated the vital parts and limbs of the terrorists. You could see if he had been hit with a Russian round or one of ours – there was no competition! A comparison between their respective hitting-power came up when, in two separate instances, the hapless victims of an AK47 round and a NATO round had hit two different men, in exactly the same place. Both men had been hit in the right leg, just at the split of the legs. The AK47 round went straight through the muscle, with a neat hole on entry and a hole about 2 inches across on exit. With the NATO round, there was no visible entry as the entire section of leg was missing – at least a kilogram of flesh had been ripped right off the leg. Impressed were we.

I have seen the damages caused by a Magnum .357 at close quarters on a human and somehow he survived. The bullet went down between the bones of the collar and straight out the small of his back. The bullet used was a full metal jacket so the holes made on both sides were small. If he had been hit on a bone, or if a hollow-point round had been used (which mushrooms quickly on impact), then he would have had a story to tell.

A black Police Reservist was shot through the head in an accidental discharge, which happened at Bindura Police Station. His colleague was unloading an Israeli 9mm Uzi and the round went off. He just stood still and said he had been hit. How it didn't kill him amazed us all. The full metal-jacket bullet hit the poor chap smack in the middle of the bulb of his nose. It travelled straight through and exited just below his skull at the back, but a bit to the left, thereby missing his spinal column. He was fine after a few months of recuperation in hospital. He was lucky it was a 9mm and not a NATO 7.62mm!

Trench Warfare:

It wasn't long before the terrorists in the Shamva area got to hating the S.I.S. We had quite a surprise one day when we were going out to be deployed. We were on a side gravel road that we often used to get into the Tribal Trust Land, as we didn't like using the main roads. Mike was driving and we had our eyes glued on the road for landmines, and in the bush for ambushes – weapons were at the ready. We rounded a bend and Mike had to put the brakes on hard. We came to a sliding, dusty halt on the side of the road, as he tried to control the Land Rover. In front of us, the entire road had a trench running right across it. We immediately jumped from the vehicle and fired some rounds into the nearest thick bush. It was on obvious setup for an ambush. What better way to stop the vehicle than a trench two feet deep and two feet across, stretching right across the road and on a bend as well! We gathered our wits and started a sweep of the area in an extended line. We came across the ambush site, which had twelve firing positions, about thirty metres off the road, and in amongst the thick bush and rocks. The evidence pointed to the gooks having stayed there for some time, obviously waiting for us to pitch up. Musa bent down and had a look at the spoor. He fingered the dirt from one footprint, brought it to his nose and seemed to breathe in the sole of the print. With a clap of hands he got rid of the dirt, stood up looked into the far distant hills.

'These gooks are asking for a hiding,' he said, and I could see him mentally wishing for a fight. Hombore was a bit taken aback by the trench and possible outcome of any ambush. He fidgeted with the brim of his hat, in deep thought. This was quite a serious display of new tactics by the gooks. I was also a bit concerned, but I believed in our fighting ability and aggression. A new chapter had been turned and it had begun to make the fight between us and the gooks very personal.

Our next stint in the bush came about through some information that had been given to us by a local farmer's labourer. The farm was next to the T.T.L and the information was that a group of Gooks had visited the labourer's compound two nights before to get food and that they had headed back into the T.T.L. We didn't know how big the group was, but we had a suspicion that they would get into the hills around Keep 1 in the North East of the T.T.L. Musa and I did a day recce of the area, with Mike as usual, and set up a plan.

The next morning I had a call from Phil saying I must get to Bindura to pick up our team's new vehicle. Wow, our own vehicle, what luxury! I sped through with Mike in his Land Rover, to be met by Phil, holding the keys to an old, green, 5-tonne, Nissan heavy vehicle. It had very little landmine-proofing; however, it did have steel plates by the driver's and passenger's feet wells, which were there to deflect any explosions. Its' load bay at the rear was covered with sand-bags, overlaid with a heavy conveyor belt. The idea behind the sandbags and conveyer belt was to nullify the blast from a landmine. However, if we were to hit a landmine with the rear wheel, I was more worried about the tonne of sand bags or, for that matter, the heavy conveyor-belt landing on us. The Nissan had a large police radio that had been hung under the dashboard by the passenger's leg area, which meant that there was little to no space for anybody to sit there. I stole a 44-gallon drum of diesel from the Bindura Police fuel station and headed back to Shamva with my prize.

Thinking about the botched incident at Keep 3, we decided to set up an ambush near the small cluster of granite rocks that had been used by the previous eight terrorists. Perhaps we would catch these guys if they were going to use the same modus operandi as the previous group.

Wildlife Shoot:

We redeployed into the Keep 3 area again and took up a position about 500 metres from the rocks where the previous group had camped out. The next day we did our usual observations in the morning, but moved down from our position and tried to find a suitable position on a path leading to the rocks. We found what we were looking for and set up an ambush position for the rest of the day. It was a great position, right next to a large termite mound with a good view of the path. Ambushing a path during the day meant we had to keep dead still for the whole day. We had to be well-camouflaged and our position had to be a defensible one, in case the gooks ran towards us. That was highly unlikely, as they normally hit the road in the opposite direction when under fire. If the gooks were going to come through, they would possibly do it later on when it was dusk. We had sprinkled some Msasa Tree seed pods on the path, which would crack when stood on. This was our early-warning device. By 18h00, the sky was dark and we knew that the moon had about an hour to come up. I had set our line of fire, making sure everybody knew for which section of the killing zone he would be responsible.

Snap, went one of our Msasa pods right in front of me. It was as dark as ink. *What do I do now, how many are there ... ah, to hell with it, let's get them.* I opened fire, with the guys doing the same. We finished our magazines of 20 rounds each, reloaded and listened. The reloading took literally three seconds. We hadn't heard any return fire. We withdrew from the ambush site and waited for the morning.

'How many?' I enquired of Musa, as usual.

'Ummm 13,' he responded, after a quick mental calculation.

In the morning we found no gook tracks, bodies or equipment, but what we did find was wild pig spoor. We had opened fire on a wild pig which had walked through the killing zone. That was it; we had compromised our position, so we pulled out. We never did find out where those gooks went, but we had made enough noise in the area that the local gook-informer would hesitate to help the gooks for the foreseeable future.

Musa in a plane:

The Member in Charge Police Shamva had been asked by Phil to help us in our endeavour to learn the layout of the Madziwa TTL. The quickest way of doing this was to fly over it in a light aircraft and take notes. The flight was arranged and Musa and I climbed aboard a local farmer's Cessna 130. The rear cargo door had been removed and so Musa sat in the seat next to the open door, whilst I took the co-pilot's position. We spent an hour flying back and forth until we thought we had seen enough. Musa was noticeably white when we returned. He had never flown before and he hadn't said much, except for the occasional yes or no answer.

'I think I will take a rest,' he said, staggering with dizzy spells when we got back to the station. I really don't think he took notes on anything we had seen, such as hills, roads and strategic OP points etc. Hombore came up, with a big grin on his face.

'So what was it like?' he enquired of his sergeant.

'I don't want to talk about it!' came the reply, as Musa went to sit under a Jacaranda tree.

The Snatch:

Our next operation was more towards what we were really here for - intelligence work. Phil and Colin had arranged what was called 'a snatch.' Colin's informer in Keep 1 was a bit jittery. The man believed that his next-door neighbour suspected him of being a police informer. This would mean sudden death, should the Gooks get their hands on him. Colin also had another twist to the story. He believed that the informer was, in fact, a double agent. The informer was really on the gook's side and only used Colin to get the money that he was paid to get information. The plan was for the S.I.S team to infiltrate the Keep at night, catch the informer, and extricate him from the Keep. He would then be relocated elsewhere and his family would be safe from any repercussions. The clincher was that the S.I.S team was to be dressed up as terrorists, in order to pretend that he had been snatched by them, never to be seen again. Colin would follow up the next day, making a great deal of noise about terrorists, and trying to follow up on the 'culprits.' I drove the team back to Bindura, where we were to plan this raid. Although it was easy to dress up the black constables to look like black terrorists, what about me? I had 'black is beautiful' cream, but I needed to cover my blonde hair. I came up with a solution and bought a ladies' hair-net, into which I tucked my hair, and a large, wide-brimmed hat completed the disguise. We dug into both Phil's and Colin's offices for various bits of Chinese, FRELIMO, Polish and Russian camouflage, etc. We grabbed mainly jackets. Phil issued us with Chinese AK47 chest-webbing and an AK each. We also managed to scrounge an RPD Russian machine-gun. We wore civilian denim jeans and dark shirts. The black guys were asking if they would get compensation for using their own clothing, to which the answer was 'in time' by Colin.

'What about the lights around the Keep?' I asked.

'We've thought of that,' said Colin, as he produced a long .22 rifle, fitted with a silencer, which I would use to snuff out two or three of the bright lights. The rifle was very long indeed. We would be able to cut through the fence without being seen. Cutting the diamond-mesh fence would not be easy, but I was to use a Russian AKM bayonet which, when combined with its sheath, made a very strong set of wire cutters. Colin gave me a drawing of the huts in the area we were to approach, with details of exactly which hut the informer was in. The team moved back to Shamva a few days later. One of Colin's men accompanied us on our mission.

Mike dropped us off on a sand road, some ten kilometres from Keep 1. We made good time getting to the Keep and arrived on its perimeter at around 22h00 hours. We sat on a termite mound and rested, whilst a cool breeze cleaned our bodies of the sweat we had worked up during the night march. The Keep was surrounded by a vast open area, where the local people grazed their cattle. There wasn't a bush or piece of long grass for us to hide behind, on our approach to the fence. We waited to take in the sounds of the area and I then crept forward with .22 rifle, with the unusually long silencer, to take out the flood lights on the South Western corner of the Keep. It wasn't difficult to shoot the fluorescent lights and I beckoned for the team to come towards my position. It really looked strange with the guys carrying AK assault rifles. The AK in my hands felt unfamiliar and I felt exposed, as I didn't have my so-much-stronger FN with me. I left Hombore, Colin's constable, and Dube at the termite mound and Musa and I crept forward to the fence. I constructed the wire cutters from the AKM bayonet and snipped the fence along the bottom for a metre, and upwards for a further metre, making a flap of the fence. The bayonet blade had a slot near its sharp end and this snapped over a metal lug on the sheath, making a great wire cutter. I couldn't cut the strong bottom wire of the fence so I left it, slipped the bayonet into its sheath, and wedged it into the top of my Chinese chest-webbing. Musa and I crept through the flap I had cut in the fence and made our way to the informer's hut. We stood motionless under the eaves of the roof, by its front door, for a few minutes, trying to listen to the sounds inside. It was so dark we couldn't see a thing. On a silent count, I burst through the flimsy door and thrust myself across the pitch-black room toward the other side, where the informer's bed was supposed to be (well that's where most people would have it – right?). Musa was right on my heels. As I ran, I pulled out the bayonet to use to threaten the informer. I got but two paces when I tripped over something soft and heavy. A loud 'umpff' came from the lump on the floor, and I landed with a crash across bodies. The informer had about six people staying with him and they were all spread out, sleeping on the floor. I wriggled my way across the now flaying arms and legs and got to the bed, where I grabbed the informer and hauled him back towards the door. A torch suddenly lit up on the other side of the room. In a flash, Musa and I were out of the jumbled room and rolling on the ground outside the hut, trying to subdue the informer. He was a big man, but he immediately relaxed when I brought my bayonet up to his throat. I couldn't utter a word because of my accent, so Musa told him to shut up and come with us. In the meantime the informer's wife, plus two others, came hurtling out of the hut with the torch and a pick handle. She didn't know that we were fully-armed and probably thought that we were some drunks coming to roughen up her husband. Things were getting out of hand and when the informer saw that he had support, he renewed his struggles. I had to release my grip on him before we got pummelled to the ground by the mad woman, and Musa and I then sped away into the night, leaving the now screaming group behind. I got to the fence first and tried to crawl through, but the bayonet's sheath got caught in the strong wire I had not cut. It took a lifetime to release myself and we both sprinted across the open grass area to link up with the others.

'So where is the informer?' asked Colin's constable.

'It's a long story,' I wheezed, as we turned and jogged off into the night. I was frustrated and grabbed Musa.

'Just hang on, let's give the Keep a rev to stop their nonsense,' I suggested.

We fired a full magazine of 30 rounds each across the roofs of the Keep, together with about the same number of rounds from the RPD Russian machine-gun. The green Russian tracers glowed in the night as they arced across the night sky. That helped me get rid of my frustrations and I eventually settled down. The guards at the Keep didn't even return fire. They must have thought the whole terrorist army was upon them. We were picked up by Mike as usual, and headed back to Shamva.

Colin did his thing by going into the Keep the next day and chasing up the people in the informer's area. He met with the informer who was, by this stage, in an absolute state, believing that he had escaped death at the hands of the terrorists by the skin of his teeth. What came out from the confrontation was that he believed the terrorists were going to kill him. His wife was adamant that a coloured terrorist was responsible. That stopped the informer's double-agent stories and he became a well-oiled informer for Colin. Colin used this man's fear to his full advantage and maintained the pressure from then on. So the action was successful in the end, but in a way none of us could have imagined.

Lemon

We once reacted to a sighting of a potential terrorist base camp. An Air Force helicopter had noted a suspicious area, as he was flying from Bindura to Mount Darwin. We were deployed by vehicle and walked through the bush for ten kilometres to get to the location. We then called in a helicopter gun-ship to give us air support: the Air Force told us to 'forget about it.' Well, we would have to get on with the job ourselves so we started to walk, in open file, straight towards the thicket of rocks and bushes where the camp was supposed to be. There was no way to approach the 'camp', other than across an open grass land area. We stopped at the edge of the tree-line and took a view across an open field of shortish red grass.

'Ishe...how long do you think it will take to get across?' asked a nervous Hombore. I could sense exactly what he was feeling – terror. Now I felt what my granddad had felt when he'd had to run across the heavily-shelled fields at Delville Wood in the Battle of the Somme in 1916. I could feel the terrorists lining their AK47 sites straight at my chest. Without answering Hombore, I signalled, 'Let's go!'

My heart pumped sooo hard I could feel the blood vessels in my neck taking strain. Every one of my senses was tuned up to maximum, as I walked briskly towards the enemy. My eyes darted from one potential hiding-place to another, in an urgent search for the enemy. My brain was telling me that this was absolute madness, as every terrorist was aiming his weapon directly at us and would open fire when we'd taken the next step closer to them. We were entirely at the mercy of our enemy, but we just carried on walking forward. Fear sharpened every aspect of my being, and I became acutely aware of everything around me. In such situations, the soldier next to you is with you all the way and I guess the only reason you put one foot forward is because he is doing so, too, and so you go on. Time stretched beyond comprehension. We made it to the thicket, sweating, and nosed our way in, fingers white against the triggers. Nobody was there, but there were a few signs that they had left the camp earlier. We called this type of operation a 'lemon', as it left a sour taste afterwards.

Special Equipment:

I was called to Salisbury to Special Branch Headquarters, where they informed me that I was the lucky recipient of some special equipment. I was to go down to Morris Depot Armoury and they would brief me there on what was going on. As I drove into the familiar training depot, I parked in amongst four other Policemen standing around on the tarmac area outside the armoury. I introduced myself to the men; they were all higher in rank than me and came from all sorts of stations spread across the country. Two of them were from the Support Unit or 'Black Boots', so-called because the normal boot or shoe for Policemen

My heavy barrelled FN with Orion night scope – a lethal combination

was brown and they wore black, canvas boots that covered the ankles. The big trend was to wear these black boots, as they had rounded soles, and no treads. The idea was that they would leave few tracks, as they had no sharp edges to leave tell-tale signs. We called them 'I wasn't here' boots. After a short while, the head armourer ushered us into the building and we came across our new equipment – a German-made Night Scope. It was an Orion passive night-sight. We sat in awe listening to the armourer explain the scope's functions and were then bundled into a Land Rover and taken to the depot's rifle range. We took turns familiarising ourselves with sighting in the scope on a rifle, and then returned to the armoury, where we were each issued with a brand-new scope. This piece of equipment must have cost the country a pretty packet. There had been 26 issued throughout the country and I was lucky to have one. I reckoned this unique equipment had travelled down some really special, dark avenues of sanctions, busting from Germany, through Israel, through South Africa and then to us. I never did find out its cost, but I knew I had to look after this thing well. The scope had a magnification of 4 times and was capable of intensifying light 50 000 times. When we were on the range we had to be careful not to remove the front rubber cover, or the bright sun would destroy the scope. Enough light bled through a tiny hole, the diameter of a pin, centred in the front plastic cover, which allowed us to use it in daylight, too. It came with a carrying-box. I headed back to my team with my new prize, proud as a pig. Watch out Mr Mugabe; we were going to rip right through your miserable army. On returning to base, I spent the evening studying every aspect of the scope and the next day took off to the rifle range to sight it on my own rifle. It weighed 1.8 kilograms and sat high up on my FN. A special 'dust cover' had been attached to the scope to allow it to be mounted on our Armed Forces weapons. The sight could only focus on objects 20 feet and further, so it had a few limitations. I found I preferred to use my left eye to look through this high-mounted sight. I could still use the normal optical sights, but I preferred to stash the sight in its little carry-bag in my backpack during the day – it was just too heavy to lug around on the weapon all the time. I also had to be wary of the battery life, as I had only one rechargeable 2.5 volt battery, which would work for a maximum of 20 odd hours on full charge. If I used it too often on extended trips to the bush, I would be in trouble. Looking through the sight was a circle, surrounding a centre aiming-point, all in green. The brightness of the aiming-point was adjusted by turning a knob. The controls were on the left side of the scope, so it worked out just fine to control the scope and still have my finger on the trigger. I was going to have fun with this thing. The lads from S.I.S were intrigued with the new scope and I gave each chap a try with it on the shooting-range, so that they would know what its capabilities were.

'With this thing we are going to have many reward beers for shooting gooks,' I said. 'The only problem is that we have to take out all your tracer bullets in the first magazine. All you have to do is to watch MY tracer and that's where you shoot – easy as that.'

Contacts Increase

Contact with the terrorists started to increase as we got to know the area and people better. We were informed that there was a group of about twelve terrorists working the Western section of Madziwa T.T.L and I got the team ready to infiltrate the area and see what we could find out. Much of the information being given to Special Branch from the local population had dried up and it was Colin's belief that the terrorists were using some very harsh tactics to stop anybody helping the Security Forces. Death and torture were not uncommon tactics used by the terrorists to keep the locals quiet. We didn't know much about the group save to say that there were twelve and they had two RPD machine guns amongst their normal AK47 weapons. We dressed up as terrorists again, but this time I took my FN with its night-sight, instead of an AK47. Alpha Charlie took up a position on a hill quite some distance from any of the kraals, so that we could use it as a base from which to operate. That night we decided to move down to a kraal about five kilometres from the hill, so we started off early whilst the sun was still up. I wanted to get to the kraal just as the sun was setting, so that we could check out the layout. The going was a bit rough, with small stones and rocks delaying our advance to the kraal. It meant we had to look down most of the time, just so that we wouldn't twist an ankle. The kraal was small, with few trees. We arrived on its outskirts a little after sunset. We had arrived a bit too late, I thought, but I was unconcerned as I had my night sight. We moved stealthily along the edge of the kraal, using a small river depression as cover. Any gooks around us would be silhouetted against the night sky. Within 30 paces of the first hut, I stopped my line of men and took a peek through the night-sight to see what was cooking. To my utter surprise, my viewfinder filled with the unmistakeable presence of gooks. There seemed to be a bunch of them, all standing in a group next to the first hut we had seen. Now, looking at the gooks through the night-scope, was like watching TV – it didn't seem real! I couldn't get to grips with the view that I had just seen and the enemy in front of me. The two scenes were so different. I dropped down and gathered my men.

'There are about 10 to 12 gooks just to the left of that hut. They are all standing and I want you guys to form a line along here and let's have a go at them,' I whispered. My heart started pounding a great deal in anticipation of the coming fight. We quickly, but quietly, formed a firing line and put a bead on the vicinity of the hut. Musa and the other chaps knew that they were to open fire on the sound of my first shot, and this time I decided to stand and take aim. The gooks were about twenty paces from us and had no idea that we were there. I waited until I had one of the machine-gunners in my sights, and fired. The night-sight hummed quietly as it gathered the images of the dimly-lit huts, as well as the terrorists. The visibility was good and I could see the buttons on their shirts. I tried to take careful aim, but the weight of the weapon, with the scope, lay heavy on my arms and it was difficult not to shake. The central, round, lit ring of the aiming-point on the scope and its central dot settled on one terrorist's chest. At this distance, I couldn't miss... Bang! From there onwards, it was difficult to see anything, as the sky lit up with tracer bullets, smoke and sparks from the bullets hitting rocks and bricks. The noise was unbelievably loud, especially in the little gully we were in. The men fired off one magazine of twenty rounds and quickly reloaded. They didn't continue firing, though, as they knew the gooks who were still alive would be high-tailing it from the killing zone. To blaze through twenty rounds takes a few seconds. I scanned the area with my scope, but couldn't see anybody. I bent down to whisper to Musa.

'I can't see anything there; maybe they went over the rise at the back of the hut.' Suddenly there was a burst of automatic fire from the other side of the hut. The tracer rounds went flying tens of feet above us. We were quite safe and didn't even flinch. It was a full burst from an AK47, and as suddenly as it started, it stopped. Then there were some explosions and another burst from two AK's, then absolute silence.

'Musa, let's get down a bit further from the hut. I'm worried about any grenade-throwing stunts,' I whispered, as I started to move the men back about 20 metres. We heard nothing further and spent the night in our new position, ready for an inspection of the killing-zone in the morning. It was a restless sleep, with the rocks jabbing my back, but we were excited to see the results of our shooting match. At first light, we were up, formed a sweep-line, and advanced up to the hill and over the other side. We came across one body, but nothing else.

'Shit, we can't hit anything!' I spat out.

'Musa, get somebody to have a look at that body, but do not move it; there may be a booby trap underneath,' I said, as I walked back to the hut to have a look at the grouping of shots on a hut wall. A number of rounds had hit the hut, but they were all at the top of the wall next to the roof.

'Ishe, I think we need to move the body over there. I think there may be something under him,' said Pedsesayi breathlessly, as he came back to brief me.

'Okay, get the headman from the kraal here now,' I told Musa. We made up a longish rope, about 2 metres in length, from bits we could find around the kraal. The resident headman had moved to the next kraal and Musa brought him up, panting, to his huts.

'Okay, get him to turn his friend over using the rope' I instructed. Pedsesayi tied the rope around the dead gook's arm and handed the other end to the headman. Whilst the dead gook was being turned over, we took up a position away from the potential blast. The headman hesitantly half-turned the body over and dropped it as though he had been burnt. He managed to run only a few paces before the blast of the booby trap went off. Nobody was injured, but the dead gook's stomach now lay five metres from his body in a jumble of bloody sausages.

'Lucky we checked that one out! Well done, guys,' I said, as we dusted ourselves off and went up to inspect the gook. It looked like he had been shot in the stomach, because we could find no other bullet holes in him. He had fired off all of the ammunition in his weapon and then set the booby-trap grenade under his stomach as he died. I guess it takes some bravery to place a booby trap right under your body, knowing you are going to die. We found no documents on the body, but at least the AK seemed to be functional. I gave Colin a call on the radio and he came out with one of his sergeants to pick up the body and AK. The terrorist would be taken back to Special Branch, where fingerprints would be taken to establish his identity and see if he had murdered anybody to date. We continued our patrol, but this time we walked in the open to show the locals we were in control - for now anyway. Funny thing about the AK we captured from the dead Gook was that it had been covered in blood and bits of flesh when we took it and, although we cleaned it thoroughly when we got back to base, we could never get rid of the smell. I guess the blood had been blasted into the wooden parts of the rifle. Anyway, we ended up giving it to the Selous Scouts at their corrugated iron fort in Bindura. I assumed the gook I had aimed at initially was wounded, as I could not have missed at that distance. I wondered how he felt with a bullet in his gut.

Gooks Stink:

One thing we found out fast was that the terrorists stank. They wore all their clothes; sometimes three sets of jeans, two or three shirts and possibly a jacket over that. Their hair was generally long and unkempt and they stank from not bathing. I know that we, too, stank after a few weeks in the bush but, gee, nothing came close to this lot! If we didn't clean our feet, or our private parts, we could end up with enough pong to chase baboons out of the trees. Foot rot was a common problem in any war and we suffered from it at the beginning, but set very strict cleaning schedules to stop this. With the miles we had to walk, we could not afford to have foot problems. Musa was the man in charge of making sure the lads were clean and he was very good at ensuring they followed our rules of survival. If you ever had to dig through a gook's backpack, you were sure to be in for a surprise, with old bits of chicken and other food stored loosely together with all sorts of foul junk lying in the depths. I just don't know how they were able to stand those conditions. I dread to know what bred and grew in those long locks of curly hair that the gooks had! The other problem they had was that their weapons always seemed to be in bad need of maintenance. If it had not been for Mr Kalashnikov inventing the robust AK47, they would have had trouble in that department as well. I never found a weapon that was in good condition, unless it came out of the grease from an arms cache. They never seemed to clean their weapons.

The pain:

One of the things that worried me a great deal was the lack of painkillers; I mean we had nothing to calm someone down if they got shot. Sure we could patch them up with a bandage or two, but that was about it. I was worried about carrying one of my men out of the bush, over some seriously difficult terrain. When we first went rushing around the bush after terrorists, we were issued one ampoule of Morphine per section but that was reduced to one ampoule of Sosagen (also a pain killer similar to Morphine) and then, later on in the war, we got nothing. I guessed we would just have to take the pain.

Tampax:

Now, one of the things that some of the 'experienced' boys had told us to carry around was a couple of Tampax (ladies sanitary device). If you got shot in the leg, you could just shove a Tampax in the hole and that would help stop the bleeding. You just had to make sure that you left the strings hanging out so, when the medics got hold of you, they would know that you were 'loaded.' We actually never carried these little devices, as I never had the courage to go into a chemist and buy a box!

The Set-up:

Two days later, we were moved to an area to the North East of the TTL. There were supposed to be around thirty gooks in this area and we had been given the job of finding them. It had been said that we were outnumbered and therefore were not to take on the group; however, we were that told we had to call for back-up if we did find them. We were dropped off on the side of the road and completed a 30-kilometre walk to a collection of three little hills – our target area. It was said that the gooks used the very large kraal, situated in the middle of these three hills, for their base camp. The night march was a horror and we arrived at the base of the most northerly hill at 04h00 in the morning. We had to criss-cross roads and take our shoes off for anti-tracking, which delayed us. By walking barefoot, our tracks would mingle with those of the locals. Anybody seeing boot tracks in the sand would know the military was in town and we always had to assume that there were terrorist informers in the area. We climbed the hill and took up a position just the other side of the kraal. It was not a good idea to let the locals know we were there. If the gooks found out we were there, they would possibly try and take us on in a gunfight. We were all dead tired, so three slept whilst the fourth took up an observation position overlooking the kraal. I hadn't even put my head to down to sleep when Pedsesayi came sneaking back from the OP position.

'Ishe, they are here just below us,' he whispered, with excitement in his eyes. The guys were up, but only Pedsesayi and I went forward to the OP position. I followed him down a line of thick bushes to a clump of rocks. There was a small crevasse just below the top rock, with some bushes in front of it. There was no way the gooks would see us from where they were; he had chosen the perfect OP position. We were no more than 30 paces from the enemy and they had no idea we were there. We were getting rather excited by this time. The morning sun started to cast light across our view.

'Shit!' I remembered something. 'Pedsesayi, get Musa to check our route up the hill to make sure nobody follows our spoor up here.' We watched the comings and goings of the local people and the terrorists. We counted thirty-two terrorists, but did not see any weapons. There were many people below us and it seemed like the whole kraal area was abuzz with activity. It was obvious who the terrorists were by the way they walked and called the locals for favours, such as food.

'Musa, that's strange that they don't have their weapons with them. Maybe we can take them out now; they will never see us coming.'

'Ishe, we are four against them and we don't know where the weapons are. Maybe we should call in support for an attack in the morning.'

'What happens if they gap it out of here before then?' I enquired.

'Ishe, these monkeys are here to stay. Look, those women have made a lot of beer. They are going to drink tonight and we can give them more than a headache in the morning.' This made sense, so I called up the Operations Room in Bindura on the radio and asked to speak with Colin. A while later, Colin's familiar voice came on the radio.

'Alpha Charlie, this is 204 - how are you guys up there?'

'We want a three-pronged attack arranged for the morning, with the following sections positioned at the following locstats before first light,' came my business-like reply. I read from our Shackle Code Book, with slow, deliberate enunciations. The radio crackled and spat, as we were on the fringe of the radio's reception. The codes had to be repeated to get absolute clarity and to ensure that no mistakes were made in the transmission.

Shackle Code

0	1	2	3	4	5	6	7	8	9
F	T	E	R	W	S	D	Z	J	K
P	O	U	A	Q	B	M	Y	C	G

Riddle Code

0	1	2	3	4	5	6	7	8	9
X	D	R	T	F	C	Y	G	V	U
I	K	M	N	L	Q	W	A	B	H

The map reference in Shackle Code (first line) would have read something like this:-

59327701   (actual grid reference)
SGREZFT   (what I called on the radio)

If one used 'Riddle' as an option, one would read off from the bottom table. There were two letters which went before each map reading, and that gave the number of the map we were using. We were told that the gooks were able to intercept our radio calls and, if they had our maps, then they would know what was cooking. The Shackle and Riddle codes were forever being compromised and we were using codes that were dated two months in advance. Each set of codes was used by all members of the Security Forces throughout the country and every member knew which dates to use. It was a very simple code and, for our small war, it was fine.

I briefed Colin as best as I could on the plan for the morning. We wanted to get PATU units to form stop groups below the hill we were on, so as to block any escape down the two small rivers that ran past the hill and we wanted a motorbike section to attack the terrorists in the kraal from the front, at sunrise. A PRAW or Police Reserve Air Wing Cessna aircraft could supply top cover and advise on the positions of the gooks, should they scatter in all directions. The plan was perfect and we believed we would have the terrorists square in a trap. I already started my mental body-count possibilities. We continued to watch the kraal for the rest of the day.

As I sat up on that hill with Musa by my side, as usual, I began to think back to the short break away from the war we'd had a few weeks before. Musa was quiet and I could hear him shuffle every now and then to ease strained muscles as we sat amongst the rocks. I looked towards the clear sky and saw the Southern Cross. A satellite crossed over in its haste to get around the world. I could hear frogs calling in the river line far below and to our left. It was a beautiful night and I missed my girlfriend and her soft, caring voice and tender manner. We had only spent a few days together, but those hours were packed with as much of each other as we could get. Murna was a nurse, and a very dedicated one, who was always looking for a shoulder to cry on with the stories and experiences she had in the casualty wing of Andrew Fleming Hospital. I had the same needs as her, so we would chat for hours and try to console each other – forever holding hands, or with an arm over the shoulder. She was beautiful and looked so pretty in her uniform and the strange white cape all the nurses had to wear. I missed her at times like this ... long black hair, with gorgeous brown eyes...

Night came and we were still stuck in our little OP position. We hadn't eaten at all during the day, save for some sweets. My eyes were eventually closing and I forced my face into a false smile, to try and keep awake. I could sense Musa was tired, so I tapped him on the shoulder and showed him my backward pointing thumb indicating we should call it a night and get some sleep before the fight tomorrow. We went to sleep to the sounds of the dancing throng below us. At four in the morning, we were up. Our body alarm clocks worked well to get us up at the synchronised time we had agreed upon. As we were dressed in terrorist gear, we would not be taking part in the operation for fear of being shot by friendly fire. We quietly switched on the radio, imagining the three groups of Security Forces working their way towards their respective positions, on foot. We had their call signs, so knew how to contact them. The sun was still below the horizon, but the red glow was already painting the clouds. We sat in our little bunch of rocks, in anticipation. If the PATU sections were in position, then the first thing we would hear or see would be the motorbike section coming haring around the corner and into the kraal. But that's not what we heard. Far in the distance we could not only see, but also hear, two heavy troop-carriers grinding their gears, as they drove slowly down the road toward the kraal. The dust pluming up from the heavy vehicles looked like an elephant stampede. They seemed to be driving at a snail's pace.

'What the hell do they think they're doing?' I asked nobody in particular.

'Give me that radio, Musa,' as I snatched the green radio handset and called the one PATU call sign. There was no answer, so I called the other, with the same result.

'The bastards are coming in without their radios on and they're coming into the kraal, without the stop groups,' I said almost pleadingly to Musa. The surprise package had been destroyed and we would not catch these gooks. The gooks had also heard what we heard and were on their feet and running at full pace down one of the riverbeds, where we had hoped to have a stop-group of PATU men. There was no way we could catch them. The PATU arrived, followed by the motorbike section virtually up their exhaust pipe. They eventually switched on their radios and I was able to speak to the relevant sections.

'PATU1, this is Alpha Charlie, both your sections are to stand to and the motorbike section is to follow those gooks down the river. Where is the PRAW aircraft?' I proceeded to give instructions as to which direction the gooks had run, and also made sure that EVERYBODY knew where we were, as we didn't want some trigger-happy farmer giving us a revving.

'He's on his way, will be with us in two minutes,' came the response from the Section Leader of PATU1.

The two trucks screeched to a dusty halt in the centre of the large kraal, men jumped out from the back doors and took up defensive positions. It was absolutely comical. The gooks had long gone and I could only laugh at this unbelievably amateurish show of force. What the hell they had expected to find in the kraal was beyond me; everybody had heard them coming from miles away. My guess was that they had been told to react like this and therefore knew no better. The locals had scampered into their houses and the area was suddenly very quiet again. The motorbike section came roaring up and, with a quick stop for directions, took off after the gooks. They were a crazy bunch, who believed they had surprise on their side, they could overtake any gook running from them. They were a bunch of farmers who were part of PATU and preferred to ride into war, rather than walk. They drove Yamaha and Honda off-road 125 and 250cc motorcycles, carrying their preferred weapons slung across their chests. Some of them carried Uzi sub-machine guns, whilst some liked shotguns. With any action taking place, they would slide the bike to the ground and quickly lie behind the bike, firing as they did so. I guess they were a bit scary, especially in the confusion of battle. We couldn't get down off the hill as we were dressed as terrorists and, with this confused lot below us, we were sure to get fired on. The sound of the scrambling motorbikes disappeared over the hill behind us and the Police Reserve Air Wing (PRAW) aircraft suddenly pitched up. I called the pilot and gave him instructions to give cover to the motorbike boys. The terrorists didn't like any aircraft hanging over them as they would be spotted, so they invariably took cover and waited for the aircraft to do its circle and then they ran on as far as they could, before taking cover again when the aircraft did its turn. This gave the follow-up motorbike boys time to make up distance. Ten minutes later, there was the sound of heavy rifle firing about two kilometres away.

'Shit, they've caught them Musa,' I exclaimed with relief. The firing continued, in spurts, for about two minutes and suddenly stopped. We couldn't tell if it was friendly fire, or from the terrorists. We could just see the PRAW aircraft circling and estimated that they were not that far away from us. The two trucks with PATU were rounded up and I sent them driving up the road, at high speed, to try and cut off the escaping terrorists. They only got about a mile down the road when the lead vehicle flew into the air in a cloud of dust. Land mine! The second vehicle came to a stop and everybody ran to extricate the passengers from the lead vehicle. No real damage was done. The right back wheel had hit the anti-tank mine and, thereafter, that wheel assembly and axle was no longer part of the vehicle, but the rest was fine. Apart from deaf ears and a few bruises, the PATU boys were uninjured.

I moved our little section of men to the north-eastern side of the hill and was rudely awakened when the firing below us made us duck behind the nearest rocks, as bullets pinged off the granite around us. What was really strange was that being in the middle of bullets from friendly fire, at that long distance, never seemed to feel the same as it did was when those bullets were coming from enemy fire. We almost had a blasé attitude about it, and taking cover was done at a leisurely pace. It was almost as though we believed that the bullets would never hit us directly and that the only danger would be from chips of rock.

Radios had been going mad all the time, and much loud calling had been heard. It was apparent that the firefight was now over. Men from the bikes were checked and a body count sweep was started, by them, on foot. Three gooks were found dead at the scene. They were armed with AKs and had obviously collected their weapons from some hiding-place on their way out of the kraal. The rest had disappeared into the bush. From the tracks, it was clear that they had bomb-shelled and scattered in every direction to escape being followed. It was also probable that they had been scared shitless, with the sudden arrival of the motorbike boys on their tails. One had to admire the absolutely brave and reckless style of the farmers on their war bikes – what a great bunch of lads they were. When I got back to the base, there was much shouting about the botched deployment and who had given the commands to 'drive' into the kraal.

A Close Shave:

We had been deployed into the Shamva area. I decided on a route that would take us along a hill range to get to our target area. The reason I chose this route was that there were a tremendous number of people living in the area and the chances of getting through the populated area, without leaving spoor or being detected, was very small. It was an arduous trip, which took us over some very rocky hills. We only arrived at the kraal area at around four in the morning, bruised and battered. Musa had taken a beating, being the lead man; he always seemed to have to walk double the distances that we did. He would stumble into a rock formation and have to work his way around until he found a way through, not a very easy thing to have to do in the dead of night. It had been a long trek of some 25 kilometres. I let the guys sleep and took the first watch and I didn't wake them when the sun came up. The view from the hill we were on was magnificent. The position we were in was not the best, though, as there was very little undergrowth in which to conceal ourselves. I sat behind the best bush I could find, whilst the guys were lying up in a depression behind me. I could see the Mazoe River far down below us, as the open valley was surrounded by a jumble of hills that rolled away from us into a blue haze beyond. The early sounds of people going about their business in the kraals below us seemed to be crisper that morning. Clucking hens gathered their young ones, dogs sniffed around the previous night's fireplace looking for scraps, and the women were out sweeping the dusty area that made up their little homes. The sun came up on my right, casting orange-tinted shadows off the hills, across the valley I overlooked. It was very esoteric and I was very relaxed. A dirt road led through the valley, connecting the kraals. Our navigation had been spot on, plus we were on the right hill, with a superb view of the kraal we were to watch. Apparently a group of thirteen terrorists were frequenting that kraal and Colin's informer in the area had told him that they were the same group who had killed a white farmer some thirty kilometres from where we were. It was payback time and we were dead keen on getting our hands on that group. Eight o'clock came and I saw a man wandering up from the kraal, towards the hill we were on. Had he seen us? I crept back to the sleeping guys and woke them up with a warning to keep vigilant. We watched as the man, carrying a stick, climbed the hill and made his way directly towards our position. He got to within a few feet of us, before his eyes caught a shocked view of four rifles pointing at him.

'Eewe muriquita chi panapa?' came Musa's question about what he was doing up there. He explained that he was looking for herbs and firewood, so we grabbed him and hauled him into the small depression. Musa began asking him questions about the terrorists, whilst I took up my observation duties again. Nothing was forthcoming from the wanderer and it appeared that he really was up there looking for wood. The problem was we could not release him, as he would definitely tell the folks in the kraals, and perhaps the terrorists, that we were there, so he stayed with us for the day. The sun beat down on us the whole day. With very little vegetation in the area, it was difficult to get any shade but the worst thing was that we drank most of our water.

It was a long, uneventful day and my butt hurt from sitting on small rocks. The lads were getting their kit together at around sunset when I noticed a line of people walking, quite quickly, parallel with the river. From the distance I was observing them, it was difficult to tell if they were armed or not. I whistled to Musa and he snuck in next to me and, peering through his binoculars, gave a grunt.

'That's them, Ishe.'

Sure enough, every now and then a glint of light from the setting sun betrayed the weapons in their possession. We watched as the column of men walked straight into the village below us, where they then just seemed to melt into the huts and surrounding area. The sun had now gone down and it was very difficult to see anything.

'That's it, let's get going,' I whispered to the S.I.S men. We told the wandering man to stay where he was and he obediently sat down with his hands over his head, resigned to the fact he would spend the night on the hill. We made our way down the very steep slope of the rocky hillside. Each step was taken very carefully, as small rocks would start to roll down the slope if we slipped. It was like we were making the same noise as a stampeding herd of buffalo. We finally made it to the bottom of the hill, where the land flattened out rather quickly, so the going was easier. We gingerly walked single file down towards the invisible black area, where the gooks had entered the huts.

The four of us inched our way down a dry, small riverbed, until we got to a position directly under the largest number of huts in which we had seen the gooks walk. We stopped, ears straining for any sound that would help us figure out where the enemy was. There were faint noises from the kraal, pots clattered and the murmured, muffled sounds of people talking was all we could make out. We waited for about fifteen minutes.

'Okay, Musa, I'm going to take a little walk up to the kraal and see what's happening,' I whispered into his ear. He passed the message down to the others and all three slunk down against the wall of the riverbed. I gave them a 'thumbs up', which nobody saw, and I gingerly made my way through the old maize stalks, peering into the darkness as best I could, weapon at the ready and safety-catch off.

Stop, listen, and don't move an inch. I continued slowly up the little rise, to a point where I could just make out the top of a hut silhouetted against the night sky. I could make out nothing from where I was standing, so I switched on my night-sight and ran a semi-circle view of the area immediately in front of me. I heard the familiar sound of the night-sight warm up with a faint whine. I could still see very little, but I could make out the outline of the hut a bit better – gee, it was a dark night. I crept forward until I was about ten feet from the hut and parallel to it. From the view in the night-sight, and the feel under my feet, I could tell that the land started to gradually dip down away from me. I decided to return to the chaps and move around the kraal a bit. Perhaps we could get in amongst these guys. If I couldn't see, it was sure as eggs they wouldn't be able to see me, either.

I made my way back to the lads and knelt down next to Musa.

Dogs are a bitch:

The one thing we were always pestered by were the dogs that the local people had. The dogs originated from Egypt a couple of thousand years ago and were, in fact, a breed of their own. They had a very curled tail that arched in a big circle over their backs, were invariably hungry and were normally as thin as rakes, with their ribs showing. Their vertebra stuck up like the teeth of a large, wood saw and they walked with a stooped gait. It always seemed to us as though they had had enough of life and just wanted their misery to end. We called them 'razor backs' because of the ridges on their backs. The local folks used them to hunt down hares and small antelope. They had a bad habit of barking at the slightest noise outside the kraals and their owners would instantly know that there was someone out there. The dogs tended not to bark as much when it was cold in winter and we would find them curled up asleep under the chicken coops. Often, as we walked past them, they would get an almighty fright as they realised we were upon them and would take off, howling and barking like mad. If we approached a kraal with many dogs, we would have to be careful not to get them barking.

Back to the story:

'I think we should go a bit further downstream and hook around the bottom of the huts and wait for the moon to come up... okay?' I whispered directly into Musa's ear. Musa suddenly raised his left hand a little, with his palm up urging me to be quiet. He then bent his index finger forward and pointed back up to where I had been standing next to hut. His head was kinked down and to the right, straining every sense to understand the sound he had just heard.

'Ishe, they are there,' he whispered back to me.

We knelt motionless. Minutes went by and nothing more could be heard.

'Okay, let's wait here and see if I can see anything as the moon comes up,' I suggested.

A few minutes passed and the moon's light started to topple over the mountains far away and touched the huts with the faintest of light. I raised my rifle and peered down the night-sight. At first it was the terrorist's brimmed hat I saw, then I could make out the barrel of his rifle – an AK47. Slightly to his left was another man, but he was in the shadows of the hut's roof and I couldn't make out if he was armed or not. I had walked to within three metres of the terrorists and they hadn't heard or seen me. I was flabbergasted – how in hells' name had I gotten so close to the enemy and neither they, nor I, had seen one another?

'That's them all right; there are two, just to the right of that hut – under the roof,' I smilingly whispered to my second in command. 'Okay, I think the moon is going to be a problem for us now, so let's just take out these two and catch the others on spoor tomorrow.'

We prepared to open fire on the two terrorists. The rest of our team had been briefed about their arcs of fire. As usual, they would open fire as soon as I did.

Bang went my first round, aimed at the shadow with the brim-hat man. All hell broke out and we fired off about 40 rounds of ammunition, reloaded and ceased fire – normal practise for us - and then we waited. A minute went by and the definite sound of a 60mm mortar tube, firing a single round, echoed through the valley and off the hills around us. *Thungk*, it went. I counted to 13 seconds in my head, knowing that the explosion would then follow. *Bang,* just 10 feet from our prone bodies, but a bit up the slope of the river bank. Thungk came another, 13 seconds, then *bang* way up the side of the hill, way off target. *Ratatatatatat,* a full burst of AK47 fire, raced over our heads. We stayed still.

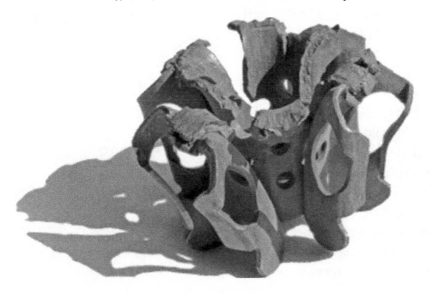

Five minutes passed and then BANG! ... a huge explosion next to my right eardrum! Musa had fired one round.

'What's that for?' I asked, not worrying whether the gooks heard my voice.

'I got him Ishe, just here in front of us, maybe 8 feet.'

I took aim with my night-sight and probed the area trying to find the body Musa was talking about. Sure enough, right in front of us lay a body. It was just too close for me to focus on as the night-sight couldn't focus on anything closer than 20 feet. I took a bead on the body and it suddenly moved and there was an audible '*Umph.*' BANG, I fired straight into it. The round ricocheted straight upward. I must have missed! *How the hell?* Then I remembered that the night-sight's point of aim was sitting about four inches above the barrel at such close proximity.

I raised the point of aim just above the chest ... *bang....* that would do it.

We waited five minutes and moved back up the dry riverbed to wait for morning. Nothing was said. We knew we had at least one terrorist. The night was surprisingly cold and we huddled up tight. About two in the morning, a hippo started grunting its way up the riverbed we were in and we could hear it munching its way around on the dry grass, not twenty feet from us.

Mils36 hand grenade - Musa called it his 'Apple'

'If he gets any closer, I'm going to give him my apple,' murmured Musa. Now 'my apple' meant Musa's Mils 36 grenade. He had been dying to lob this thing, having carried it for many miles in his front webbing.

'Forget about it, Musa,' I retorted. Eventually the beast wandered off looking for grass, leaving us with very little sleep left before the sun came up.

As the day dawned, our little group inched our way back to where the firefight had taken place. The kraals were dead quiet. Everybody knew they had to stay indoors, as the soldiers were around looking for the terrorists.

Lying prone on the ground was one dead terrorist, Musa's victim. We searched him and removed his weapons. I picked up the tail fin of the 60mm Chinese mortar bomb that had nearly wiped us out.

'Musa, it's your special magic that made this little bomb miss us, hey?' I said, holding the fin up for all to see. No other trace of the terrorists could be found; they had hastened away from the village, leaving very few tracks indeed. We rang up Bindura Police Station on the radio and had a chat with Barbara, telling her what we had accomplished. Colin and his men were on the scene within a few hours and that was that for us. We left Colin to his interrogations of the local folk and headed back home.

We hit this little group of terrorists again a week later. It was Sunday, October 22nd 1978. They had moved from the area they had been thumped in and were trying their luck in the farming area. We guessed they might have gone back to the farm where they had killed the farmer in the Matepatepa area. We were dead right.

Sally The Tracker Dog:

My night-sight came in handy with this next action. The approach to the farm compound was not too difficult, as the moon was down and both the small shrubs and the darkness shrouded us in a cloak as we got up real close to our targeted position. I was able to get the team right up to a corner-post of the fence of the farm compound. As the moonlight peeked over the trees, it began to shine its ghostly light everywhere, which made us feel a bit exposed, so we moved down into a small ravine. Very quietly, we took up a firing position facing the fence. As I peered through my night-sight, I could see three terrorists standing at the corner of the fence. They were brilliantly lit up by the moon. I could see the detail of their faces, the shine on their cheeks. I was even sure I could smell them. Sometimes you just know someone is watching you. Have you ever turned around for no reason and spotted someone staring at you – you subconsciously knew they were. Well, I swear the terrorists felt or 'knew' we were there. They hesitated in their movements and turned to peer down towards the ravine. There was no way they could see us. We were in the ravine and in darkness, and also between them and the moon. We didn't make a sound. The terrorists thought nothing of it and continued with their mission of getting food from the locals. I searched each visible man to see if I could pick out the leader or machine-gunner and found him when he turned, with his weapon held vertically - the unmistakable legs of a Russian RPD machine gun. I whispered right into Musa's ear, who in turn whispered to the next lad.

'Right next to the fence pole, that's where they are.'

We prepared to open fire on the area I had indicated to them. My first round went off, followed by a plethora of rounds from the lads. I immediately re-aimed and literally saw a hat in mid-air. There were no humans visible. Gee these guys can move fast. I called 'cease fire' after about 80 rounds had been fired and stood up to scan the area. I saw nothing by the corner-post, but caught a fleeting glimpse of someone running away and put a round after him, but probably missed as the bush was thick and this chap was doing the 100 metre in record time. We moved back from the fire zone and called Bindura. A decision was made to send a dog to follow up on the tracks – now that was a first for us. As these terrorists had killed a farmer, they were put onto high priority for murder. At first light, we searched the contact area for bodies, but found only a bit of blood and odd bits of equipment. Whilst we were busy doing the search, the small tracking team arrived by Land Rover, together with a young dog handler with a 'puppy' called Sally. She was a bloodhound and was no more than a year old. With Sally came a killer dog, an Alsatian, pitch black and obviously rearing to go. He was on a short leash, whilst Sally had a longer one. Each dog had its handler. Sally's handler was young and wore brand-new camouflage gear. The killer-dog handler was older and had constant trouble keeping his dog from chewing off one of our legs. We had a quick chat with the dog teams to establish the rules and let them get on with their work. Sally was quick off the mark and found her tracks – actually we could see the tracks, but I guessed Sally needed more information from the smells. After 10 minutes we started off on the tracks, not knowing what to expect. We had dumped our backpacks in the tracking team's Land Rover and carried only killing equipment, which was our weapons ammunition, radios, water and medics kit. We had started the tracking of the gooks at a fast pace, but the tracks were all over the place. It seemed that the terrorists had run in all directions at the firefight. It took time for Sally to get the general direction of the gooks and we would often have to wait whilst she moved back and forth, with her nose flat on the ground. Having found her mark, we would be off again, but at a quick trot to keep pace with her. The further we got from the farm, the more problems Sally had, with the bush having undergone a big burn a few days previously. There was black ash from burnt grass and bushes everywhere and she had trouble breathing through this, as it clogged up her nose. We were able to pick up the spoor visually more often than not, and trotted on. The idea was that Sally would lead us to the terrorists and the killer dog would be sent in to investigate difficult and thick bush areas that may potentially be harbouring somebody. It seemed like he was expendable. Sally had to have water every now and then, as I guess she was losing a great deal working in this dry and ash-filled terrain. At any rate we did not stop and traversed a huge tract of land, before we crossed into the Mfurudzi Wild Life Reserve where the bush began to get thicker and where the fire had not been so active. We ended up travelling along riverbeds more often than not, ever-conscious of possible ambush from behind the huge rocks and in the ravines we came across.

Around 25 kilometres into the chase, we were spread out along a thickly-vegetated river when Sally spotted the terrorists' backpacks amongst the rocks and bushes on the side of a hill. The killer dog was let loose and we took up positions for any potential firefight. There was nobody up the hill, just their backpacks. Equipment was scattered everywhere. We did a quick

search through everything to see if we could capture litera-
ture or weapons, but there was nothing of interest. Each pack
seemed to have the same stinking bits of unwashed clothes and
a few bits of food, and one had a basic medic's kit. We left the
packs there and continued following the tracks. It took a while
for the killer dog to be leashed again. The tracks were generally
following a thin path and we were clambering down in-between
some huge granite rocks in the middle of a steep ravine, when
the first burst of gunfire deafened us. I found myself in-between
two huge rocks, with the firing taking place just around the corner, unseen to me. Musa was in action and I flung myself around
to join him. I fell over Sally's handler as he hugged the ground,
with Sally protected under his clutching arms. Musa was standing and firing into a small cave to the left. I didn't open fire, as I
could see nothing. The noise was unbelievable and the smell of
cordite and smoke lay heavy, when Musa and the killer-dog handler stopped firing. Musa and I crept forward with guns at the
ready, not a word spoken. In the dark recess of the small cave,
we could make out the bloody body of a dead terrorist lying flat
over his RPD machine gun. We did a quick search of the area to
see if we had other problems, but that was it - one really dead
terrorist, full of holes. I had never seen so many holes in a body;
there must have been 40 in all. The killer-dog was nowhere to
be seen. He had obviously broken free from his handler because
of the extreme noise, and bolted into the bush. We had tried to
call in a Fire Force support team from Mount Darwin when we
had found the backpacks as we knew the gooks were close; however, were told without ceremony to 'get the hell off this radio
channel'. It was obvious we would have to sort out this situation
ourselves. What we didn't know was that a large Air Force and
Army operation was underway in Zambia. The Army was busy
bombing the hell out of Westlands Farm, where a huge terrorist camp had been found. We were way down the list for Fire
Force support. The Rhodesian's were attacking Joshua Nkomo's
ZIPRA bases near Lusaka in Zambia. The Air Force had effectively taken over the air space around Lusaka, whilst the camps

North of Zambia's capital, were being bombed and thereafter our army took out the terrorists in their camps. They were hitting at Nkomo as payback. He had authorised the downing of a Viscount aircraft carrying civilians from Kariba to Salisbury. He had allowed the shooting down of people going on holiday; men women and children...that didn't matter to him. The few survivors had been bayonetted to death in the most gruesome way. The Rhodesians were as mad as snakes at this barbaric action and were in the mood for blood and revenge.

The sun was beginning to disappear behind the hills and we realised we were far from home with no food, sleeping-bags or anything else, so decided to head back to the farm. We took a look at the map to try and work out exactly where we were and discovered that we were 36 kilometres away from the farm! We had a look on the map and found a road running to our North, about 15 kilometres away. We decided to head for that and called Colin on the radio, giving him our situation report and asking for an uplift. We had no idea exactly where we would get onto the road, so asked him to have a couple of vehicles run up the road there at around ten o'clock that night. We eventually linked up with the vehicles and collapsed in a heap - exhausted. We had left the terrorist where he was, having recovered his weapon. I guess he still lies there in that cave.

'Those are the guys we got at the farm last night,' I said to Musa. I worked out that the terrorists had been wounded during the night's firefight and that this man had been left behind, as he'd probably been too badly wounded. If we hadn't seen him, then the terrorists would have come back for him later, but we were so hot on their tails that they were running like rabbits. He must have been in extreme pain the whole day as he was hauled through the bush by his colleagues, but obviously he must have become too much of a burden to them and he'd been left in the cave to look after himself, or to act as a delaying tactic. I don't believe the terrorists ever knew we were on their tracks; they just knew they had to get as far away from us as possible. They could have been just around the corner when we hit the wounded man; we will never know. All told, we had walked - no, in fact, had run - a total of 51 kilometres on spoor, had had a firefight at the end of it and then still had the 15-kilometre walk to the road. We were a real fit team. The little water we had with us had to be shared with the dogs, too, during the day and we were only too pleased to get big gulps from the pick-up teams' water bottles. We vowed we would get around to the other side, ahead of the terrorists, the next day and see if we could pick up their spoor, as the river we were on exited the Umfurudzi Wild Life Reserve.

The killer dog pitched up at a nearby farm a week later and the relieved handler went out to pick him up. The dog was in a bad way and apparently never worked in the bush again; he was just not up to it anymore. However, Sally had been everything she was supposed to be. She had worked tirelessly the entire day under the most extreme conditions and taken us all the way. What a dog!

We were whisked off to check out the Mazoe River-line the next day, still with sore feet. We again walked for miles, searching every river and path we came across. We didn't find any spoor and, in fact, the area remained clear of the remaining terrorists for quite a while. They must have given up and moved elsewhere.

Propaganda:

The Rhodesian Government was dead keen on stopping inflated reports from journalists being printed in the international newspapers. There was a host of efforts made to try and clean up the news being printed in the international newspapers. One of the many aspects of this anti-propaganda campaign was in the form of an airmail letter. I sent one to Trish, my sister, in Johannesburg. I didn't expect her to be influenced by this, but it kept her in the 'know.' The Government also printed little book-lets with pictures and stories of the atrocities the terrorists had committed. I had seen some of these atrocities myself when I had been in the Zambezi Valley and these ghastly inhumane acts had been performed by modern-day men - so-called Freedom Fighters.

Operation Enterprise

We were called in to assist in a huge operation called Operation Enterprise. The main JOC command was stationed at Enterprise Country Club. This was the local country club built by the farm-ers in the Enterprise area, just North East of Salisbury, and it came complete with an 18-hole golf course and club house. There were tennis courts, a cricket/rugby field and a bowling green. The farmers in that area were relatively well-off and had not endured the hardships that the farmers in the Centenary and Mount Darwin areas had suffered for the past four years. The location was chosen because of its proximity to an area which was now riddled with gooks. It was a staging area for the gooks to hit targets in Salisbury and the plan was to route them out of the area. If attacks continued on Salisbury, the morale of the en-tire population fighting the terrorists would plunge and that was not good for all sorts of reasons. The operation included many facets of the Armed Forces, including the regular Army, with a number of different units, the Air Force and various sections of the Police. The Selous Scouts had their sections to infiltrate. It was a well-co-ordinated plan and essentially the strategy was simple. We knew that the area had been subverted by the resi-dent terrorists and that, should any Government forces wander around the area, the terrorists would know about it via their ex-tensive network of informers and Mujibas. There was also the chance we could get our hands on Mudzimo Nderinge, my old enemy from SIS training days. There were a great many patrols out during this operation.

Dear TRUTH

No doubt you are worried about the situation in Rhodesia, particularly in view of all the sensational headlines and horrific articles which appear in the Press. The psychological war being waged against Rhodesia through many of the news media of the world has escalated to such proportions of misrepresentation that many observers outside this country find it difficult to separate fact from fiction.

Daily examples of deliberate distortions and half truths are carried in the headlines of the world's newspapers and radio and television networks. The initial feelings of unease which assailed the people of Rhodesia and their friends abroad have now turned to anger at the perpetrators of these attempts to undermine the morale of our country and its supporters.

Scores of journalists from all over the world have descended upon Rhodesia and, believe it or not, are hard put to find enough to do or see. There are no massacres and bloodbaths, there are no massive terrorist force build-ups, there is no panic or hysteria, and there are no queues of people leaving the country. Many of the photographs and Press reports which have been sent to us by our friends bear no relationship whatever to the real situation in Rhodesia. In fact, some of the photographs and film were not even taken in Rhodesia!

Instead, these journalists find themselves in a country where they can travel safely with no fears of bomb explosions. They can walk through the cities at night with no fear of being mugged. They can spend a day in the country and watch the soil being tilled and the crops gathered. They can go to restaurants or a nightclub and pay less for better food than in many other countries in the world and they do not find sandbags or steel shutters over the windows of their chosen venue, nor are they searched before entering.

They find black and white Rhodesians mingling peacefully together and carrying on with their day to day jobs as they have done for many years. They find that there are sporting events, theatres, cinemas, horse racing and many other facets of entertainment available to them as they would elsewhere. They do see troops coming and going from their barracks, because there is an anti-terrorist war being waged on our borders, and there are shortages of things like razor blades, black pepper, light bulbs and the more exotic foods and toiletries.

And, some are disappointed, because every journalist lives on the hopes of scooping a disaster. And so, stories are made up — and elaborated upon to make them more sensational at editorial desks thousands of miles away. What much of the world Press does not wish to print are the true facts about Rhodesia. That she has weathered the last 10 years so well, in terms of internal peace, productivity, growth and racial harmony, despite the effects of boycotts and sanctions.

We do not deny that Rhodesians are going through difficult times — difficult but not drastic, and compared with most countries in the world today Rhodesians have much to be thankful for.

Well take note of the above raised by the Government. These are things with you. Thank you very much for the news of longs that you sent me. You must think this I am a long thing. They did not fit

One of the tactics the guys came up with worked like a charm. We were deployed into one small area, essentially as an observation post. Other units had the same tasks, whilst others were actively operating overtly and showing their presence. Four sections had been placed in strategic locations with extreme care, so as not to arouse the local informers, and they were instructed to lie very low. After four days of ripping up the area and showing our strength, all units were pulled out with trucks, leaving behind the four concealed units.

We hoped that the terrorists would be hungry after four days of hiding and would make their way to food outlets at a number of kraals. The plan worked. Within four hours of the main body of troops being pulled out, the first contact took place on one of the terrorist groups. A number of terrorists were shot dead and the rest captured. One PATU unit was lucky enough to have the entire senior command of the terrorists walk past their ambush position in broad daylight. The group included Mudzimo Nderinge, and his entire section, which totalled 7 men. They were so confident of their abilities and the information that all troops had been withdrawn, that they were walking with their rifles over their shoulders. The PATU members opened fire, instantly killing 3 of the group. Mudzimo was one of them. Two others were shot at a distance of between 5 and a hundred metres, and the remainder were captured about a week later. Our S.I.S team went to uplift the bodies in a Land Rover and took the corpses to the Selous Scouts Fort in Bindura. Mudzimo's hat had a hole in it from a PATU bullet and Hombore grabbed this as a souvenir. Mudzimo had been shot through the head with the bullet that had made a hole in his hat, and one of the lads ripped his silver chain from his neck and unceremoniously dumped it into the scrambled hole left by the bullet.

'Guess your luck just run out, you murderer,' he said and walked away. Hombore wore this hat everywhere. We had often tried to get Mudzimo and it seemed right to Hombore that he now had Mudzimo's soul.

The Army Doc and his humour:

When Alpha Charlie was pulled out, we were told to remain on standby at the military camp. I was suffering from veld sores and needed to get them treated, so I went searching for the resident Army doctor and asked him to attend to them. I had approximately six patches of about two inches each, all over my legs. Veld sores, or bush sores, are really just a fungal growth on the skin, caused by many weeks of work in wet conditions in the bush, where we had no bathing facilities. Little grass seeds that burrowed their way under the skin were quite often the cause of this infection. It was generally treated with a fungicide and cleared up after about a week or so, although the spots where the fungus had grown were often itchy for months afterwards. The makeshift medics-room was a green army tent, with a plastic sheet floor, a couple of beds and a few cabinets full of bandages and other stuff. I was chatting with the doctor, as I sat being treated on the bed, and found him to be well-travelled. If I remember correctly, he was an ex-American Doctor who had served a number of stints in Vietnam. He knew exactly what to do about my condition. He had obviously treated hundreds of Americans with the same problem during his time in Vietnam. Later, I heard he was a bit on the crazy side and was prone to playing jokes on people. One of the terrorists who had been captured had been shot in the right leg, just below the knee, and Doc decided to amputate the leg. He then took the leg and plonked it upside down in the sand bunker, at the fourth hole, and balanced a golf ball between the toes! Now the story gets even more involved!

Churchill pops in for a visit:

The main communications tent housed a number of women soldiers and volunteers, who sat in front of their radios and typewriters. They operated the vital communications radios and telex machines. On the same day the leg was made into a statue on the golf course, the women were busy performing their duties when in walked Winston Churchill - well, his grandson anyway - complete with cigars under his arm. Keith Samler (2 i/c in charge of Selous Scouts Intelligence) escorted him around. He had come on a visit and when the ladies were introduced to him, they all burst out laughing thinking that it was some sort of joke. Anyway, Winston made his way to the army section, accompanied by about twenty senior-ranking military men, when they happened to pass the 'statue'. You can imagine the big brass and their response when they saw what the Doc had done! I never did find out if there were further actions taken, but it was a good, light-hearted story that lifted the spirits of the troops a bit, in a time that was very tough for all of us.

Keith Samler with Winston Churchill and reporter at Operation Enterprise (Photo author unknown)

Putsi flies

I suffered from a batch of Putsi fly infestations on a number of occasions. Putsi flies had a bad habit of laying their eggs on your clothing, especially when they had just been washed and hung up on the washing-line to dry. The eggs would hatch and the little larva would burrow into your skin. The first sign you had of this problem was a few red dots on your skin. They weren't itchy, so it was normally brushed off as being a rash from grass. A day or so later, the larva would begin to get bigger and it was then that you knew you were in trouble. There was no way to remove them whilst out in the field. You had to let the larva eat their way to maturity and then, when they were ready to pop out, you could squeeze them out and have your vengeance. You couldn't kill them whilst they were in your body, as they would fester and you would get rather sick. The larva would be around a centimetre long when they were mature. The holes left when they popped out were raw, so we always tried to use some antibacterial ointment in them. As ironing clothes kills the eggs, Kenneth was instructed to iron all clothing, especially my underwear. I didn't want any problems there!

Fuel tanks ablaze:

One night, when Alpha Charlie was on operations, we saw a huge glow to our South in the night sky. It seemed like the sun was coming up at two in the morning! We later found out that the glow was from the huge fire caused when a couple of the fuel reservoirs in Salisbury had been blown up by terrorists. The country was desperately short of fuel and we were back on rations again. At one stage during the ration period, most folks were issued coupons according to the distance they travelled from home to work. One coupon meant that you were allowed to buy one gallon of fuel. Most folks were issued with only one coupon per month, so we often clambered into one another's cars for a lift if we were travelling anywhere.

Ghetto blaster:

Terrorists were forever raiding farm stores and stealing as much as they could carry away with them – effectively acting as criminals. They stole radios, bicycles, shoes, boots, hats, clothing and food. We had had enough of one group, who were really stealing a great deal from one of the farms neighbouring the Mfurudzi Wildlife Reserve, so we decided to install a small bomb, using PE4 plastic explosive, into a radio. The civilian radios we had in those days used two types of battery. One was large and the other half its size. The larger lasted twice as long. We used a large battery and stuffed the PE4 explosive into one half and kept the battery section in the other half active. Then we connected an electrical detonator to the dialling system and arranged it so that they would have to change the channel to tune into their favourite channel and, in so doing, would bring two wires together and complete the circuit. The store was raided, as predicted; however we never got to hear whether we'd blown off someone's head, or not. The stealing stopped, so we guessed it had worked.

Every feeling you can imagine:

Through my years fighting in the bush, I found that with every contact I would experience many phases of emotion. On first seeing the enemy, there would be a surge of excitement and anticipation. Knowing that we had a chance of killing some or all of the terrorists, induced in me an eager, concentrated attitude towards the imminent firefight. Young and 'invincible' as we thought we were, we would take them on with little regard as to the consequences. Amidst the noise of the fight, I found that I was able to think and direct the plan I had made for my team to be effective. Yet, mixed in with the sweat and dust, in the pit of my stomach I was always aware of the dangers we were in. On occasion, fear of losing the use of my legs was one of the worries

I contended with most. I would often pull my legs up towards me if the mortars were mid-air and on their way towards us. I knew that we would make it through but, more importantly, my main concern was about my guys and whether they were okay. After the contact, there would be a phase where I would run through the chaps' names and check that everyone was alright and only after that would I relax and plan according to the demands of the new situation. I imagine that a boxer would have similar emotions leading up to, during and after a fight.

Bad news:

Our little team was travelling back from Chiweshe TTL through the Matepatepa farming area of Bindura, when we heard some disturbing news on our Police radio channel. Apparently a Police Anti-Terrorist Unit had had a contact with terrorists at one of the farms early the previous evening. In the morning, the unit had started a sweep of the area and the terrorists had opened fire on them, killing two of the PATU men instantly. The terrorists then took off for the hills. One of the PATU men shot a running gook at about 450 yards. Now that was a good shot. When we arrived at the scene of the battle, I was traumatised when I saw the two dead farmers in the back of the Land Rover. I should never have looked, as for many months thereafter, I had recurring nightmares about battles. I felt so sorry for the families of the dead men.

The stars:

The stars and the moon meant a great deal to us in the game of survival in the bush. Musa and I would use the stars to guide us across the bush, deep in the middle of the night. We would study our map of the area and establish the direction and distance we would need to walk to get to our destination. The calculations were simple. At night, we would use the Southern Cross to establish due south. By keeping that position, say on our right shoulder, we knew that we were heading east. The Southern Cross was not always visible, though, so we then would have to use the Orion constellation as an alternative. Orion comes up in the East, but wasn't always around either, especially in winter when he would go hunting in the Northern hemisphere. The moon was almost always there and that was a synch to use. During the day, we would use our watches. By pointing 2 o'clock towards the sun, we knew that due north was approximately between the hour hand and the figure 12. We calculated, after many nights of route marches, that we would generally walk 25 miles in 8 hours at night.

Musa and I would often chat about the stars and the moon. They had such an influence on our wellbeing that they became integral and as one of our 'must have' items in the bush. The moon could either be your friend or foe. Walking at night under full moon was easy, but we could also be seen by the enemy in its silvery wash. We used the moon to time our approaches to kraals, or areas where we thought we may be seen walking. By timing it just right, we could be in position just before the moon lit up the area and we would have the advantage. Anyone mincing around after that was clearly visible to us.

I remember sitting high up on a granite rock, with the full moon shining off the Mazoe River, one night. Musa was right by my side and we whispered our thoughts to each other about life and family. He had a deep-rooted love for his family and the splendour of the scene below us aided him in his emotional description of the times he'd had with them. He missed them, just like I did mine. We made a pact right then.

'One day, when all this is over and we are old men,' I whispered 'use Orion or the Southern Cross and we will find each other again.' We sat quietly, pondering our thoughts. Musa was a special man and my friend.

S.I.S days are numbered:

Phil called us into the Special Branch offices and gave us the bad news that the SIS units were being disbanded. We had no idea why, but guessed the manpower requirements in other areas was too high and we would be needed there. We handed back our spook's equipment (another name we gave the gooks, because they were difficult to find) to Colin. The Special Investigations Section had been a year full of action for us and there were many stories to tell. However, more were to come with the setup of a specialised unit, which was to comprise some strange characters. When we handed in our kit, I stood outside the Special Branch offices and couldn't do anything else but give each one of my guys a hug. We didn't say much, as we knew in our hearts that we had been through a great deal together and that our memories would last forever. I missed them deeply the minute they had turned the corner to go back to their normal Police duties.

What a bash

A few days later, I arranged to have a farewell party for the S.I.S. team at the Police pub. I stuffed all the money I had into the kitty behind the bar counter and said to Never, the barman, that everyone could drink on me until the money ran out. I don't remember getting home to bed, but when I woke up the next day I found my money under my pillow. On enquiry, I found out that Mac, from the Selous Scouts, had paid the entire bill...gee, what a guy.

It was at this stage that I collapsed. I had been driving my body so hard and that, together with the limited food supplies we had in the bush, meant that my body was in a state of severe malnutrition. I had terrible headaches and felt very weak, so I was told to go and see a doctor, with the result that I ended up in the Morris Depot hospital for 6 weeks. I weighed 70kgs when I was admitted.

8

Pachedu (1978)

On the 1st June 1979, Bishop Abel Muzorewa was elected, in a general election, as Zimbabwe Rhodesia's first black Prime Minister. This was after a negotiated settlement between himself and Ian Smiths' ruling party. There was now a plan to incorporate the military parts of Muzorewa's political party into the new government's Armed Forces. The new 'irregular' unit was to become known as the Auxiliaries or Pfumo Revhano (Spear of the People). A number of so-called terrorist leaders and other black leaders, including Chief Chirau, made up a new government, which was not accepted by the international community. One of the things that really didn't help was when the Nigerian Government refused to accept tender offers from Britain for some rather large contracts, if Britain accepted the new regime. With economic pressure, the Thatcher Government was forced to not accept the validity of the new mixed-race government. We had hoped that Nkomo and his ZIPRA would join the new government, but that didn't happen. Both ZIPRA and ZANLA didn't want anything to do with the new peace initiative. Over 4 million pamphlets were dropped around the country, saying that the country now had a peaceful settlement and that all 'freedom fighters' should come home. An amnesty was issued and the hope was that the terrorists would hand in their weapons by the drove. It didn't happen. Muzarewa, Sithole and Chirau didn't control the fighters they bragged about; they didn't come close to having the local support they wished for. Initially, the

Selous Scouts were tasked with training these new members of the military and deploying them into tribal areas. The idea was that the Pfumo Revhano would take over security duties in those areas, so releasing the regular military to concentrate on other tough-nut areas. With the small number of terrorists coming on-sides, it was apparent that there were very few 'fighters' willing to change sides. A plan was hatched to flood the new unit with anyone who showed willingness to fight on our side. Busloads of local men were recruited and summarily dumped at training farms, for incorporation into what became known as The Auxiliaries.

Special Branch gets involved:

Detective Inspector Ken Stewart was a tall man, with almost Scandinavian, blonde looks. He walked into the SB offices, Bindura, where Phil and I were chatting about the local soccer match we'd had over the weekend. All the policemen had gotten together on Saturday and had had a great day playing against each other. Many goals were scored on both sides, mainly due to the fact that beer had been allowed on the pitch during play to keep the thirst at bay.

'Howzat, Phil,' greeted Ken, as he plonked a briefcase onto the table and pulled up a chair to sit next to me.

'We were just talking about the soccer,' replied Phil. 'You missed a good match.'

'I think I'm glad to have missed it. What time did you guys get to bed at the end?' asked Ken.

'It must have been around four in the morning. We all went to join Mac and the boys at the pub afterwards,' replied Phil.

'Well, to business,' said Ken as, he leaned forward on his chair to open his briefcase.

'Keith, you're coming back with me tomorrow to Doug Tapson's place. We have a funny farm and I want you to help with the instructing,' said Ken.

'Bring your civvies and your bush kit. You'll also need your rifle and stuff, but don't worry too much about ammo - we've got it all at the farm. I'll meet you here at 09h00 hours.' With that, Ken seemed to indicate that he had finished with me and wanted to talk to Phil about something else, so I left the office and headed back to the Patrol Officer's mess to sort out my kit. What about Kenneth? I told Kenneth to pack his kit and come with me in the morning; I couldn't do without my Batman.

Retreat was just like any other farm in the Bindura district. It had one main house, some sheds, a cattle race for dipping cattle against ticks and a couple of thousand acres of land that had been farmed with maize some years before. The farm would also have had a compound where the farmer's workers lived together, with a rudimentary school, with one teacher, to teach the children primary education. The old lands were now overgrown with grass and weeds and it seemed like the farm was not so active. I drove up the dusty road leading to the farmhouse security-fence and was shocked to see an armed man standing with his rifle at the ready. He wasn't even dressed in uniform, but wore jeans, a brown T-shirt and what looked like a terrorist cap. His one trouser leg was pinned up at the belt and I realised he only had one leg.

'Ishe,' whispered Kenneth, as he slunk down nervously into his seat next to me. He didn't utter another word, but just stared at the man. It was very odd indeed to be talking to a person who, for all intents and purposes, was a terrorist.

Gumbo the one legged ex terrorist at the gates to Retreat 'funny'
Farm (Picture author unknown)

'I am PO Chisnall.'

'Good morning, Sir' came the reply, as the man jumped to attention, saluted in a Russian manner and spun around very acrobatically on his good leg to unlock the chains on the fence. The soldier hobbled aside, using a handmade crutch. I parked under a shady tree at the back of the farmhouse.

'Better stay by the car,' I instructed Kenneth, not knowing what else to tell him. I walked through what appeared to be the back door to the house, made my way past a number of people busy sorting through a pile of boxes and looked for Ken Stewart. He was the only man I knew there and I found him on the verandah. There were clothes and weapons everywhere and the faint smell of a stew wafted past my nose.

'Morning, Sir,' I initiated as I spotted Ken, placing my rifle and webbing next to a chair.

'Hi Keith,' came the response. 'Hope your trip was okay. Come, I'll introduce you to the other guys,' he said, leading the way back to the jumble of people and boxes. The names flew past me and I would have to remember them again at a later stage. The scene was so different to Bindura or Centenary Police Station. I felt very out of place surrounded by Russian and Chinese camouflage clothing, East Block weapons, radios and all sorts of things that made it impossible to walk freely around the room.

'I've got my batman here. Where can I send him to pack away his kit?' I asked, once the introductions had been completed.

'Set him up with Moses, the cook. If he can cook, he is welcome, otherwise he will be a trainee,' came the response. I danced my way around the boxes and returned to the car.

'Come with me, Kenneth, and meet Moses. You can stay with him.

You have to start cooking here for all the officers, with Moses,' I said.

'What about all the bags, Ishe?' Don't worry, meet Moses first, and then take my bags through to the verandah. Moses was a large, black chap, with a big, smiling face and an obvious sense of humour. He lumped a pile of washing into the bewildered Kenneth's outstretched hands and muttered something about new boys trying to take away his job. He turned and walked away to the oven, with a smile that showed his bright, white teeth, as he wiped his hands across his white apron.

The old farmhouse was a hive of activity, as everybody was just settling in. I got stuck into fixing the radio equipment, running aerials and organising a desk so that we could work on something. There was the mandatory telex machine and three radio sets; one was a TR48, which had huge receiving capacity. The TR48 could pick up civilian radio stations in South Africa some 1500 kms away. The aerial for the TR48 had to be a 'T'-shaped affair, so I put up two gum poles and strung the aerial across them. There were spare batteries and a battery charger for the TR48. The other radio was a large, desk-based one, which I was familiar with and which would be used to communicate with other operations groups as far as 300 kms away. There was a small FM-based radio, which could only receive and transmit within line of sight or approximately 10 – 15 kms, depending on the terrain and the weather. The last, smaller radios were the types we often used when on operations. Electrical storms played havoc with radios. I tested the reception of the TR48 with Barbara at Bindura, and the reception was strength 5, which meant that we had a good signal. I then tested the desk-based radio, with the same result. I was proud and stood up, hoping that someone would notice my expertise, but nobody was interested and I sat down again to look at the maps thrown across the table. I peered out from the radio-room window and was surprised to see two of the odd-coloured Land Rovers, into which I had installed radios about a year earlier.

Afrikaans Theuns:

I met Theuns and a few of the other support staff over the busy day. Theuns was a short, dark-haired chap, who was South African by birth. He and his brother had been gold prospecting in Botswana, when some of the Rhodesian Special Forces did an op into Botswana and knocked off a couple of the ZIPRA commanders there. Theuns and his brother were suspected of helping the Rhodesians with information and therefore had had to high tail it out of Botswana as fast as they could. They packed a few things and drove like wild men through both Botswana and Rhodesian border posts, at high speed, knocking down booms and poles as they drove, and immediately volunteered for service in the Rhodesian Army. Theuns joined the Selous Scouts and became quite a character in that unit. He'd only been able to speak Afrikaans when he'd first come to Rhodesia and had struggled to learn any English. When I met him at Retreat Farm, his English was much better and he had a vocabulary of around fifty words which, when placed together in sentences, did not always come out the way they were supposed to. Half of those fifty words were swear words, anyway. Shame, I felt sorry for him when he struggled to describe something and he would often not say anything at all, so that he wouldn't be laughed at. He was, however, a very dangerous man. That day, Theuns was busy digging a huge hole in the front garden, some 8 paces from the front verandah. The pit he had dug had three steep, almost sheer, walls and one wall with a gradient. He had four black staff with him, digging through the red soil.

'What's this all about?' I enquired.

'Dis my bomb shelter and there is no way any f..cker is going to get inside, but me,' came his puffing response. When he had finished, a few days later, he laid railway sleeper logs across the top and piled earth on top of them. The sheer walls were then carved so that shelves appeared, and his bed, cupboard, grenades, ammunition, flares, machine guns and the like followed him into the dark pit. He never ran electricity into the pit, as he was frightened the static build-up would detonate the stockpile of explosives and detonators next to his bed. He booby-trapped the entrance with explosives every time he left the hole. As he said, 'No f..ker is getting into my hole!' I guess Theuns didn't really like us and preferred his own company. He came from a long line of Afrikaners who had fought the British (twice) in South Africa, in what had become known as the Anglo-Boer wars. The Boers had won the first war, but were eventually subdued in the latter war, which had ended in 1902. We did learn that he was very materialistic and would horde all sorts of things down in his pit. He was also dead keen on using explosives and was the type of guy who would throw a thunderflash into the toilet whilst we were using it. The rains came later but, although it became damp, he was never flooded out of his little pit.

The Pachedu Camp:

Most of the guys bedded down on the verandah that night, whilst Ken took up a room. I felt it was cooler on the verandah, but there was nowhere to store my kit so I commandeered a very large and heavy steel trunk and dumped all my spare kit in there. The steel trunk lay next to my stretcher bed. The camp was relatively unguarded in that there were no trenches or outside firing positions, so we would probably have been in for a hell of a time if we were ever attacked. There was a six-foot, diamond-mesh fence around the entire main house and there were armed guards, so I felt safe. I slept well that night, after Moses's stew; it had been a long day.

Pachedu was a unit primarily set up to train a new section of the military called the Auxiliaries. It had been running for a little while, when I joined. The political agreement with Bishop Muzarewa, the then Prime Minister of Zimbabwe-Rhodesia, meant that all his armed followers would now come under the control of the government. One day, they had been the enemy and the next they were fighting on our side. The idea was to get as many 'pro' forces into the field to combat the increasing number of enemy. Just like in Vietnam, as soon as the forces left an area, the enemy would go straight back in. We needed to keep our guys in the field and in as many parts of the country as possible. At the beginning, we had T-shirts printed with the logo of the unit on them. It was important that the men saw themselves as a single unit. The training was not up to the very high standards of the Rhodesian Armed Forces, but essentially gave the recruits a basic idea of the way we worked and how they were to conduct themselves in the field of operations. To do all of that in the short time we had to train them, was going to be a tough one.

Training Starts:

The next day was spent deciding on tactics for training the recruits and setting out a plan. We had arranged to get up early to go down to meet the troops. It was 04:30 hours and, after a quick visit to the bathroom, shower and shave, and a rushed cup of coffee Theuns and I headed off to the old farm sheds. The guards walked with us, six of them, all armed with AK47s. The guards and/or instructors were all ex-terrorists. Theuns and I carried hand guns. We rattled up the trainees and they came pouring out into the open area in front of the sheds. There were 500 of them and they formed a rough square, facing us. The idea was to take volunteers from areas, train them up, arm them and reintroduce them back into their home areas, so that they could protect their own people. We had 6 weeks to complete this arduous duty and we were assisted by 20 or so instructors. The instructors were all ex-terrorists from ZANLA/Bishop Muzarewa's lot, who had been captured - 'turned', as we called it - by the Selous Scouts and were then considered to be on our side. They were actually a fine bunch of guys. They were very experienced and were a real asset to our efforts. Most of them had had at least 5 years of military training, far more than any of us in the Police.

Auxiliaries being trained by two instructors at Pachedu Retreat Farm (Picture author unknown)

The instructors rushed up and down the line in an attempt to get the 500, principally uneducated men into some semblance of order. The language spoken, or more descriptively shouted, was Shona. The drill routines had to be done in Russian format, which were foreign to me, so I followed the lead of the instructors with regard to orders, as they knew the drill backwards. The senior instructor came to attention before me and saluted, with his right arm horizontally across his chest and slapping the front grip of the AK47 he carried.

'Ishe, everybody has been counted and we are ready.'

'Carry on,' was my uncertain order, assuming that the next order would be for physical training - it was. Up ran the instructors, separating the men into squads of about 50 men. They were

Some of the instructors and trainees at Retreat Farm
(Picture author unknown)

unarmed and dressed in an array of clothing – all civilian. Piles of Rhodesian Teak railway-sleepers awaited the recruits and, in a melee of legs and arms, these were manhandled up onto shoulders and the men were off down the road, towards a hill about two kilometres away. Each sleeper had three men to carry it. The sleepers were solid, rectangular hunks of wood, and Rhodesian Teak was well-known for its hardness and, of course, weight. They were by no means easy to carry and one could see the sets of three men trying to change shoulders whilst on the run. The instructors hounded each and every one of them. With threats and sticks, they walloped the men's legs, urging them on. The run lasted about 25 minutes but, on returning, every man was physically done for. The logs were unceremoniously dumped onto the pile again and the recruits formed their panting, sweaty squads again. Stragglers were pursued by respective instructors, until they collapsed on the makeshift parade ground. There were injuries galore. Shoulders were bloodied and fingers injured – it was a tough initiation for the recruits. The instructors did not let up and had the men down on their stomachs for 100 press-ups and subsequent 100 sit-ups. After that, the recruits were excused for thirty minutes to wash up and get ready for break-fast. Twenty of the recruits, mainly the physically incapable, had been weeded out to perform mess duty and had prepared the food, which was gulped down by the sore and exhausted men.

'Johnson,' I commanded, calling the lead instructor to my side, 'I need to know about any medical problems that any of them have. We don't want men who can't perform in this unit. I want one squad at a time to stay on the parade ground and the rest must start to clean the barracks and the parade ground. I also want to start building better toilets. Theuns will help with the toilet construction.' Theuns came up with a really good idea for the urinal. He constructed a decanting tin which dumped wa-ter evenly across a wall. Below the wall was the trough, which led to the French, drain-toilet system. All orders to the instruc-tors (who spoke good English) were in English, so there was no misunderstanding.

The terrorist instructors:

I learnt, over the next few weeks, that the instructors had origi-nally been supportive of Bishop Abel Muzarewa's faction of terrorists. Now, Bishop Muzarewa had been head of one of the factions supposed to be fighting for the liberation of his coun-try. He didn't have much support within the country and was regarded by the other two major factions as a sell-out to the cause. Muzarewa had once visited a ZIPRA camp in Zambia, where he was seen trying to lift a light machine gun in the air and chant war songs. He didn't manage the lift it and, from then on, the ZIPRA men called him 'Heavy, Heavy.' His men had been trained in China, Libya and Tanzania and were some of the first operatives to be harnessed into the liberation struggle. They had been in Zambia when discontent between the various factions of the struggle had started, and they had ended up on opposing sides of each other. The landmine which had blown up Herbert Chitepo, one of the most senior men within ZANLA, had caused an enormous stir. Chitepo had been killed by an SAS man living in Zambia. Actually, this assassination was to help the Rhodesian Security forces for a long while. Infiltrations almost ceased in certain sectors. The Zambian Government had a whole bunch of the terrorists arrested, believing it was fighting between the different terrorist factions which had had Chitepo killed. Tempers between the various factions increased overnight. What happened was a power struggle within the top ranks of the different liberation factions, and the lowly soldiers ended up with the bloody sticks. Battles between the factions were commonplace and an incident in Zambia was narrated to me by one of the men who had been there. Two factions had faced each other in the bush and the Zambian Police and military had tried to intervene, to stop any bloodshed. On Johnson's side was a female commander called 'She Bitch', who stepped forward and egged the soldiers to attack the opposing faction. She was shot stone-dead by the Zambian Police. This didn't stop some bloodshed but the instructors, plus a few others, became disillusioned and fled back to Rhodesia only to be arrested and 'sorted out' by the Selous Scouts. They were now willing soldiers on the Rhodesian side. They had seen some terrible things and experienced extreme hardships, so they were tough soldiers. Their training had been extensive, but not one of them had committed any acts of terrorism in Rhodesia, so they were ideal candidates for this new force.

Russian drill:

The training routine was rigorous, with physical training and parade-drilling taking up a large part of the day. Political indoctrination was also part of the recruits' education, together with medical training, bush survival and combat tactics. The instruction style was all based on the Russian military way of doing things - very different to our military way. At first, the recruits had to fashion wooden 'play' weapons from wood and these were later replaced with a variety of Communist weapons, including AKs and SKS rifles. No machine guns or grenades were issued. The weapons came from captured stockpiles in the Rhodesian inventory, together with a huge pile of munitions supplied to us by South Africa. The South Africans had apparently captured a massive Russian supply ship off the coast of Angola, which kept our armoury full to the brim. The supply shipment was destined for the MPLA (Movement for the Liberation of Angola) forces fighting South African-backed UNITA forces. The South Africans had enough Communist weapons for themselves, so they sent the rest to us. Brand new weapons and tonnes of clean, grey boxes of ammunition were delivered to us. None of the recruits had access to ammunition, except when they were on the improvised firing range and, even then, we kept a very close count of rounds of ammunition. One could never be too careful, as any one of the recruits may have been ZANLA plant who could take it upon himself to pop off an instructor.

RENAMO:

We had amongst us a special number of 'recruits.' Members of RENAMO were with us doing some training. RENAMO had been created as a joint venture between the Rhodesian Special Forces and some of the local tribe's people of Eastern Mozambique, as an aggressive venture to harass the FRELIMO and ZANLA forces in Mozambique. There were a number of ex-Portuguese soldiers, who had fought against FRELIMO in Mozambique, to kick-start the movement and they worked well with the SAS in Mozambique to stir up trouble. We had a chap called Charles from RENAMO with us for a while. This chap once borrowed our clandestine 'civilian' white Peugeot 404 to nip into Bindura to do some shopping and had rolled it. Not a great move on his part. The Special Air Service or SAS were the chaps mainly involved in the RENAMO work and operated with them in the heart of Mozambique. The tribes around the Tete area of Mozambique were not all in favour of FRELIMO, and the Rhodesians took full advantage of their dislike of the communist force. RENAMO still exists to this day and they demonstrate their opposition to the Mozambiquean Government by means of the guerrilla tactics and hit-and-run methods they learnt so many years back with the Rhodesian Special Forces.

'Dear God, how can we be brave for the dead' (Heather Silk):

On the 12th February 1979, the shocking news of the shooting down of the second Air Rhodesia civilian aircraft was transmitted to us via telex machine. Joshua Nkomo's ZIPRA thugs had shot the Viscount down with a SAM 7 missile. There were no survivors from this. The country was in shock and experienced intense anger, as the passengers were returning after having been on holiday at Lake Kariba. The rest of the world said nothing and didn't condemn this horrible act. We, however, were all in a state of shock and I phoned my parents, as I knew they would have been helping the tourists. My mother had been working for UTC in Kariba at the time and had loaded all the people into the bus, wished them a safe trip and had waved them goodbye, before they'd boarded the aircraft. As she wrote in a letter to my sister, which she posted two days later:

'Dear God, it's happened again – all those people killed, it's just too ghastly. No survivors this time, just nothing left of that happy crowd we put on the buses yesterday afternoon. And even before I closed the office to go home they were all dead. .... Amongst them was Mr Ebben, the new owner of Anchorage Marina, the wife and two children of the new manager of Caribbea Bay, the son of a Casino chap, four young wives whose husbands ran the gauntlet of the convoy', a young Army chap who bought a bus ticket from me at the last minute and so the list goes on ... I posted a long letter to you yesterday but fear it must have been on the plane.'

Such a terrible shame; we felt so sorry for the people and their families. Everybody in the country knew someone who had been killed in the two Viscount disasters, so it was now, more than ever, a very personal war. We had been hurt and we wanted 'payback'!

At the going down of the sun and in the morning we shall remember them!

Charlie Small... the bomber:

Some friends arrived in a cloud of dust at the base, driving a white Land Rover. As they rounded the corner of the house, Theuns recognised the occupants in the vehicle and promptly shot and punctured all four tyres with his pistol. It was his friend, Captain Charlie Small, from the Army Engineers. Theuns knew Charlie from operations they had carried out, deep in Mozambique. The vehicle came to a sudden stop, with dust billowing out.

'Hey, hey, hey!' came Theuns's welcome. What we didn't know was they had just been ambushed up the road and were not in a

*Some of the first Auxiliaries at Retreat Farm were issued
communist weapons (Picture author unknown)*

state of mind to be shot at again. Upon hearing of the ambush, a bunch of the Pachedu guys jumped into our large troop carrier and mounted our 4 GPMG machine guns on each corner. Long belts of ammunition were rolled out across the floor of the vehicle, so that we would have plenty of food for the guns. We took off to see if we could avenge our friend's nasty surprise. We fired heavily into the thick bush going up the hill, but the terrorists had legged it. No follow-up was done and we headed back to the base at Retreat Farm. Everybody migrated to the bar and stories and lots of drinking took place that night. The visitors bedded down with us on the verandah, as it wasn't a good idea to travel around at night in case we got ambushed.

The next morning, Theuns was up early and decided to clean his sniper rifle in the lounge. Now this was one of his loves - weapons. His scope was carefully taken off and a little cloth was used to clean every speck of dust from the lenses. Just as he was placing the scope gently on the table next to him, a thunderflash came whistling through a window and landed right at his feet. The fuse burnt with a blue smoke and Theuns knew he had seconds to escape. He was up and over the chair with his weapon in hand, but the scope fell to the floor. The thunderflash burnt for another second and 'phsssst' ... Nothing happened. Charlie, being an army engineer, had defused it before hurling it at Theuns. Theuns was now in a state and was threatening murder. Everybody evacuated the building in a hurry, including Charlie; you didn't want to be around Theuns when he was fired up and in a mood. It all worked out fine at the end, and it was really payback for Theuns having shot the tyres on Charlie's Land Rover. Charlie was later killed in a terrible helicopter crash, deep inside Mozambique, when he was on a huge military action called Operation Uric, in which many sections of the army, plus some South Africans, were involved. (Read Neill Jackson and Rick Van Malsen's emotional book called 'The Search for PUMA 164.')

The songs of the war:

We sang our hearts out, with a mixture of revolutionary lyrics. The songs had migrated down from training camps in many African countries, where the terrorists were being trained. Singing as the recruits did physical training, kept their spirits up and I imagine it's the same for the United States Marines and other units the world over.

A ZANLA song used in promoting their cause during the bush war:

Chimurenga

Hondo takayirwa na mbuya Nehanda bakomana Nehanda
Chimurenga takapinda nambuya Nehanda bakomana Nehanda
Ini ndakafamba nesanago rinemindzwa inobaya
Nesango, Nesango, Nesango, rinobaya
Nasi nonayi bamwe bakagarika
Zwabo munyika yeropa
Nasi wonayi bamwe bakagarika
Zwabo munyika yeopa
Isu tinotenda mbuya Nehanda, bakomana Nehanda
Nasi takagarika nemaka yenehanda
Barume Nehanda
Nasi tintenda Nehanda, bakomana Nehanda

We fought the war with the men of grandmother Nehanda
The freedom struggle was entered with the men of
grandmother Nehanda
I went into the bush full of thorns and injuries from stubbing
Bush, bush, bush, stubbing
Look today others are free and settled
In our country of blood
We thank you grandmother Nehanda, the men of Nehanda

Today settled because of grandmother Nehanda
Men of Nehanda
Today we thank you grandmother Nehanda, men of Nehanda

(Nehanda was one of two spiritual leaders who rose up against the Pioneers during the initial colonisation of Rhodesia.)

Pachedu expands:

The demand for Pfumo Revanhu exceeded supply, so it was decided that we would open up a second 'funny farm' up the road. I left Retreat Farm with my twenty one instructors and all the equipment I believed I needed, to start up a new training team. The new farm was about twenty kilometres from Retreat and was an abandoned farmhouse, with old tobacco barns set nearby, with similar buildings to those at Retreat. I was joined by Brian Timmer and Clive Dredge. My ever-faithful Kenneth came with us. A lot of work had to be done in a few days, including securing the farm buildings and making a fortress as best we could. Brian was a stocky, blonde-haired fellow, with a huge sense of humour. He was a Policeman with Special Branch, but had worked directly with Superintendent Mac Macguiness within the Selous Scouts 'Fort' at Bindura Police Station. Clive was a tough ex-sergeant from Support Commando Rhodesian Light Infantry, a specialist soldier. All the staff had exceptional skills and we worked as a great team.

Again, the farm had all the normal buildings; however, this time, the buildings were backed up against a small, granite-covered hill. The main house overlooked old disused fields and, on the left, were the old tobacco barns. There wasn't a soul living within ten kilometres, so it made the ideal place for training.

Camp defence:

'Don't you think we should strip all the barbed wire from around the farm and use it to bolster the defences?' suggested Brian. It was a great idea and we set to it with vigour. We used the heavy-armoured troop carrier (called a Crocodile), as we had to haul the bundles of wire we collected back to the house, from every corner of the farm. On one of the wire-collecting trips, Clive was driving. He couldn't see too much out of the small openings on the armoured cab and he really needed some help in reversing. I was sitting on top of the cab, with my legs dangling down through an escape hatch, almost on top of Clive's head and I was cradling a 7.62mm MAG machine gun, with a belt of ammunition fed into it. A bunch of the ex-terrorist instructors were in the back, amongst the barbed wire. Clive was trying to reverse the cumbersome truck and I was shouting out instructions on which way to turn.

Obediah, Brian Timmer and Clive Dredge
constructing the new 'Funny Farm'

'You're okay, keep coming,' I said, peering backwards, as Clive increased the revs and reversed. I didn't see the huge, antbear hole at the back, right-hand wheel and the truck lurched into it with a massive lift to its front end. I instantly lost my balance, fell backwards off the cab roof, and my right shin scraped along the raw metal plating as I headed for the ground some ten feet below. I landed on my back, holding the machine gun at arm's length to cushion its fall. I was more worried about bending the weapon's barrel than the injuries I was about to sustain to my back. The result was two 'dislocated' wrists and a massive wound to my right leg, but the gun was safe. After the initial shock, all the instructors burst out laughing. I immediately saw red and, without blinking an eye, opened fire on the truck, wrecked wrists or not; I felt no pain, just anger. I pumped 50 rounds at disappearing heads and saw rounds thumping off the heavy steel-cladding at the back of the truck. I slumped back, with the gun smoking blue and hot. I was more hurt from embarrassment, than anything else. My anger was dissolved when the pain in my hands struck me and I let the gun drop across my chest. Clive jumped out of the truck and, with some effort, we managed to get my hands working again. The instructors didn't say a word on the way back to the farmhouse. A month of pain later, I realised that there was something wrong with my back, so I dropped into the Morris Depot medical unit and had it X-rayed. I had broken my L5 vertebra in half. The bone healed; however, it caused me some problems over the years that followed.

The camp came along quite fine and the arrival of the recruits, 500 in all, added to the workforce we could allocate to making this a tip-top training base. A similar toilet system to the one that Theuns had made was installed, together with a fine cooking area, under some corrugated sheet metal. It must have been a great house in its day but now that we had taken over, there was little regard to the condition of the paint on the walls and the once-pretty garden. At the back of the house was the hot-water 'Rhodesian' boiler.

Our first batch of recruits:

*Our first recruits at the new training farm – issued with G3
rifles the old tobacco barns can be seen beyond.*

The first thing we did with the new recruits was to sort out the
'can dos' from the 'can't dos'. We had the men running up and
down the old maize field, carrying rocks. Within a short time,
we established who would continue doing physical training and
those who would act only as administration support, or cooks.
We also had to sort out any characters who didn't want to continue training, or those who were too big for their boots and wanted
to take control. One chap, who was a good 6' 8' tall, was hauled
out of the ranks. He was a big, strapping man, with muscles to
back him up. However, his attitude towards us was vividly aggressive and we had to bring him down to size to gain respect,
before we could continue. He seemed to be the 'hero' of the recruits and was not going to take orders from us. We had to fix
him NOW. As he stood towering over Brian and myself, I called
Lance, one of the smaller instructors, to my side. Lance had a
mild manner, but he had an unbelievable fighting ability. He
knew exactly what I needed from him and he lashed into this

giant with a thousand words. Lance's face was level with the giant's chest. At one point, Lance stopped his vocalisation and suddenly reached up with his hands, grabbed the giant by the throat and proceeded to choke him. The giant's instant reaction was to grab Lance's hand away from his throat, but as he did this he fell to the ground unconscious. What Lance had done was to stop the blood flowing to the giant's brain and when the grip was released, the blood rushed to his brain and thumped so hard into it that he was knocked to the ground. Now that was impressive! From there on, there was no more upheaval from anyone. There were about 35 men who could not make the training due to physical problems, and they were set into a squad of their own. Training men who had little education was difficult and required a different tactic to training folks who could read and write. The majority of instruction was done in Shona, because the instructors did most of that. Marching drills were commanded in English, although the drill manoeuvres were Russian. Training in the use of radios was also done in English. Not all of the recruits were uneducated, but the majority were from rural areas where running a farm the old subsistence way was what they knew. We had to bring the men down mentally until they were rock bottom and then bring them up again, at the same time maintaining a very superior position to them whereby we would gain their respect. That was the answer - gain their respect and trust and, at the same time, have them increase their sense of teamwork and confidence. The training schedule we put together was very, very hard. We ran these men into the ground. The first five days of training were dedicated entirely to physical training and included getting the men up before the sun rose, ordering them to run with logs for an hour, followed by press-ups, sit-ups and then the dreaded obstacle course. The obstacle course was our pride and joy. There were a myriad tree logs to jump, vehicle tyres to squeeze through, tunnels to navigate and so on. The recruits had helped to build it and Brian and Clive had really enjoyed creating the most difficult of obstacles. The recruits' first attempt at the course was weak. They completed it, squad by squad, with each squad being timed. Unbeknown to them, the instruction there-after would be that they were to better the course time, as an entire squad, by 15 seconds, every time, or they would repeat the course until they did. Every man had to be across the finish line for the time to be noted. This meant that the strongest went back and helped the weaker men over the course. The squad's sense of pride in itself and its identity was compounded. Squads took up nicknames for themselves and made up war chants to spur each other on. Any physical injuries, and there were many, would be attended to with the best bits of medical equipment we had. The most common injuries were cuts and bruises and these were not really a worry; however, sprained ankles meant the recruit would join the medically-unfit cook section and this was not what they really wanted. We had to show we cared for them, as men.

Very quickly the men started to work together as squads, and this helped tremendously with the camp's morale. Morale had to be high as the recruits slept in the barns, on the ground, with one blanket each. If morale dropped, we could have a trying time with these men. Their food was very important to them and a great deal of time was spent trying to improve the quantity and quality of this. Their daily Sadza - a stiff form of porridge made from maize meal and water - was cooked in huge pots, and meat was high on the list of things that made them happy.

Every now and then, we would take time out of training to allow for sport and recreation. With the inter-squad rivalry so high, we had to stop some of these games out of fear of starting full-out battles. The one game they were banned from playing was called Murder Ball. The old maize field in front of the house was the venue, and the recruits were divided into two teams - about 250 per side. You have never seen such a mad game in your life. There was a wooden pole at each end of the field, about 100 me-tres apart. The object was to touch the 'ball', which was a sand-filled, plastic, water-bottle, onto one of the poles. There were no boundaries and no other rules. We added another bottle to the game, as there were just too many bodies trying to grab the one 'ball.' Only one goal was scored when about 50 men formed a block and barged their way through the opposition. It was very funny to watch, but it caused a hundred small injuries so we stopped it. The 'balls' were absolutely destroyed in the process. It was mayhem; there was blood and snot everywhere. Someone suggested we use a telephone pole instead of a 'ball', but we wisely decided against that as we could very well imagine the destruction that would cause. It was one very tough game!

Most, if not all, the rural black folks could not swim, so part of our aim in training was to help them overcome their fear of deep water, and we used the water reservoir at the back of the house for this. It was ideal in that it measured 20 feet across and was 5' deep. All those who could at least stand in the water were thrown in, 50 at a time. We helped the non-swimmers in and, with their companions, almost all began to quite enjoy this activity. No horseplay was allowed. Later, we added a large pole for them to hold. We also made a make-shift diving board, which proved a hit with the comedians amongst the men. They had no style at all and, the more dramatic the jump off the board, the more applause they got, which made for some serious comedy. All of this was to boost their confidence and morale.

The recruits were taught tactics to be used in bush warfare: ways to walk through the bush, weapons handling etc., which was identical to the training at Retreat Farm. We had six weeks to turn civilians into basic soldiers and we tried very hard to do that. When it came to teaching them the 'art' of surviving an ambush, we discussed the basics in that it was better to charge full pelt into the ambushing team and overrun them, rather than running away, as the latter increased the time the enemy had to get a shot into you. By attacking them directly and aggressively, the idea was that they would tend to keep their heads down. It takes a great deal of courage to run up a small hill and attack an entrenched enemy. We thought we would test the recruits, once we thought they had the story right, so we sent them with the instructors up into the hills to do some marching exercises. In the meantime, Obediah, Clive, Brian and I set up a huge ambush on the return path. We had a couple of machine guns to add firepower, plus thunder-flashes to bring up the decibels. We could hear the recruits coming down the hill. Our instructors knew the ambush was coming, so they were prepared. We let the first twenty men get past the ambush-killing ground and then opened up with everything we had. We must have been ten paces from them and we were expecting to be overrun by the recruits, as they had been instructed to do. They didn't have any live ammunition, as this merely a training-exercise. The idiots didn't do a bloody thing they were taught! The entire lot took off at a gallop, and were gone within seconds. Not one of them followed the instructions we had tried to drum into them. One chap ran all twenty kilometres back to Retreat Farm. We found three of the recruits in the old cattle-dip, hiding, with just their noses sticking out of the water. We would have to do a great deal more training for these guys to become soldiers!

Our bunker outside the house with our fake 75mm recoil-less rifle – two ex-terrorist instructors with Keith – I have a Chinese RPD 7.62mm machine gun

Initially, Russian SKS rifles were issued. This ten-round, carrying-capacity rifle was commonly used by terrorists, although they far preferred the AK47. All the communist weapons we had were captured weapons from engagements with the enemy. We took off the bayonets, though, before issuing them. Later, we took these weapons back and issued them with German G3 Heckler and Koch rifles, which took the NATO 7.62 x 51mm round. The 'tinny' G3 rifles were definitely not as strong as the AK47 or FN rifles, but at least they were 'friendly' weapons. The magazines were designed to be discarded once used and, being made from very thin metal, they were useless and forever being damaged. We wanted to change the weapons, because the recruits looked more and more like terrorists and we had to change their weaponry urgently. The main Pachedu team still kept their Russian RPD machine guns and AK47s. I still had my FN and so did Brian. Kenneth had his little baby UZI 9mm, but he wanted to carry an AK as well, which I refused.

How far away was that shot?

An exercise we considered important was to try and estimate the distance at which the enemy was shooting at you. A squad would be placed facing a hill and, stretched out down the valley, would be the instructors, at differing distances from the men. Each instructor would fire a round over our heads and we would ask the trainees how far away the shot had been fired. We would hear a click as the round clipped overhead and then hear the sound of the rifle. Quite a scary exercise, but worth it in what it taught us.

Mortars:

As always, we had to consider security. Clive took off for Salisbury with the Land Rover one day and returned with 16 boxes of 60mm mortars, 'donated' by his mates at the Rhodesian Light

Infantry RLI Support Commando ordinance stores. We had a Portuguese 60mm mortar tube and so set about constructing two pits to house the weapon. We were in dire need of more fire power, so the mortars were a welcome addition to our small arms collection. We built up a variety of bunkers above ground, and included a lookout post on top of the low granite hill behind the house. The lookout post had a ring of sandbags about three feet high, into which we placed a very peculiar 'weapon.' We assumed that the terrorists in our area had bigger weapons than us, so we converted an old, steel, corner, fence-pole into a cannon. The 'barrel' was made from the main pipe of the fence-pole and also had the ideal diameter, measuring 76mm - the same calibre as the Chinese anti-tank recoilless cannon

Portugese 60mm mortar

at Retreat Farm. The side braces of the fence-pole were used to act as legs and we fashioned a chamber from an empty 5-litre plastic bottle, stuck it onto the one end of the pipe and painted the whole thing black. The entire 'cannon' looked awesome and the barrel stretched a good 8' into the air, giving us 'immense power' over the area. Deceptions like this were used by us on many occasions to fool the terrorists or, in fact, ordinary, everyday people from the area, into believing something else. Every now and then, we would cover it with a tarpaulin to pretend to protect it from rain, etc. The 'weapon' was so convincing that when the Senior Superintendent from Special Branch Salisbury did a camp inspection, he was completely fooled into believing that it was real.

'So now explain this to me. Where did you get this weapon and why is it not on the camp inventory?' was his question, as he stood right next to it. He had obviously never fired a weapon in anger in his life - well, not that big anyway.

Gooks in the area:

We had a couple of interesting episodes in and around the camp. One day we had a visit from one of our farming neighbours. He arrived in an Isuzu pick-up truck, brandishing a very long-barrelled Magnum .44 revolver. We had a chat about the rains and, as always, the security situation. He said he was very happy having us as neighbours.

'I met some of your boys up at the top fence gate the other day. I nearly had a heart attack when I saw them, as they looked just like gooks to me, but then I remembered you guys were here and that they were probably just a security patrol.'

'When was that?' I enquired.

'Last Thursday at around noon.'

'We didn't have any of our guys out at that time. How many were there?' I quizzed.

'Ah, around fifteen I guess.'

'Did any of them have a machine gun or RPG rockets?'

'Ja, there was one RPD machine gun, but I really didn't see any rockets.'

'I can't believe it. You met up with a real bunch of terrorists and they did nothing to you. What did they say?' I was now on the edge of my seat. Brian just sat there, his mouth hanging open in amazement.

'They said 'Good morning, Sir' and carried on walking.'

Now that was something, I wonder why they didn't just shoot the farmer. They were miles from any retaliatory force. The only thing we could think of was that they were a new and inexperienced group, en route to the outskirts of Salisbury. We changed our tea-drinking to beer, to celebrate the miraculous survival story.

Hell from above:

Clive had been itching to test-fire the mortars. We cleared the firing area of people and the three of us, Clive, Brian and I, crouched in a mortar hole with the mortar. The second hole was right next to this one and was really there for escapes from danger in the firing hole. We ranged the mortar as best we could, trying to hit a tree some 400 yards away. This was not easy, as the mortar was a simple tube with no legs, base or sights. We used the carrying-strap as the range finder. The idea was that you sat on your bum, pulled the middle of the mortar back towards you, and pushed the strap out with one of your feet. There were brass tags on the strap indicating range so, if you wanted 400 yards, you would push the 400-yard tag onto the ground just at your foot. The ranges were really inaccurate and if you used booster charges on the mortar, then that would be even worse. We ran through the drills with Clive; neither Brian nor I had ever fired a mortar before. We took it in turns to hold the tube, trying to get the aim right. We got quite good at aiming, and Brian was triumphant when, on his third shot, he hit right at the tree's base. Thereafter, boredom set in, so we decided that we would try to see how close we could get the mortar rounds to land to the hole we were sitting in, by firing straight up into the air. The idea was that if the mortar landed in the firing hole, we would have already jumped into the neighbouring one to escape the shrapnel.

Well, we got closer and closer, with some of the rounds hitting just outside the hole. The problem with this game was that when we looked straight up, it was very difficult to judge exactly where the mortar bomb would land. We had but one choice and, if it was wrong, well then, we would meet our Maker. There was one dud round, which Clive defused. I said I wanted to chrome-coat the round and keep it as a souvenir, so we left it soaking in a bucket of water for a week, trying to get the explosive to dissolve. We had to pull the bucket quite some distance away, though, because the explosive had produced Nitro Glycerine, a very unstable explosive. The diffusing worked but, when I took the round to Dennis Thompson (one of Pachedu's support guys) in Salisbury to have it chrome-plated, he was insistent that the whole factory be cleared of staff whilst he burnt the round in a fire to rid it of any explosives. He threatened me with death if there was a problem, but I knew that Clive had done his stuff on the round to make it safe. The mortar came out beautifully, with a mix of copper- and chrome-coatings, and it looked like a winner's cup.

The sprint for beer:

Brian and I decided to bet Clive that he couldn't drive to Retreat Farm (20 kms away) within 20 minutes and get a crate of beer for us. It was dark and the road was hazardous, with rivers to cross and hairpin bends to navigate, not to mention the possibilities of there being an ambush, or a landmine. The rule was that he had to get someone at Retreat to radio us, in order to prove that he had made it. Watches were synchronised and Clive was gone in a cloud of dust, in his Ford Bronco. To our amazement he got there in time, so we ended up having to pay for his beer. Such were the mad adventures we got ourselves into.

Thumbs and bombs:

There is one thing that we had to watch out for when driving around in a war zone and that was the health of our hands. As the driver of a 'landmine-protected' vehicle, we could be alright if we hit a normal Russian or Chinese landmine, although that was definitely not something we wanted. Some poor guys did die from landmines, but the Rhodesian clever guys were forever improving the technology to counter them. While we may have ended up with a few bumps and bruises, or perhaps a broken bone here or there, our safety and well-being also depended on a lot of luck. If the landmine was boosted with petrol, or a double landmine was laid for us, then we would be in mighty big trouble. Reports came around that the terrorists knew how effective our vehicles were, so they would dig a deep hole, lay a landmine, then place a 25-litre tin of fuel on top of it and then another landmine on top of that. Although all the military vehicles in Rhodesia were modified to handle landmines as best they could, we would come off second-best with a multiple landmine. Some of the inventions on

Brian Timmer with our door mounted GPMG 7.62mm machine gun and a huge drum of ammunition

modifying vehicles to reduce casualties in that war are still used to this day. The main idea was to have a "sacrificial wheel", where the portion of the vehicle which detonated the mine would disappear, but would leave the main body, where the passengers were, intact ... but maybe a bit deaf. As the drivers, we had to learn to keep our thumbs outside the internal part of the steering-wheel. Gripping the wheel in a monkey grip meant that if the vehicle hit a 'tin', the steering-wheel would twist very fast and break or dislocate our thumb, if it was hanging on the inside. The other thing to watch out for was loose stuff lying around, which could become a missile in the blast. We also had been warned against roadside bombs, which could be triggered by a trip wire. These were lethal, in that the Land Rovers we humped around in had little to no side protection.

Another report came through that the terrorists were making their own anti-aircraft devices. Their idea was to dig a hole around 16 inches across and about 30 inches down, lay some TNT in the hole, layer a lot of earth above that, place 6-8 Chinese stick-grenades in a wagon-wheel effect on top, and then connect all the grenade pull-strings together, and peg this off firmly on one side of the hole. When an aircraft flew overhead, the explosive would be initiated, which would send the grenades flying upward, with their strings having been pulled. After a few seconds the grenades would detonate at around 800-1000 feet in the air, causing mayhem to aircraft passing overhead. Well, that was the idea. We tested the theory, but kept blowing the strings clean off, so the grenades didn't detonate. Not wanting to be admit defeat, and given that we loved playing with big bangs, we dug a hole two feet deep, laid some PE4 explosive at the bottom and layered this with about 4 pounds of maize meal. The end result was a smoke ring, which went straight up for hundreds of feet and must have reached 30 feet in diameter... what fun!

Three Zero Romeo Nine:

Muzarewa (our Prime Minister) decided to visit his Auxiliaries at our farm and give them moral support. Our heavy vehicle was at Retreat Farm, getting supplies, so a convoy started off towards our training-camp along the dusty, dangerous road. The reason it was dangerous was that it was lined by heavily-wooded Msasa trees, plus there were countless granite hills through which the road wound. Anywhere along this 20-kilometre road was prime ambush territory. The convoy had Muzarewa in the lead Land Rover, then our heavy vehicle followed, then a number of support Land Rovers followed them. After about ten kilometres, the convoy was busy winding its way through a series of small, granite hills when suddenly there was an almighty bang as our heavy Bedford vehicle hit a landmine. Fortunately, the tyres were half-filled with water to reduce the explosive effect, plus the cab was armoured underneath, so the front left wheel took off into the hills beyond, but there was not too much further damage. Muzarewa

Our first group of trainees in front of the farm house
– note the bunker top right

was not too keen on hanging around and instructed his driver to head for the safety of our base as fast as possible. Not such a smart idea, because there could have been another landmine further along. Anyway, he arrived in a cloud of dust and headed straight for the house, with his bodyguards in sweaty pursuit. He sat down and told everybody how he had been miraculously saved from death. Kenneth had been instructed to make tea so, without celebration, he smartly marched in, carrying the tea-tray with some biscuits as a bonus. Muzarewa took one look at the cups and asked for a mug of tea. The question came, 'How many sugars?' and his answer was 'If it's a small mug then three, but if it's a big one then nine spoons, please.' The muffled laughter in the kitchen really had to be controlled and thereafter, he was known by us as 3or9 (Three Zero Romeo Nine).

Muzarewa decided he was not going to travel those dangerous roads and ordered a helicopter from Salisbury to haul him out of the operational area and take him back home.

The record to beat:

The final few days of training was left to inter-squad champion-ships and reruns on vital aspects of the training schedule. The in-ter-squad championships was really a final morale-booster and a way to see how well we had prepared these men, physically. There was no running; we just concentrated on the obstacle course, press-ups and sit-ups. Each squad was run through its paces and the times taken. One squad had been outstanding throughout the whole training period and, when it came to the press-ups, we had seven chaps who completed over 1000 press-ups. Directly after-wards, they went into the sit-ups phase and one chap exceeded 1400 sit-ups. We immediately radioed Retreat Farm and passed the challenge over to them, to beat that. They, of course, didn't believe us.

'Just impossible!' – 'You have got to be joking!' - 'Have you been drinking?' etc., came the responses. We knew we had a good bunch of guys - physically, anyway.

Passing out:

The first bunch of recruits were now ready to face the war. We had trained them as best we could with the facilities we had and with what we knew. A full parade was arranged and speeches were made full of gun-raising bravado. A combination of Rhodesian and Russian military drills and tactics were drummed into their heads and we hoped that these would be enough to get them through any battle, unscathed; however, we knew, deep down in our hearts, that they would never be able to put up a fight in a full-on battle, with a well-organised opposition. They left, in Bedford trucks destined for a variety of homelands far away, cheering and waving their rifles in the air as a final salute to us. They carried very little equipment with them - just a few clothes, maybe a spare pair of boots, their webbing and their beloved rifles. To all the remaining instructors, they looked just like a bunch of terrorists. The next batch of 500 men was already in-bound for their training and we would start the whole thing all over again.

Obediah the terrorist:

Some of the instructors we had in Pachedu had some hair-raising stories to tell. Obediah once had been an integral part of the terrorist network of informers in an area called Mazoe, just some 25 kilometres North of Salisbury. He was on the opposition side to us. He reported to the gooks on aspects of Security Force movements, informers on the government side and also organised things for the groups, such as food and medical supplies. Essentially he was a Mujiba. One night, a new group of terrorists had come through and they had been spooked by a contact with the Rhodesian Army. One of Obediah's enemies within the terrorist group, chose this time to tell the other terrorists that Obediah was, in fact, a double agent and it was he who had told the army where they could be found. The terrorists grabbed Obediah and beat him to a pulp with sticks, rifle butts and anything they could lay their hands on. They then tied his hands and feet with wire and threw him into the Mazoe River, believing him to be dead. Now the Mazoe is quite a large river and Obediah would have surely drowned within a minute, if luck hadn't been on his side. In the first place, he couldn't swim but, with his arms and feet tied, he would never have been able to surface if the water was deep. Being night-time, the terrorists inadvertently had thrown Obediah onto some rocks, which were just submerged, and he was able to breathe. He lay where he was until the terrorists left and he was able to move. He managed to wriggle his painful way out of the river and started the slow and very painful journey away from it. He just continued wriggling through the bush like a worm, until he reached the main Mazoe to Bindura tar road, where he fainted from loss of blood and exhaustion. He lay there throughout the night and it was by chance that a member of Pachedu (Pat Walsh), en route to Mazoe, saw him lying in the bush next to the road. He stopped the Land Rover and tentatively worked his way toward Obediah's seemingly lifeless body. Finding him still alive, Pat untied him and tended to his wounds as best he could, and then carried him into the Land Rover, Obediah grunting with pain, as his ribs had been broken in several places and he had massive internal bruising. After a journey to Salisbury Hospital, Pat got just enough information out of Obediah to understand what had happened, and he made up his mind that Obediah would be a very good candidate for changing his allegiance. Obediah spent nearly five weeks in Hospital, until he was strong enough at least to walk. Pat made a point of bringing him chocolate and other things to brighten his spirit. Obediah was now so angry with his previous gang of terrorist that it was a cinch for him to change sides. On being discharged from Hospital, he was brought back via Mazoe to Retreat Farm where he was clothed, given shelter and food and, most importantly, a bunch of chaps who would befriend him. It wasn't long before he was up and strong again, and became a fully-fledged member of Pachedu, as an instructor. He had been trained by the terrorists, but Pachedu took the training further and he soon learnt most of what was to be known to train recruits for the Government project of Pfumo Revanhu. Obediah was a typical example of the turned terrorists, who made up the bulk of our team. We trusted them implicitly and the feeling was mutual. The ex-terrorists were a huge advantage to us. They revealed many of the tactics used by the terrorists and we were able to use this information when we ourselves 'turned terrorist'. Pachedu operated a great deal as pseudo-terrorists and infiltrated many terrorist networks. Our biggest problem was getting updated information on the terrorist tactics, so we were always on the lookout for 'freshly-turned' terrorists to supply us with this vital knowledge. The terrorists knew that the Rhodesians, and especially the Selous Scouts, were posing as ZANU or ZIPRA combatants and so were forever implementing defences against this method of attack.

Rebellion:

Some months later, the training facility shut down. I guess the supply of Auxiliary forces had reached saturation levels. I was posted, temporarily, to a Tribal Trust Land, to support a team of Pfumo Revhano near the outskirts of Salisbury. This was to be a very lonely and trying time for me. The camp was a rundown, old, Rural Administration building, surrounded by 30 or so brown, ten-man tents. A rickety, 6' diamond-mesh fence, masquerading as a security barrier, formed a perimeter around the base. In reality, that fence could scarcely keep out the local goats, never mind anything bigger. There wasn't a blade of grass anywhere. There was a double gate for vehicle access, a 5000-litre water tank and a few long-drop toilets and that was pretty much it. I was joined by a Police National Serviceman who was doing his one-year stint for his Country. It was during this time that I genuinely thought I may die. Many of the 'soldiers' at the camp were openly rebellious, which fuelled a potential explosive situation. I quickly realised that I was facing a hazardous situation, one that would need to be handled with *extreme* kid gloves. The vibe was sour and tense. A core group were brazenly terrorist supporters and it was clear that they had had plenty of opportunity, and intent to incite others. It would be imperative to weed out these trouble-makers, or the entire camp would collapse. With there being only one other person, two counting Kenneth, whom I could trust, my position was precarious. This was a serious challenge - over 200 of them, all fully armed ... I needed a fucking miracle. What was even worse, on evaluation, many in this group were clearly lazy layabouts, not willing to participate in the smallest form of exertion. Many were openly insolent.

The daily routine was to get the men up early and parade them for inspection. Teams would then be allocated to patrol different sections of the local area. Periodically, they needed to stay out for a couple of nights. During the first few weeks in particular, I would survey the paraded rabble in front of me and inwardly heave a heavy sigh. These were not soldiers; they were louts. Their demeanour was slovenly, and their attitude toxically insubordinate. As a man with a background of being drilled in discipline, it was an anathema for me to see such disarray. The belligerence was one thing, but what caused me untold gall was the craze that many adopted to don wide-brimmed hats, similar to those the terrorists wore, combined with an assortment of cheap, imitation gold chains, draped haphazardly around their necks, and finished off with an assortment of clothing that defied description. To me, they were beyond redemption. If I could, I would have thrown the whole lot back into training to relearn the principles of self-control and teamwork. Deep in my heart, I believed that there was no way they were actively patrolling in the field. By my reckoning, they probably advertised their presence to the terrorists, so as to ensure they would not have an encounter or a scrap. It was also very possible that they were in cahoots with the enemy.

'Where is the commander?' I called out.

A short, fat individual meandered across to me from his position against the only tree in the camp. He didn't salute, or show any acknowledgement of my rank. I'd had a brief meeting with him the night before, so I knew that he could speak English.

'Right, let's get two squads of 20 men out on patrol today. They are to carry only their weapons and water for a three-day patrol. I want the others, under your command, to start digging trenches along the Eastern fence-line. After the parade, I will come and show you where they are to go.'

He didn't even answer. I clenched my teeth.

'I want to see you in my tent as soon as you have given my instructions to the men,' I commanded, as I turned on my heels to go to my 'office' in the tent. I was sorting out the tables and chairs when the commander walked in and stood waiting for me, near the front opening of the tent. I launched into him with a ton of commands and enquiries. He just stood there, without responding. His nonchalance told me that I was wasting my time. I walked out of the tent and beckoned him to follow me, as we headed to the place where I wanted the trenches to be dug.

'Where are all the picks and shovels?' I asked, as we walked across the dusty ground.

'We have five picks and about ten shovels.' He could talk!

'Okay, that will do. Get about 50 men on the job and they can work in shifts. I'm taking the two squads on patrol,' I instructed. I showed him where the trench-lines would start and end, how deep and how wide they were to be.

I left him standing at the corner post of fence, looking on vacantly at the bush beyond. I walked back to the tent to collect my rifle and webbing belt. I always carried my Walther P38 9mm pistol, plus two spare magazines on my belt, *just in case*. With facilities being non-existent, I had no safe in which to keep my personal weapons, so they lay on my bed for the moment. I had stripped the weapons down so that they could not be used by an unauthorised party. The RPD machine gun stood on its "legs" next to the bed that Kenneth had made up for me. My AK47 lay on the bed. Bits and pieces of each weapon lay in and around the bed. In that moment, I sat down on the side of the bed and cupped my face in my hands. *What in hell have I gotten myself into this time?* I thought. I was in virtual isolation.

Standard patrols were sent out from our miserable camp and the reports I started to receive from local people began to worry me. Report after report flew from my type-writer to headquarters. It seemed that the men under my command were not sticking to the rules and were harassing the locals for food, money and other favours! I pulled all the troops back into camp one day and gave them a verbal hammering. After my harangue, I went back to my tent. I was sickeningly aware that with no support, any power I may have wielded was compromised anyway. I knew I would have to do something soon, before chaos descended. I was looking down at the ground, pondering deeply about the situation and wondering what I could do to change it, when suddenly my head shot up, as a loud bang came from very close by – unmistakably, a rifle shot!

"You are now going to DIE, you white pig." At the tent opening, shouting venomously, stood a Pfumo Revanhu soldier, his AK47 pointed directly at my temple. I couldn't see him well, as he was silhouetted against the light, but the barrel of his gun now stuck against my head made itself abundantly clear. Perilously poised between life and death, my mind raced. Son of a bitch! I sure as hell was not going to go down like a sitting duck. Just as I started to rise in fury, there was a loud smack and the man fell to the ground. The National serviceman had cracked him across the head with the butt of a weapon. The rebel had not seen him when he had come in to kill me. A desperate wrestling match ensued. The policeman had the man pinned down on the ground. I prised the AK from him and threw it clear across the room, well out of the way. Seizing my Walther pistol, I now pointed at the soldier's head. "Stay still," I warned him. It had all happened so fast. Jesus, I was so lucky to be alive. Kenneth came running through the opening in the tent cradling his Uzi sub-machine-gun. I learnt later that Kenneth had seen the man coming and had rushed to get his weapon and had pushed the barrel through one of the openings in the tent in an attempt to protect me. By now, though, the immediate situation was under control. We hoisted the man to his feet to search him for hidden weapons. I could smell alcohol on his foul-smelling breath. He was rapidly hand-cuffed and ordered back down onto the floor. A small crowd of about 20 armed soldiers had gathered outside the tent and when I stepped outside, I was instantly aware that I faced more trouble. They were not there for sight-seeing; they also wanted my hide. Fortunately, I had my AK47, now fully operational, with me.

'What the bloody hell is going on here?' I bellowed at them. 'Get the hell away from here, move back.'

On seeing I was in no mood for bullshit, the soldiers shuffled back a few paces and then, as their numbers swelled, they moved forward one pace. They started to mumble amongst themselves and I could sense that the situation was going to deteriorate rapidly. I had to do something fast, or I would end up dead. Rising to my fullest height, I strode purposely right between them, through to my office tent.

'I want everybody to form a parade NOW, outside this tent, on the DOUBLE.' I shouted, with my back towards them. Somehow, I think they had expected me to be cowered by their combined confrontation and had not expected such an aggressive stance, or for me to appear to be ignoring their threatening position. I turned as I got to the tent, some five paces from them. My strategy was to split them, with the National Serviceman and Kenneth on one side, and me on the other. Without realising it, they were surrounded. With my wrath palpable, and well-knowing my ability with an AK47, they lined up in a loose formation as instructed.

Keeping the pressure on, I hollered. 'Right, I want you men to follow me to the cells. You are ALL under arrest.' They started to follow me, but then were undecided. They stopped and started to chant war songs. By then, I'd had enough. I threw the metal cell door open with a load bang and walked away from it. I raised my rifle and pointed it at nobody in particular, but in their direction.

'Get into the fucking cell, with or without your weapons, RIGHT NOW!!!' I meant business and they knew it. With large eyes, they stopped their chanting and moved into the cells, still carrying their rifles. I slammed the door shut and locked it. I stormed back to my tent. Theuns had given me some spare explosives, which I was now going to put to good use as additional security. With my knowledge of these devices, I quickly had the perimeter of the cell hot-wired, ready to explode in a jiffy if disturbed. I threatened that if anybody tried to exit the cells, they would all be 'flying fucking high'. To the last man, they knew this was no joke. I headed back to my tent. Kenneth was there waiting for me, with his weapon still trained on the soldier who had first attacked me.

'Kenneth, guard the open area to the front. If anyone or anything moves, tell me.' He nodded and stood just inside the tent, looking out. There were potentially more out there. I could not tell. I hoisted the handcuffed soldier up firmly by his hands and hauled him off to the cells. I threw him in, still handcuffed. Things were far too volatile to take any chances.

I reached across to the National Serviceman's hand and shook it. "Thank you," I said, from my core being. We both knew it had been a very, very close call. I radioed Salisbury and explained the situation. They promised to get a team out first thing in the morning. There was no further activity that night, but I didn't sleep a wink. There was far too much running through my mind. The truth was that I was bloody lucky to have survived the day. The rebels got no food that night.

In the morning, the sort-out team arrived. They couldn't believe their ears when I told them the story and shook their heads in disbelief that I had not been taken out! They told me that a group of 500 Pfumo Revanhu had rebelled in another district as well, and that there had been several hundred resultant deaths. The Fire Force had had to be called in to quell it. It was reported to me later that the soldier who attacked me had been jailed, whilst the rest also had received lengthy jail sentences for their part. After the uprising, it was apparent to Headquarters that greater manpower and equipment would need to be brought into the camp to sustain the status quo regarding Pfumo Revano.

At my camp, the seeds of rebellion had begun before my arrival; I, the National Serviceman and Kenneth had all played our part in sorting it out. It was now over to the Army. I requested a transfer out and this effectively ended my stay with Pfumo Revanhu.

Pachedu - new role in the war:

Pachedu regrouped into a 'safe house' on the outskirts of Borrowdale suburb in Salisbury. All the guys were there and I was so happy. We were joined by a bull of a man named Jerry Webster. Jerry, Theuns and I took up residence in a ten-man army tent. It was well-furnished, with a 9 x 12 foot carpet placed directly on the ground right, on top of the grass. The main house became the operations area, with two offices and an armoury. All the spare equipment we had from the Pfumo Revanhu days was stuffed into the armoury and, on surveying this, we had every type of Russian, Chinese and East European weapon, probably in excess of 250 rifles. We had thousands of rounds of ammunition, radios, medic's kits, grenades, anti-tank weapons, machine guns and our 75mm recoilless Chinese cannon. We couldn't move in that place, it was so full. The main lounge became a mixture of a meeting-room, a briefing-room and a bar. We built a really large bar counter and had two fridges, in which we kept our beer. Moses, the cook, was with us and so was Kenneth, so we had good food. We could not have asked for anything better.

Then the hard work started. We were being pushed into all sorts of call-outs and found ourselves out on patrols in many parts of the country – all the time. From then on, every operation performed by us was in terrorist attire, and covert. We sure looked like a motley crew when we were all dressed up with our jeans, terrorist jackets, communist weapons and webbing.

The unique Pachedu shoulder patch

Once the training of recruits ended, we went operational. Call sign AC was my section, whilst Jerry took up the call sign AW. We could take whomever we wanted into the sections, so I chose my men from the instructors we had. Jerry had a mixed bunch and had included Theuns for the first couple of bush trips. Jerry didn't get on to well with Theuns, so that partnership soon dissolved.

Operational:

In the Hartley area, the two sections of Pachedu were called in to sort out a group of ZIPRA terrorists that had been raiding farms in the area and then escaping to the relative safety of the nearby Tribal Trust Lands. ZIPRA was better trained than their ZANLA counterparts, so we knew we could be in for some interesting fighting. Call signs AC and AW deployed to two areas and then gravitated towards each other, hoping to chase up this group. During the patrol, we were walking in broad daylight and ambushing known footpaths at night. Eventually we were about three kilometres from each other. We had radio communication, so knew exactly where each team was. The going was relatively easy, with the fresh, short green grass at the beginning of summer making a carpet across the rolling hills. Here and there were outcrops of granite rocks and typical savannah trees broke the patterns, with clumps randomly spread around. Jerry, Theuns and his lads were following a three-strand fence down towards a crossing at a wet, vlei area. They were very surprised when they spotted twelve terrorists walking up the same fence-line toward them. They quickly took cover behind some termite mounds and bushes, and set up an impromptu ambush. We had no idea what was happening and the first thing we knew of the confrontation was when we heard a barrage of gun-fire. It lasted for thirty seconds and stopped. I thought we would support Jerry with the action by keeping the terrorists' heads down, so we set up our Chinese 60mm mortar tube (I had swapped it for the Portuguese one, as it was lighter) and fired three rounds on the side of the rise where we thought the terrorists would be running. I fired the mortars, but the tube kept on sinking deeper into the soft soil of the vlei. I had no base plate. On each occasion, the blast from the mortar going off hit my hands and I could hardly move them after the third round. One of the lads pulled out the now sunken tube from the mud and we called Jerry to see if we could help. My hands were numb from the explosions and I felt a bit stupid that I hadn't considered the recoil. The terrorists would use a shoe as a base plate, as they didn't want to carry a heavy plate around with them. Actually, in another incident, three terrorists firing a mortar had had the same trouble with a sinking tube and the last round had gone straight up and down ... and wiped them out!

'Ah.... AW this is AC, over,' was my call.

'Ah... AC AW, roger if you see the fence-line make your way along it and meet us at the top of the hill. Just be careful of possible wounded as you come,' came Jerry's instructions.

We made our way up towards Jerry and came across them, whilst they seemed to be caught up in a mixture of heated argument and laughter. We spread out and I had a quick chat with Jerry. The gooks had walked straight into the ambush position, without having had any clue that they were in trouble. They must have been five metres from Jerry, when they received the full blast from five rifles. The first or lead terrorist had been hit three times in the chest from a burst from Theuns and had run away, after dropping his rifle. Theuns was absolutely livid - although the others couldn't stop laughing - that his AK47 didn't seem to have had any effect on the terrorist! Jerry had had a shot at one, who'd jumped behind a termite mound, and had then shot the Makarov pistol the gook had been firing, straight out of his hand, a great shot at more than 300 yards. We retrieved the Makarov, but no terrorist. The others seemed to have disappeared into thin air. What we found funny was that they had run clean through the three-strand, barbed-wire fence in their efforts to get away. That took some doing; I think they fled without concern as to what was in front of them in their utter haste to escape the bullets chasing their rears. At least there were two confirmed wounded and our guess was that a number more had been seriously cut up by the wire.

'How the hell did they all get away?' I asked and the laughter broke out again.

We caught the same group again a few days later, when they ran across the road in front of our vehicles. Four of them were caught in a hail of bullets, fired by one of our guys from the twin-mounted machine guns atop one of our vehicles. After that incident, I really had to question the strength of the AK47.

Tuberculosis:

One of my chaps, Willie, started coughing incessantly and we had to leave him at the base every time, as he would compromise our position if we took him out on patrol. We didn't want to make these kinds of sounds in the bush, or the enemy would be upon us in no time. Our 'tame' Doctor Black came out to visit us in the field to give us a medical, as he sometimes did. After examining Willie, Doc Black told him to cough, and took one look at the gunk brought up.

'Tuberculosis - that's what he has,' came Doc's prognosis. Thus, we lost the field services of this ex-terrorist, one of my best lads, but he stayed back at camp and was able to do chores there. We had to give him an injection once a day for six months and eventually he recovered. Tuberculosis is a serious and increasingly problematic, infectious disease, which affects huge numbers of people in Africa.

Land mine

On the same trip we were sitting in our make-shift base camp, when we heard a huge explosion not four kilometres from us. Jerry and I scrambled into our vehicle, armed to the teeth, and headed out toward the explosion site. Jerry took the steering-wheel, whilst I slung a GPMG machine gun, with 250 rounds of ammunition, on the passenger side. The other lads were in a follow-up Land Rover. The cause of the explosion didn't take much to find. The first thing we saw was a huge tawny 'lion.'

'Holy shit, Jerry, did you see that lion?' I cried with shock, then realised what it was as soon as I'd said it. The lion was actually a rather large dog ... gee, but the mind really plays tricks when under stress.

Suddenly the Land Rover came to a dusty, skidding stop, as Jerry realised there was something on the road ahead of us. About 20 metres ahead, we could see what had caused the explosion. A cow had been blown in half from the force of a landmine ex-plosion. It lay off to the side of the road, right next to the huge hole atop a storm-water, culvert drain. We immediately jumped out of the vehicles and spread out, expecting to be ambushed. Nothing happened. The thick smell of dust, blood and explosives hung heavy in the air. We started a slow walk towards the hind-quarters of the cow, whilst looking at the bush all around us for any sign of movement. Simultaneously, we had to inspect the ground and mind our foot placement, as there might have been anti-personnel mines that had been laid, just for this type of re-action – but there was nothing. The ZIPRA gooks had obviously gotten tired of us running after them and tried to take us out with the landmine. Thank you, poor cow; you saved our skins.

Twisted testicles...the pain:

Two days later, Jerry called for an evacuation. We were both out in the bush, hunting gooks again, and he was busy climbing over a barbed wire fence. The way we did that was to use our rifles to push the top strand down and leg it over the fence. In this way, if the gooks decided to have a go at us, we could still use our rifles to shoot back, but if this happened the top wire could spring up and snap at your private parts. Anyway, this was the best way and that's how we always did it. Jerry had just done his wire-crossing trick when he fell to the ground in severe pain.

We had no idea what was wrong and so had to get the support team to pull him out. It turned out he that had twisted one of his testicles and I guess the pain must have been like having a set of pliers permanently applied to the area. Shame, he really suffered from that one and wasn't able to join us on operations for a good while. He said he had a great time at the hospital with the nurses though – typical Jerry. He later married one of the nurses who had attended to him.

'Take the pain away, but keep the swelling!' he used to say.

The loss of Trust:

On an operation that was hastily put together, we did a night approach on a cluster of huts which had been indicated as being a resupply point for the ZIPRA terrorists. Five metres from our target kraal, was a line of small bushes. We took cover in them and waited to hear if there was any movement within the huts. One of the buildings was not the typical mud-and-thatch hut, but a small, brick house, with a corrugated metal roof. I used my night-sight to search the area, but found nothing. We could hear the faint sound of talking within the brick house. I sent Obediah and Trust (a Matabele and ex-ZIPRA terrorist) to knock on the front door. They were just out of sight from where we were. Immediately, the sky lit up with green tracer and the noise of automatic firing was deafening. Within seconds Obediah was by my side, but Trust was not behind him. We didn't open fire until we ensured that Trust was nowhere near us and only then did we let the house have it, firing a hundred rounds into it.

'Cease fire,' I instructed.

'Come, Obediah,' I ushered, as I tugged at his webbing. We made our way to a large window on the other side of the house from the door. In the dim light coming from the moon, I showed Obediah that I wanted him to lob a grenade through the window. He had a Russian fragment-grenade, whilst I used a Phosphorous grenade. On the silent count of three, we threw our grenades. They both bounced off the window and landed at our feet.

'Shit!' Within a second we had picked them up, smashed the window with rifle butts and sent the grenades through the now broken window. We were flat on the ground instantly.

Bang....

One grenade went off....

Bang... the other.

We ran back to our little temporary position, with excitement boosting our ungainly sprint.

'Let's pull back,' I told the lads and we backtracked about 10 metres into thicker bush, to wait until daylight.

Morning came, with the typical cockerel giving everybody a waking crow. We were dressed up as terrorists, so stripped down to our civilian clothing and dumped our webbing in the bush. The sun was just peeping over the trees as we formed an open line and walked toward the site of the night's battle. Nothing! There was nobody to be seen and the entire area was now devoid of people. We checked out the huts and the surrounds, and gave our lads at the base a call to come and help us out. We found where we had fired and also the empty cartridges where the ZIPRA terrorists had been firing. There was no sign of Trust, however, so we started looking for tracks. There were many - some coming to the house and others leaving, in haste - but we couldn't find Trust's tracks at all. The terrorists had scattered in all directions. We estimated there had been ten but, strangely, we had found no blood. The Land Rover with our backup team arrived. They also searched the huts for clues and tried their luck at the tracks – same result. In the meantime, one of the black chaps decided he was going to try his luck on a bicycle that was standing on the verandah of the house. He climbed on and started to pedal madly around the yard. Within a second he was off the machine and had both hands clasping his butt, yelling his head off. I grabbed him and took a look at what was happening to his rear end. The phosphorous grenade I had used the night before had exploded on the verandah, having passed right through the house and out the front door, and some of the phosphorous had landed on the bicycle seat and burnt its way into it. At some stage, the lack of oxygen had stopped the burning, but when he'd placed his butt on the seat, it had activated the phosphorous again. It wasn't bad, and we had a great laugh. We left the scene and headed back to camp. Later that day, I went up in a Cessna aircraft to see if we could pick up any sign of Trust. Nothing. We spent a good three hours criss-crossing the area, hoping he would give us a signal as to where he was. We never saw him again.

SAS and Selous Scouts guys join us:

We were joined at the Borrowdale Camp by some really experienced soldiers. They would assist us and were paid by the special slush fund of the Selous Scouts and Special Branch, headed by Mac McGuiness. Ian Suttil was an ex-British soldier who had come to Rhodesia and joined the Special Air Service (SAS) and was a tough and wiry character. He didn't live on the base, but with his wife not far away. Most of his time was spent with us, so I don't believe he had a tremendous home life. Ian had been shot and wounded several times during the war and the scars on his arms, chest and legs were evident. He had blonde hair and spoke with an English accent. Across his chest was a huge tattooed rat. He had been involved in many of the actions in which the SAS had participated, in Mozambique and Zambia. Ian believed in fire power – the more lead you laid down the better, he said. His favourite weapon, whilst with Pachedu, was a shortened RPD Russian machine gun. The butt had been cut off and the barrel made shorter. This weapon was amazingly short but still seemed to weigh as much as a normal one, because Ian carried a long belt of ammunition attached to it. He had used the same weapon whilst with the SAS. Billy Grant, a tough, red-haired soldier, was also an ex-SAS man and good friends with Ian. Gary Lewis and Jake Harper Ronald joined us a few days later. Jake was an ex-British Paratrooper, who had taken the pictures of the dead at Bloody Sunday in Northern Ireland. Jake had served in both the SAS and the Selous Scouts. The four of them, plus Theuns, made up a solid reaction team. We had great confidence in these very experienced men and we learnt a great deal from them. The tactics learnt from so many different Special Forces helped Pachedu operators get through some sticky times. Ian taught us a great deal about Special Forces' explosives techniques and much of what we learnt came into use later in special operations. Billy was a true soldier, with an iron gut, as tough as they came. He taught us tactics. Theuns was a rough-and-tough bush soldier, who taught us many things in the bush environment. For a short time, we had the good services of Jannie Meyer, ex-SAS, a quiet but tough soldier, too.

Theuns goes to live in the armoury:

Ian Suttil's sawn-off RPD

Theuns decided to move into the armoury and away from our tent. He felt safer there, or maybe less harassed by being on his own. His bed was made in between the rows of rifles and ammunition boxes; Theuns was a very tense character. One day, Jerry went to knock on the armoury door to ask Theuns if he wanted to come with us to the pub. Three 9mm rounds hit the wall, just next to Jerry's head. I guess the answer was NO.

On the second night, we were at our new camp with our new support team of Special Forces guys. Everyone came together for a briefing and Ken gave us a rundown on our general tasks. There was a discussion about our camp security and other issues and then, once all the formalities had been completed, we retired to the bar to celebrate our new station. One thing led to another and we proceeded to get really loud. A guard had been positioned at the main gate on a 24-hours position and he came in at around midnight to say that there was somebody at the main gate to the property who wanted to talk to the owner of the house. The visitor was really angry because of our loud music and noise, and was shouting threats at us from the gate. Ian let rip with a few rounds from his Russian Tokarev pistol and that was the end of the visitor's shouting, as he took off at high speed. No one ever came to complain about noise coming from the base again.

Pachedu was now under Special Branch Headquarters' control and, as such, we were being used more and more for 'funny' actions. In March 1979, the Officer Commanding Special Branch Salisbury and Mashonaland Assistant Commissioner, Jock Waugh, was replaced by Chief Superintendent Danny Stannard. Things began to change. The entire team of Pachedu now numbered something like 43. Many of the men were still with us from the Retreat Farm days, including most of the chaps who helped us with all sorts of things, including procurement, driving, radio watch, administration and the like. If the operations team needed anything, the backup guys would arrange it – just like that. We still had all our heavy and light vehicles, so were also very mobile.

Many clandestine operations were conducted from the safe house, with the vast majority being done with the guys posing as terrorists. By now, the operational teams were well versed in these types of operations. Jerry headed up one team, whilst I was in charge of the other. Our teams were made up of four-man units, with the other soldiers being ex-terrorists. The seriously tough backup team of Ian, Billy, Gary, Jake and Theuns was more than adequate to help us in any situation.

The pub that didn't serve beer:

On one operation, we worked with our Special Branch friends in Bindura again. Phil and Colin had come up with a great deal of information, which had led to further contacts taking place in the Chiweshe Tribal Trust land area and areas around Bindura. On one such operation, we had pulled out of the bush and stopped off at an Internal Affairs camp to refresh ourselves at their pub. The entire operational set of two Pachedu units descended onto the camp. We must have stunk to high heaven after some time spent in the bush, but our thirst for a good beer exceeded our desire to smell nice. We had dumped our terrorist kit into the back of our transport VW Combi and were dressed in normal Rhodesian camouflage. We walked up to the bar and could see the barman behind the counter. He was alone, but was soon joined by four Internal Affairs men who wanted to see who had arrived at their camp. I guess they didn't often get Special Forces in their pub and they were inquisitive. The place was really nice, with all sorts of decorations on the wall and what appeared to be a couple of full fridges.

'Beers all round,' was the call from the Pachedu men.

'I'm afraid we're closed for stock-take,' came the answer from one of the Internal Affairs men. That was not the right answer to give. Ian hauled out his Tokarev pistol and proceeded to shoot each bottle on the shelves behind the barman. The five Internal Affairs men took cover behind the bar as best they could. Theuns and Jake joined in and, before long, the once neat-looking pub was covered in broken glass and holes were splattered on every wall. The Internal Affairs flag was ripped down from the wall and became a souvenir. In the end, no drinks were served from that pub. The pent-up energies of soldiers all over the world are the same and, on this occasion, it happened to be the Intaf Pub that got the brunt of our anger. The Internal Affairs boys just didn't get it - all we'd wanted was a beer.

Gold in the Mazoe River:

Theuns joined AC section on an operation on the Mazoe River, just for a bit of extra fire power. The walk into the designated area in which we were to work was again classed as a 'frozen area', so we knew there would be no government troops running around. All of us were exhausted by the time we reached the Mazoe River. It had taken fourteen hours of hard, difficult terrain to get there. We were very conscious of making our entry into the area as clandestine as possible, so we used all our experience in anti-tracking.

'Listen, that's the Mazoe River, boys,' I whispered, as we came over the last saddle between two hills. We could hear the rushing river as it cascaded over rocks on its way to Mozambique and we quietly made our way down to its edge. My backpack shoulder-straps were cutting into my shoulders ... aah the pain! We hung back about twenty metres from the river and took up a defensive position. I slumped down and the relief from taking off the backpack was immediate. It was broad daylight, so we didn't want to approach the river without checking around for terrorist or local Mujiba presence. After an hour, Theuns made his way down and filled his water bottle. We watched the other side of the river for any movement. He balanced his bottle on a rock next to him and we could see him reaching into the water. He plucked something from the rushing water and turned, picked up his bottle and came back to us.

'What did you find there?' I asked him, as he slid next to me.

'Ah, it's nothing just a rock.'

We picked up our gear and moved on downstream. We decided to set up camp a little back from the river that night and split up for our night's rest. Before we did, I asked Theuns about his 'rock' he had found. He reached into his pocket and pulled out three small gold nuggets. I was intrigued as I looked at the match-head-sized nuggets.

'If I can pick up gold this size in the river then there is a lot more here. Remember, I did gold-panning in Botswana before I joined the Selous Scouts'

We made a pact there and then to come back to this spot after the war and start our own gold-mining company. We shook hands and looked into each other's eyes in a disbelieving stare. Naturally, we would have like to spend the next two weeks knee-deep in the river making our fortune, but the war took preference. We never did make it back there and, in 1985, the headlines of The Herald newspaper showed pictures of the river being system-atically scoured for gold, with hordes of people panning. It was a huge find and I never forgave myself for not doing something about it.

The Seychelles Debacle:

Back at base in Borrowdale, the entire Pachedu team was having a beer in our pub. A couple of mercenaries we knew popped in to join us. A couple of them had operated in Angola and were famil-iar with the sell-out of the teams operating under CIA guidance (refer to a book called 'Fire Power' by Chris Dempster and Dave Tomkins). We were just talking generally about the war and then it became apparent that they had something to ask us. They were offering US$5000 cash payment up front and US$5000 after a big job was done. There was no interest until they told us what the job was. They were working for Colonel Mike Hoare, the well-known mercenary leader who operated throughout Africa, and they were organising and recruiting for a coup in the Seychelles Islands in the Indian Ocean. Mike Hoare was a real character, having run a number of mercenary operations in Africa. After quite a bit of debate, the Pachedu lads all turned down the offer. If we knew about it, then half the military guys in the country would know about it as well. We carried on drinking, so that ended the recruitment drive from the mercs. In 1982, the attempted coup took place and was a complete flop. We heard that Des Botes (a world champion karate expert, who had once trained us in Karate in Bindura) was left behind to fend off the 'enemy' on the beach. We could just imagine him taking a karate stance and trying to fight off the whole Seychelles army. What a mess. We were all thankful that we hadn't gone. (Read the book 'The Seychelles Affair' by Mike Hoare.)

Nylon the terrorist:

We reacted to a lot of different terrorist activities whilst we were in Borrowdale. We seemed to be wanted all over the place, including in the far South of the country, when a bunch of terrorists - under the leadership of a gook called Nylon - managed to kill five Selous Scouts. He had apparently laid an ambush in an open vlei, deep in amongst the long grass, and had a clear view of the Land Rover carrying the Scouts. The road snaked in an 'S' shape and Nylon was in the middle. The Scouts had no chance. One of the unfortunate men was Johnny Whitfield from Umtali. We never did find this Nylon guy and his lot, but we sure tried hard. We used everything in our experience to locate the gooks, but I guess they high-tailed it out of the area knowing there would be military boys after their sorry arses. The loss of so many Special Forces in one contact was a big blow to all of us.

In trouble with the law:

We were called to the Sinoia district to sort out a terrorist group that had been causing trouble in the area. They were ZIPRA terrorists. We ended up in trouble with our deception tricks, as we took all our vehicles through the familiar farming town with a huge show of strength, which scared the pants off the locals and put them into a panic. The idea was to show the terrorists that we meant business. The local Member in Charge of the Sinoia Police Station was not too impressed with our parading down the main street like that, and he summoned us to his office to tell us that this was not the Wild West. We even had a trailer, with a long pipe covered by a tarpaulin complete and with wheels, pretending that we had a huge cannon with us. A 20mm cannon that we did have, mounted on the back of a roofless Land Rover, was fired just outside the town. The deception tricks worked for us on many occasions to not only scare the terrorists into zero action, or the opposite, by pretending to be a weak military unit to get them to show themselves. We must have looked like a real band of renegades, with our mixture of weaponry, different camouflage uniforms and vehicles that virtually bristled with fire power. This state of affairs was not really appreciated by the conservative section of the Police.

October 1979 – SAS prisoners:

The peace talks between the Rhodesian Government and the two terrorist organisations were to take place in England, and were to be hosted by the British Government. Everybody could feel that the intensity of the war had increased. The warring sides were hell-bent on beating the shit out of one another in order to position themselves well for the peace negotiations. The SAS, RLI and Selous Scouts were pounding external terrorist bases in Zambia and Mozambique, and the Gook Organisations were trying their best to get as many of their cadres into Rhodesia as possible.

Pachedu was engaged flat-out with operations in the bush every day.

One day we were relaxing at our Borrowdale safe house after an operation, when a few of our colleagues from Special Branch arrived with three civilians, two white men and a young boy. The story was that the SAS had dropped a rail bridge over the Chembeshi River in North Eastern Zambia. The SAS were on Operation Cheese. The idea had been that by dropping bridges with explosives throughout Zambia, it would limit the movement of ZIPRA troops and their quest to launch a conventional attack on Rhodesia. The Lancaster House Peace Talks were to take place, so disrupting the Zambian economy would make their President, Kenneth Kaunda, put pressure on the ZIPRA command to attend and sign an agreement that would bring peace to Rhodesia and therefore relieve the huge drain the war was having on the Zambian people. The three civilians had been in the wrong place at the wrong time. The SAS didn't want to release them in case they informed the Zambian military and, with the operation so far away from Rhodesia, the SAS would have had a problem, with no backup available. The young boy had just had his birthday and, as a treat, had been travelling with his father on the trip of a lifetime through Africa. The two men were from the East Block and were brothers.

We were asked to look after the prisoners. At first we had serious doubts about the men, as we were concerned that they would attempt to escape, or even try and overpower us and use our weapons to blast their way out. The safe house was not designed to be a jail, so we had to come up with a plan. Jerry and I did the first night guard duty. We kept the prisoners in a spare room and Moses had to make extra food that night. The next day, after some chatting in broken English and some sign language, we got to know them a bit better. It turned out that they couldn't care less about our little war and were truly no threat to us. They had been overwhelmed by the SAS operations in Zambia and thought that they were due to be executed at any time. They just wanted to get home and away from this ordeal. We relaxed our guard and, over the next week, we became good friends. One of the chaps had played tennis for his country, so I took him down in our Peugeot to watch a provincial game. We had a great time. After three weeks, it was considered time to send them home and negotiations were made for their repatriation. It was a sad day when we said goodbye. I tore a Z$20 in half and gave the signed other half to my new tennis friend, saying that we would join the note together and buy a beer when we met again. We hugged and they were gone.

The last battles:

Near the end of the war, information came in that there were fifty terrorists running around the Concession farming area, not far from us. They hadn't caused any trouble as yet and I thought that they were just cruising, as the Government had been in peace talks with all the terrorist organisations. A ceasefire was due to start in ten days, after an agreement at Lancaster House in London saw all the parties sign on the dotted line to stop the war and have free and fair elections. Pachedu decided that the war was still on and deployed to a farmhouse, owned by the Carr family, in the Concession area just North of Salisbury. We set up base and raised the Internal Affairs flag that we had stolen from the 'pub that served no beer.' It was important that the number of operators in our unit were not counted by the locals, or any terrorists brave enough to stop and look at us, and that most of the time they were to wear civilian clothes, almost as if they weren't in the military. The general idea was to get the terrorists to believe that this influx of people was not serious and had no bearing on their successful survival to the end of the war in a few days. The raising of the Internal Affairs flag, in the garden of the farmhouse, also boosted the perception that we were of zero threat since, for the most part, the Internal Affairs folks were not considered 'operational' by the terrorists. The local Gooks were fooled and they swallowed the ruse, hook line and sinker.

On the first night, both Jerry and I took our teams out on patrol to neighbouring farms. We made contact with the terrorist group by setting an ambush, but unfortunately didn't score a hit. We were out every night for the next six nights and fought with them on every occasion. One night, I spotted them in the local compound of a farm and fortunately I had Theuns with me as additional support. Using my night-sight, I saw the terrorists making merry with the local people at the bottom corner of the compound. I whispered into Theuns's ear, asking him what he thought we should do and he suggested that we approach the terrorists from the direction of the compound itself.

'Come, let's go through the houses and get these bastards,' he whispered. Now that was different. We had never started a contact by intentionally walking into the middle of the party, but our confidence was high. We made our way up to about midway of the compound and entered the cluster of huts. I used my night-sight constantly, trying to see where the gooks were. The five of us spread out a little, until we came across a brick-walled hut. I signalled to the others to stop, whilst I took another view through the night-scope. I could only see some people walking down by the party area, but then Theuns came up to me and whispered in my ear, 'I think some of the gooks are in this hut right here.' His English was getting much better!

We listened intently and, sure enough, could hear the sound of male voices. I signalled to Obediah to come closer and see if he could work out what they were saying. He stuck his ear against the metal door and listened. In the meantime, Theuns moved around to the side of the house and sat under a window, acting as a guard. Obediah, in his efforts to hear better, leaned too far against the door and it creaked a little. The talking inside stopped and suddenly there was a mad scramble, with people jumping out of windows. Theuns was knocked right over, as a terrorist fell across him in his effort to get away. He picked himself up and we ran after the terrorists in pitch darkness. Theuns was swearing blue murder. How could someone have the cheek to knock him into the dirt? He was in the mood for a fight, immediately. The rest of us were in fits of subdued laughter as we sprinted downhill and into the fight.

We didn't have to go far literally to fall in amongst them. There were people running all over the place and we opened fire. One terrorist was hit by Theuns, not five feet in front of him. He walked forward and put his foot onto the wounded terrorist's back, whilst he casually reloaded and carried on shooting at the Gooks. The noise was intense as we opened up with everything we had. The position we found ourselves in meant that we were firing at running terrorists from a circle. One terrorist lay in front of us, with an unexploded Czechoslovakian anti-personnel rifle grenade sticking out of his stomach. We had to watch out for that one. The dust and sweat only became apparent once we had stopped firing. There wasn't a sound. During the contact, the wounded terrorist breathed his last breath.

The reaction team of Ian, Gary and Billy arrived in a Land Rover within twenty minutes, as they had heard the gun battle from the base camp. We had one dead terrorist and three civilians who had been wounded in the cross-fire. I nearly collapsed when I saw a young girl injured near the road. I lay down next to her and tried to get a drip into her arm by using the flame of my cigarette lighter to create enough light so that I could find a vein. I got it in just as Ian and the lads arrived. They took one look at me lying down on the ground and thought I'd been shot. The girl was taken to hospital, together with the two other injured civilians. We didn't involve ourselves in interrogations. We knew that the war was nearly over, and so headed back to base on the next farm.

We had one more day of war left, but made the decision to

hammer the remaining terrorists. I took my team out and we made our way to another farm compound, not too far from the base, and couldn't believe the amount of noise coming out of the farm compound. I shuffled my three guys close to the huts and we listened to the clamour coming from within. After a while, I decided that I'd had enough and didn't really want to get into another firefight. We had had six contacts in the last six days. I was tired. I grabbed an Icarus flare and fired it up into the air above the compound. I had said to the lads that if they had a positive sighting of any terrorists, they were welcome to take them out. The flare hung heavy in the dark sky and swayed as it started its decent. There was nobody to be seen in the airy light of the flare and the compound was suddenly very quiet. It was a very strange feeling. It was almost like nobody wanted to shoot, make a noise, or move. After a few minutes, the flare burnt itself out in its hissing swaying way and we relaxed a bit. I decided to move the team back, away from the compound and rest up in the bush for the night. About a hundred metres from the compound, I thought, *To hell with it* and opened up with a full magazine over the top of the compound, hoping that the terrorists, if they were there, would fire back. Nothing happened, so we just nestled down and slept the night away.

A really Bad day

21st December 1979:

In the early hours, I took my team back to camp as it wasn't a long walk and we would arrive just in time for breakfast. Jerry and the reaction team decided they would take the Land Rover up the road to visit the farm compound I had revved last night. The time was 07:15 hours on a bright, sunny morning. I went across to the Carr's farmhouse and they offered me breakfast. I sat down and was just about to take a mouthful of maize porridge, when there was a huge explosion. I turned my head toward the dusty road leading away from the farmhouse and saw a plume of dust and smoke around the Land Rover that Jerry and the lads were in. My spoon, full of porridge, dropped and I rushed to grab my rifle, webbing and as much first aid kit as I could. The rest of the chaps grabbed any available vehicle and drove like madmen down to the crippled Land Rover and crushed passengers.

My thoughts were, 'Please don't let there be any fatalities, please!!'

The last casualties of the war

I stopped the small convoy about fifty metres from the landmine scene and told the guys to spread out and be very careful, as we made our way as quickly as possible towards the injured. The guys spread out with one eye on the ground looking for anti-personnel mines and the other on the mess that was ahead of us. My heart was racing and I could feel it hitting hard against my ribcage. I was carrying the medic kit and looked this way and that for any trace of anti-personnel mines. There weren't any, but I didn't want another explosion taking place. The scene was surreal and I had to take in the many confusing thoughts rushing through my racing brain. There were bits of Land Rover, tools, backpacks and debris from the explosion everywhere. I slid next to Jerry, who was lying with his back up against the rear of the Land Rover. His knee was in a mess and his left leg lay at an awkward angle. He was okay for the moment, but I guessed he was going to be in a load of pain shortly.

'Get to Billy, he's in a bad way,' came Jerry's instruction, as he directed me with a slowly raised arm.

I rushed across to Billy, where Jake was holding his friend's hand. Billy was lying with his back up against the graded edge of the road. He was covered in blood and looked like he had been badly burnt. Jake seemed to be fine, although he was also covered in dust and blood. As I knelt next to Billy, I looked up and saw Ian standing near the front of the damaged vehicle with Pete Lawrence, one of our support guys, next to him. I turned my attention back to Billy.

'I'm going to get a drip in your arm, mate,' I said, lifting up his right arm. As I prepared to insert the needle, I could see that he was beginning to shake.

'You better get that thing in fast,' he said. 'I can feel shock coming on.'

I wiped the dirt and grime off his arm. I tried and tried to get to the vein with the needle. What I had to do was get the needle into the vein, then make sure blood came out the open-ended needle when I pulled the plunger away. Only when I saw the blood was I going to attach the life-giving saline drip, by connecting the flexible clear pipe to the needle. I tied a bandage around his upper arm, flicked the skin at the bend in his arm to get the vein to show – nothing. I was getting frustrated in my attempts. *After all the times I had done this before, I couldn't do it to my good friend.* Billy had lost a lot of body fluid and he was getting thirsty from the loss. I could feel his temperature dropping, as I continued in my attempts to get the drip into him. I shuffled my feet and tried again.

Just then all hell broke loose, with rounds going off right near us. We instinctively hit the dirt, but realised that it wasn't true firing from a weapon. Billy didn't move; he just lay there, with his arm in my hands. I let his arm rest across his bloodied chest and stood up, rifle at the ready. I peered across in the direction of the noise. Ian was still standing in the middle of the road, looking across into the grass at his webbing. He had a habit of leaving his ammunition and webbing in the spare wheel attached to the front of the Land Rover's bonnet. I turned to look in the same direction as Ian; his webbing was lying on the ground about ten feet from us. It was burning and I could see that a white, phosphorous grenade had exploded and the explosion had set off the ammunition from his RPD machine gun. The rounds had started to cook off and explode in the heat of the fire and they continued to explode like popcorn in a pot. I knelt back next to Billy and tried to get the drip in again, all the time thinking that there could be another grenade explosion, so I kept my head down a little lower. I changed needles, as the first one was getting blunt. Just then, another Land Rover pulled up and a medic climbed out and slipped in next to Billy. He struggled a bit, but then got the needle in and the Saline drip started to do its job of filling Billy's veins again. I stepped back, a bit more relaxed. It seemed that everything was going to be okay. In the meantime, I had a look at Ian.

'I'm okay, just a sore right-hand side, that's all. Have a look at Pete,' was Ian's comment. He was still standing - what a tough guy. Pete was now lying down and was semi-conscious. I didn't realise it at the time, but Pete had suffered severe brain damage. His eyes were bulging out of his head and huge, blood-red patches were showing the possibilities of severe brain damage.

By this time an old friend called Charlie Hand appeared, as he had been working in the area not three kilometres from the landmine incident. Charlie had heard the explosion and knew from experience that it was a landmine. He had called for a helicopter casevac from Mount Darwin, from his radio in the Police Land Rover he was driving, but it was taking too long to arrive. Eventually, he decided to load the wounded men into his Land Rover and drove them to Andrew Flemming hospital. Thank God for Charlie. We later found out that two Air Force helicopters had met Charlie on the road and managed to airlift the casualties to hospital. The whole thing felt like it had happened in minutes but, in fact, it had been a full hour before the lads were on the vehicles and helicopters and off to hospital.

I stayed behind to clear up and secure the base. The guys were in a bad way, with injuries that would have them 'man down' for a good while. My biggest relief was that they had survived.

'Mighty fine thing to happen, hey?' I said sarcastically, to nobody in particular. Another Land Rover drove up to the landmine scene and a number of army engineers climbed out. They came across and shook hands with everybody, then got into the hole where the landmine had exploded. Their job was to try and identify the type of mine used. It seemed all so senseless now that the war was officially over.

The Land Rover was a complete wreck and I stood next to it, gazing out across the open grass land to the hills a few kilometres away.

'I wonder if those buggers are sitting in those hills,' I said and I turned and headed for the radio in one of our vehicles. I called up Bindura and asked if it was possible to get a tracking team down to us, with a PATU section.

'Ah, AC, this is 204,' came Barbara's sweet voice. 'You are to pull back, there are no teams available, all units are to stand down, Ceasefire is now on,' came her instructions.

Well, that was that. The remaining Pachedu soldiers returned to the farm base, where we loaded up everything and headed back to Borrowdale base. The engineers had hauled the Land Rover back to town and had established that the mine had been a Chinese box mine, made of wood. This type of mine was impossible to find, if you used an electronic detector. I was glad that the gooks hadn't packed a drum of fuel under the landmine to act as an incendiary device, as well. They could also have packed two mines together. This had been one of their tactics more recently, after the Rhodesian Security Forces had been getting rather smart at building vehicles that could handle mines quite well. If that had been the case, we would have had a very bad situation indeed.

The men of Pachedu were the last casualties of the Rhodesian war. Having gone through so much in all the years without anybody being killed or injured, was a miracle. Just our luck to have this happen to us right at the end of the war ... shit! It was as though somebody higher than us had lent down and said, 'Oh, boys, I forgot about you lot; have some injuries before you go home!'

What a wonderful world:

Everybody had been singing the song from Louis Armstrong 'What a wonderful world', at the top of their voices when the mine had exploded under the front left wheel. Pete Lawrence had been driving. Billy had been sitting in the middle seat and had rocketed through the roof and ended up under the vehicle's engine. Ian had broken ribs and a broken collar bone. Jerry had his entire knee smashed and his leg was pushed upwards by a good six inches. His leg had been resting on the metal plate just outside the vehicle, literally inches from the full blast from the mine. Pete had serious damage to his skull and suffered major concussion. Jake, who had been standing in the back of the vehicle, came off the best and was not too badly injured. He had a broken wrist. Billy was the worst off. He had 65% of his body burnt with 3rd degree burns. What was amazing was that all the lads had seen Billy under the engine getting burnt. With broken leg, broken ribs and collar bone, with skull bashed in, the lads had heaved the Land Rover off Billy and saved his life. This was a remarkable act of selfless courage to save their friend, and considering their injuries, quite a remarkable feat.

The camp back at Borrowdale was not the same. Almost all the operational special forces support team, plus Jerry, were out of action. It took a while but Ian, Jake and Theuns came back to camp after a short time in hospital. I remember Ian saying that he was sick of being shot up. He had been shot and wounded several times during the war. Billy and Pete's injuries were more severe and they never came back to Pachedu after that.

We take off for South Africa

The lads were shattered after many years of war. We decided to take off for a holiday in South Africa. Five of us jumped into Jerry's Peugeot 504 and headed south. Jake and I stayed at my sister's flat in Braamfontein in Johannesburg, whilst Jerry, Ian and Billy drove all the way to Cape Town. I reckoned they were going to drive off the end of the continent! We came down fully-armed with our AKs and Russian Tokarev pistols. Ian and the lads were nearly arrested in Cape Town when they were spotted in a bar with pistols. The reacting Police SWAT team surrounded the pub and burst in, guns at the ready. I reckoned it was lucky Ian wasn't his normal self, with his quick draw action, as there could have been a very serious gunfight. Anyway, all ended well and the SWAT boys ended up drinking the night away with weary Rhodesian soldiers.

Jake and I wandered around Johannesburg and even watched 'Apocalypse Now' on its first showing, which raised the hair on our backs. We couldn't adjust to the bright lights, music and girls of Johannesburg. We stuck together and spoke to few people – we seemed alone in this mass of civilian life. We went to a pub, where a long-haired musician played the saxophone on the steps just outside. The beer was good, but we were in a strange place with strange people, food, sights and sounds and felt very foreign. Trish's flat was a retreat, where we took refuge to get away from the confusing place.

Ian, Billy and Jerry arrived back from their long journey to Cape Town and we bid Trish goodbye and headed back to Rhodesia and an unknown future. We were mentally exhausted and, on the way back, got arrested three times by the South African Police for various offences, but were released with no charges after it became known who we were. I guess they felt sorry for us. At one Police Station in Louis Trichardt, the police said, 'Just leave and don't come back – you were never here, okay ... and, oh, by the way, good luck to you.' I believe the South Africans felt sorry for us, as we had basically just lost our Country.

Our last night in South Africa and at the small town of Mussina, on the border between South Africa and Zimbabwe, we slept in our sleeping-bags after a long night of drinking. I guess we drank five bottles of whiskey, two crates of beer and ten litres of wine between us. We fired off a few hundred rounds from our pistols at the empty bottles we placed on a small wall next to our sleeping spot. Police from the town didn't react to the guns blasting away. Drinking was our escape-mechanism. In the morning, we couldn't find Ian anywhere. Eventually we jumped into the Peugeot and drove on the road back to Johannesburg, after we had spoken to a local who said he had seen a chap walking next to the road. Ten kilometres further on, we found Ian who was intent on walking back to Cape Town. He got back into the car, after much persuasion, and we crossed the border back into Rhodesia. At no time did the South Africans ever question us about our weapons. Our appearance must have told the whole story.

We crossed back into Rhodesia and were about 200 kilometres north of the border, when we came across about 150 terrorists, walking on the road in two long files. Jerry stopped the vehicle and Ian was all for taking this lot on. After much discussion, we decided it wasn't a good idea and drove between the two lines of terrorists with fingers tight on triggers. The ceasefire was in full swing and the terrorists were making their way to the prearranged assembly points. The Rhodesian Army and Air Force had to stand down and were basically confined to barracks, whilst the terrorists were ushered into 24 assembly points stretching across the Country. Elections were imminent and the Country was going to go through a very delicate stage in its History. I was now going to be involved in stuff that was mentally testing. The war was over - for some.

9

Central

Intelligence Organisation

The war was officially over and all troops had been pulled back into barracks. The Police still had police work to do; law and order had to be maintained. This meant that I was still operational, but not under the control of Pachedu. I fell under Special Branch Salisbury jurisdiction. The terrorists were now to start moving into assembly points. Essentially, all Armed Forces were being separated from each other. It was now the job of the Police and other Government units to assist with the gathering of the terrorists into their respective Assemble Points.

I was sent to Chirundu to man the Special Branch station. Chirundu is the smallest of towns, with a customs and immigration station at the border with Zambia, together with a single hotel, a few shops and a few houses. The Chirundu suspension bridge spanned the Zambezi River and linked Zambia with Rhodesia. The Police Station was right next to the border post, with the Special Branch office in the same building as the customs and immigration guys' offices. In that office were two tables and two chairs; on top of one table was a really strange grey machine. I had just laid my eyes on my first fax machine. This was considered a top secret device and was good enough to send encrypted information back to CID and SB Sinoia Headquarters.

What you did was make your normal phone call to whomever you wanted to send a fax to and, at the same time, you inserted your A4 sheet of paper 'landscape' ways into the machine. On joint agreement, the receiving officer would push his button at the same time that I pressed mine on the machine and it would start rotating the sheet of paper on a securing tube, similar to what you would find on a typewriter. The reading head would then start to move across the document and transmit the information to the receiver. To send a single document took a minute – if you were lucky. The crackle from lightening, and the static noise on the telephone line, would often scramble the information to the point that it would be illegible on the other side. It would sometimes be so bad - and after soooo many attempts to send the information had failed - that we would often just read the information out to the receiving officer. A frustrating machine indeed!

With the help of some of the chaps at Customs, we were able to nab a number of people importing illegal stuff - from weapons to fake money. One Indian fellow had US$27 000 stuffed in a bag … and all of it was fake. We also found 15 Kruger Rand coins hidden under the bottom flap in the same bag. When he tried to bribe me with one of the coins, I had to be restrained from giving him a hiding!

It was during this time that the bulk of the ZIPRA terrorists and their equipment started to pour into Rhodesia from Zambia. Truckloads of vehicles, inflatable boats and tanks, with accompanying men were convoying through. Some of the ZIPRA High Command accompanied some of these convoys and it was interesting finally to meet some of the men who had been our sworn enemies. After a short period, I was transferred back to Salisbury.

Being friends with the enemy:

I was instructed to take a heavy troop carrier (called a crocodile) and join another Special Branch chap and his similar vehicle, with the task of picking up a group of 24 terrorists from the Bindura area and transport them to their Assembly point. We were accompanied by a 'Liaison Officer' from the military wing of ZANU PF. We picked him up at Special Branch Bindura and headed to a kraal, where we were to meet the terrorists. He was dressed up in some new colourful and fancy camouflage we had never seen before; he looked like a walking daisy! I had to wear a badge, which disguised my unit, so I had hand-stitched it onto the right shoulder of my camouflage shirt. I was called a Liaison Officer.

Now, I had heard that the terrorists were very nervous and the slightest incident would start a firefight. My Policeman friend and I were horribly outnumbered. We came to a stop at the kraal and stayed in our vehicles, whilst the Liaison Officer went forward to call the terrorist group out from the bush. They had a quick discussion and formed a rough parade, where they sang a few songs. I leaned out the windowless vehicle and beckoned the Liaison Officer to get the show on the road. The terrorists split into two groups and I was joined by 12 of them and the Liaison man. We had a quick chat and started on our way. As I drove, the terrorists were full of questions. Some of the questions were really strange and showed how little they knew about their enemy. One of the questions was 'Why do the aircraft change gear when they are about to attack us?' or 'What was the really big gun the Rhodesians used?' I was getting tired of the questions and the atmosphere was very tense. The stench from these gooks was unbelievable; they hadn't cleaned their clothes or bathed for weeks. Their hair was long and lay flattened under their customary wide-brimmed hats. They were all heavily armed and wore an assortment of jeans and jackets. As I rounded a corner on the dusty road, a Land Rover approached from the other direction AND a military Alouette 3 helicopter just happened to fly over us. In the middle of the bush this was sheer coincidence, but with 24 very nervous terrorists with you, it became quite a problem. It took everything the Liaison man had within him to calm down the terrorists. The Land Rover pulled up next to me as I made space for him to move on and my good, friend Dave Cox, recognised me and wanted to chat, not knowing what a dangerous situation we were in. I just waved and sped on, much to Dave's disgust. He understood when I caught up with him on a later day and explained. I had switched off my radio, just in case the terrorists thought that I was setting them up for a hiding. We eventually made it to the Assembly Point, dumped our cargo and sped off back to town. When we got back to the office, I asked my Special Branch friend how his trip had been. He told me that the terrorists had been absolutely gobsmacked when he'd been able to identify every member of the group by name. He was the local SB man in the area and knew this enemy backwards. It amazed me, too, but showed how efficient our intelligence systems were.

Special Branch transfer:

I was moved to Special Branch 'E' Desk and joined the Special Operations Section. I worked with various characters I had met and worked with on and off over the last few years. Jake was with me and his job was essentially support on a number of operations, including photography. He had been the main photographer for the British Paras when the well-known Bloody Sunday shootings had taken place in Northern Ireland. He was well-versed in photography. Some interesting stories took place during this time. I was thrown into intelligence-gathering of a different kind. I was responsible for collecting information from the Salisbury University and had on my payroll two characters with some influence. One chap was the President of the Students Union, a likeable, black chap, and the other was a junior in the same organisation. Having two informers in the same organisation was a good tactical move, as it enabled us to confirm whether the information we were being fed was correct. The two informers didn't know the other was on our payroll. Away from the University, I also had a Catholic Priest to deal with. He had been caught red-handed having a sexual relationship with a black chap and was now passing information, via me, to Special Branch on the activities of the Catholic Church, which was known to be sympathetic to the terrorist organisations.

I was also involved with the installation of listening devices and subsequent monitoring of some new targets. One was the local travel agents known to be linked with the Cuban government, whilst the other was the Russian Embassy. Jake and I worked together on numerous occasions on these projects.

Special Branch Desks

The Intelligence part of the Rhodesian Government was made up of a number of units/branches/groups. Essentially, all fell under Special Branch Head Quarters. SBHQ was made up of two distinct groups, namely Central Intelligence Organisation CIO (Branch 2) and SBHQ (Branch 1). Both groups were further split into various desks, or areas of responsibility. SBHQ had regular CID Polices officers and civilian technicians, plus registry staff. SBHQ controlled a number of desks including:

- 'E Desk' - European or Counter-Intelligence desk, which was responsible for the monitoring of immigrants or visitors into Rhodesia. They also had to monitor any influences of Communist origin, whether these came from European or the countless aggressive African countries. This desk became a sub-department, run primarily by Branch 2 civilian staff.

- 'C Desk' - This was originally the Communist Desk, but later became the Economic/Sanctions Liaison Desk.

- 'A Desk' - The Nationalist Desk was responsible for monitoring the Black Nationalists groups and was very involved in supplying the Government with key intelligence into dissident activities.

- 'Technical Desk' - This was also called 'B Desk' and was responsible for interception, by various means, including radio broadcasts, newspaper and electronic surveillance and so on. Anything that was of a terrorist or potentially damaging nature to the Government, from any source, was their baby. This was a specialist desk, with some very clever people.

- 'Terrorist Desk' - This was initially part of the Nationalist Desk and its task was support of all of the Defence Forces, with information relating to terrorist activities.

- 'TU Desk' - The Trade Union desk was concerned with the monitoring of these unions.

Listening to Cubans:

We had to place a radio transmission device in the Travel Agencies' offices, which apparently had links to Cuban Intelligence, from which we could listen to their conversations from our offices in Special Branch nearby. Their building was a block away from Salisbury Police headquarters; it was a four-storey building, with their offices on the top floor. Phil, Jake and I planned the installation and, late one night, climbed over the property's back wall, went up the fire-escape steps and used a duplicate key which Phil had obtained from the cleaners, to enter the building on the top floor. We all carried Tokarev pistols, not that we were really going to use them. Our biggest fear was setting off an alarm, to which the normal Police would react. We had our listening-device and a few tools. The idea was to place the device inside one of the lounge-suite chairs. We crept forward and peered over the stairs, down to the ground floor far below. We could just make out the shoulder of the security guard as he sat in his chair, reading the newspaper. We quietly moved into the offices using one of Phil's keys. The room was reasonably well-lit from the street lights below. I got to work removing the back piece of material from the three-seater lounge suite. I stuck the small device onto a piece of supporting wood and closed up the back again. Fortunately it was easy, as the fabric had been secured with tacks, so it was a quick and seamless in and out job. We left the same way we had come in. The device had a voice-activation system and a battery life of 1000 hours, so we started to get conversations recorded on big tapes in the Special Branch offices. Most of the talking was of no interest, but all of the tapes were sent to a translator. I don't know if the information received was of any use, but a week later Jake and I were called in to Phil's office.

'The transmitter that we installed in the travel agency has gone on the blink, so we have to go back in and check it out,' Phil said.

That night we were back in the agency's offices but, to our utter disbelief, we realised that the lounge suite, in which I had positioned the radio transmitter, had been replaced with a new one made of wood. There was no way we could install a device in that lounge suite, so we left. That was the end of that. We wondered if the Cubans had picked up the transmissions and removed the lounge suite. Somewhere out there, there is a lounge suite with an expensive listening device in it. I remembered the frequency was 138MHz FM.

Listening to Russians:

The Russians, like many other countries, were opening up embassies in the new country of Zimbabwe. With the new Government soon to be elected, the rush was on by foreign governments to make political and economic connections and trade deals. They had placed their embassy not too far from the already existing American one. Some of the lads from CIO, with the help of the CIA, had already installed listening devices in the Russian building and had placed them under the window sills and in various other positions throughout the building. I'm sure they were issued by the Americans to our guys. The units were voice-activated and would automatically transmit conversations to receivers monitored by the CIO lads. I was responsible for collecting the tapes that had recordings on them and bringing them back to Special Branch. The tape recorders, three in all, were in a bedroom of a ground floor flat which overlooked the Russian Embassy. CIO had rented the flat for the monitoring of the Russians. Jake was often with me, ready with his camera to take photos of people coming and going from the embassy. One of the tape recorders was linked to the telephone and we could establish what number was being dialled out by holding the two big tape reels and letting the reels slip slowly through our fingers as we counted the clicks made by the numbers dialled. The telephones were analogue systems. We would have to write down the numbers and refer to the counter on the tape recorder so that when we sent the reels in for translation, the translators would be able to give a full report on the conversations, including the numbers the Russians had phoned. I am sure the Russians knew they were being watched. We would often see them wandering around the garden in conversation, but we couldn't monitor them there.

Running after Russian KGB:

Whilst at Special Branch Daventry House, the entire 'E' Desk team was pulled into a meeting. Two KGB men were coming into the country and we had the job of assisting with the monitoring of these guys. We were told one of the men was the head of the KGB Africa Division - a very senior man. The two men shared a room at Meikles Hotel and we knew that both the CIO teams and the CIA had adjourning rooms, with all sorts of listening devices installed. Our job was to follow them when they left their room and to watch where they went and who they met. Jake was with me on most occasions, as we sat in our unmarked, grey, left-hand-drive Fiat. We had cameras and small handheld radios. There were other teams around as well, so we could alternate on both the stake-out and the pursuits. I must say it was rather boring sitting in the car, under a Jacaranda tree, and munching on a plate of chips covered in tomato sauce. Our call to duty came when the two were seen taking the stairs down to the bar, where they then wandered out of the hotel main entrance, heading towards the main street of town. One of them was carrying a black briefcase.

There were mad and frantic calls on the radios to go after the two. The briefcase was of major interest – why and what was he carrying in the case? Three teams of two SB people were up and on their feet. We had a selection of people to use, one was a lady, one was a black constable and the rest were white males. All were dressed in civilian clothing and everyone carried a newspaper to cover the handheld radios.

The whole scene played out like this: The two started a slow walk along the pedestrian curb to the main part of town. The three SB teams split up, with one team walking faster on the other side of the road to get ahead of the KGB guys. The other team crossed the road, but held back a bit. The main follow team tried to keep a 'safe' distance of about 20 or 30 yards from the agents. The two KGB men started to walk faster and it now became an almost quickstep to keep up with them. They turned right down another road, and then left into the next road to get to the main street. The 3 SB teams were trying hard to position themselves so that their target was always in sight. A few things were imperative, like: do not lose sight of them, check out anybody they met and include them in the pursuit, understand why the briefcase was being carried, etc. The two KGB men arrived on the main street and turned right again. Just on that corner was a large shoe shop called Bata. The corner of that shop had two huge windows that the agents could see through to the other street. The KGB agents stopped immediately after they turned the corner and looked back to see who was moving faster than other people wandering around. They spotted both the teams, which were behind them. One of the things that blew the teams' cover was the fact that it was unusual for a person to be speaking into a newspaper. Once the KGB boys had turned the corner, there was mad calling on the radios to get the lead team to turn back and take over the pursuit – caught red-handed we were.

The two KGB men had identified 4 of the 6 people following them; had they spotted anyone else? The two teams following them turned around and quickly made their way around the office block to approach their target from the front, on the main street. By this time, the KGB men had entered a fast food restaurant and had taken a seat to have a meal. Again, calls went out that the front team must now get their butts into the restaurant and monitor what was happening. The briefcase was placed on the floor next to one of the KGB agent's feet. The lead team had just sat down. The briefcase carrier pushed the briefcase across the floor to his colleague - Holy Moly, now that was real espionage stuff! Just as the waiter arrived to take their orders, the KGB men were on their feet again and out the door. They turned at the door and spotted the two SB men getting up from their table. Simple as that, the entire team of SB guys had been identified. Needless to say, we were pulled off the case and didn't take any further part of the KGB/CIA/CIO incident. We had to admit we were complete amateurs compared to the KGB boys. We had never been trained for that sort of action – that was our excuse anyway!

Follow me:

One of the laborious tasks we had was following diplomats around to see where they were going and to gather as much information on certain characters as possible. The task was simple.

We had to hang around outside an Embassy – say the Cuban Embassy- in our little Fiat car. If a particular car came out with a particular registration number (such as CD501344), we were to follow it and record everything that happened until they went back to the Embassy. Any vehicle with a 'CD' prefix would be from an embassy. We were very often caught by the target, as they had no problem looking left as they turned right out of the Embassy – spot which cars were down the road and go from there. We decided to use a single chap, with a radio, who would have to wander around the Embassy gate and then have the pursuit car try and catch the target a few streets up. A couple of problem arose from that type of surveillance. Firstly, the target could double-back and we would never catch them and, secondly, the number of cars driving around the streets was minimal, so the target had no real problem seeing what type of cars were around and whether they were following them a few streets down. I don't know; we never seemed to have the upper hand in all of this espionage stuff.

Airport Intelligence:

I was called to Salisbury Airport to man the Special Branch offices there. My job was checking incoming flight manifestos against a list of 'enemies' on a list we kept in a file. The office was in the Arrivals Hall at the airport and had two rooms. The main room was essentially a desk with a typewriter, telephone and files. The back room had all our photographic equipment and more files, with names on them. If someone came in who was mentioned on the list, we would pick up the entry form that they had submitted to Immigration and forward this information back to headquarters, for potential follow-up by other teams. Any other individuals who caught our interest on the forms, would also have their information punched through to Main Office. Another job was to photograph people as they entered the country, if they were on the list, or when we were asked to do so. I remember I had Jake and another Special Branch chap helping me to try and photograph Russians who were going to the embassy. Jake was on the first floor of the building, using his 600mm mirror lens to capture images of the three Russian gents in the entrance area below. He was spotted by one of the Russians and, before he knew it, the chap was next to him, grabbing the camera from his hands and ripping out the film. We were hauled over the coals for that one - it nearly caused a major Public Relations blow-up for the new Zimbabwe Government. We also monitored a couple of the chaps working at the airport. One of these guys became very friendly with the Russians and was often seen carrying gifts from them, either when they arrived or left the country. He worked in the Immigration Department and, after a few messages of caution to Head Office, he was suddenly removed and we never saw him at the airport again. We guessed that he had been visited by the CIO boys.

In the Departures section, we had a mini office, just behind the wall where the baggage for people flying out travelled down a conveyor belt to the aircraft. Our job was to monitor people leaving and search relevant luggage for information. In the tiny room, we had three walls covered with every type of key, for every type of suitcase. We had a set of lock-picking tools and generally were able to open all suitcases and relock them, without anybody being any the wiser. I had taken a course on lock-picking and found that I was able to open most locks with our special equipment. I practised a lot and opened just about every lock I came across. We had a photocopy machine that we used to copy documents, together with a small camera to photo any items of interest. Passenger names would be attached to the reports we sent through to headquarters. On one occasion, we were phoned from CIO offices to say that two Cuban diplomats were about to leave on the London flight. Instructions were that we had to copy everything in their suitcases on the photocopier. All went well with being able to identify the two Cubans. Not only did they dress differently to most folks, but we also received a wink from our friendly Immigration Officer as to whom they were when they checked in. We had their bags in our secret room as soon as they had turned the corner on the conveyor. Now we had to get into them, without damage or sign that we had been there. We identified the make of the suitcases, used the right keys, and we were in. To our horror the cases were full of documents, surrounded by smelly socks, shirts and the like. We had limited time and space in our little office, but got started right away. We were sweating within minutes, but managed to get through about half of the documents in one case. Suddenly, a knock on the locked door broke our routine and we were told that the check-in counters were about to close for that flight. I suppose the easiest thing to have done would have been to make the bags 'lost luggage', which would have given us plenty of time to do the works, but our nerves got the better of us and we repacked the cases, locked them again and sent them off on their journey. We never did find out whether we had managed to get the juicy parts of the documents. This was typical of the type of information-gathering we did. At that time in the history of our country, many folks were leaving the country for good and the amount of gold coins and weapons we found was astounding. On many occasions we would let stuff go through, knowing that it belonged to an ex-soldier or farmer. After a while, I started feeling very guilty about going through other people belongings, but it was the Russians and Cubans we were mainly targeting.

Mugs and Machel:

During my time as the Special Branch rep at the Airport, we had Samora Machel come through on a State visit, with much pomp and ceremony. Mugabe treated his neighbour from Mozambique with lots of typical African fanfare. Machel had been the leader of FRELIMO during the war in Mozambique and he became its first elected President. FRELIMO had worked hand-in-hand with ZANLA during the troubled times, so they were generally good friends. After a few days, it was time for Machel to leave and they had his aircraft on the main concourse – with a red carpet running from it to the airport building. In front of the Mozambiquean aircraft were three platoons of ex-ZANLA men, paraded and ready to give the salute. I happened to be standing behind Mugabe and Machel, as they gazed across the troops and waited for the customary flypast of military jets. The three platoons were standing to attention and suddenly the blast of three hunter jets, screaming across the roof of the airport at high speed, deafened everyone. They were supposed to fly *up* the runway, but this time they flew from behind the airport building and over the control tower 200 feet above the three platoons. Well, the ex-ZANLA terrorists had seen years of bombing and their first instinct was to take off for the hills. All three platoons broke

ranks in all directions – it was absolute chaos! Mugabe didn't have much to say, although I did notice that he got as much of a fright as I did when the jets zoomed past.

10

Top Secret

Operation Zebra

It was during the ceasefire, and leading up to the elections in Rhodesia, that Operation Zebra came into being. Just prior to the first elections, the political scene was hyped-up and talk was rife about a coup d'état by the Rhodesian Light Infantry, Air Force and the Special Forces units. Rumours abounded within military circles that the Selous Scouts, Special Air Service and Rhodesian Light Infantry were to be involved in the coup by seizing key installations. We, at Pachedu, never received instructions of any kind to be involved in any coup, but we had heard about it through the grape vine. A cease-fire had placed all combatants involved in the war beyond conflict situations. The military men of the political wing of ZANU (Zimbabwe African National Union) and the same for ZAPU (Zimbabwe African People's Union) had been moved into predetermined locations within the country, i.e. into so-called Assembly Points. The Rhodesian regular Armed Forces were also placed behind barracks. A cloud of mistrust between all political parties and military camps lay heavy across the land. The situation was left wide open for clandestine operators to wreak havoc. A few 'third party' actions could change the political and military future of the country. African politics has always been plagued with murders, harassment of voters, ballot-fixing, intimidation and the like. The same uneasy state within military units was apparent, too, since the circle of wild, unsubstantiated stories and second-hand information kept everybody on the brink of mental collapse. The lower-ranking men on both sides relied heavily on directions and information from their superior officers and would believe anything they were told. The rapidly-developing political situation was confusing for those in the lower ranks.

The general undertakings and clandestine operations generated by the volunteers involved in the Operation Zebra, was to seriously disrupt the viability of the ZANU and ZAPU forces, and their respective political leaders' attempts, to lead any new government in the new Zimbabwe. The goal was to generate beliefs that the 'freedom fighters' were incapable of running a government, and that the rift between these organisations was wide. We were to attempt to intimidate both sides into believing that the other party was untrustworthy and that each was attacking the other, in order to win in the race to take over the country. We also tried to create havoc, which we trusted the media would use, to instil a belief in the local population that, by voting for either one of the terrorist groups, there would be a collapse of Law and Order. To vote for a more moderate, middle-of-the-line political party (which included blacks and whites) would perhaps be the best option for those voters sitting on the fence. The idea was to show that neither of the 'liberation' parties trusted the other, that there were elements within each that were prepared to attack the other's supporters and leaders and, finally, that the support held by both parties amongst the local population was not as high as expected. It was hoped that by creating an environment where it was 'obvious' to the world, and more especially the new uneducated electorate, that *neither* ZANU nor ZAPU were capable of running the country, that votes would be cast favouring the more moderate Bishop Able Muzarewa camp. Muzarewa had run the country with a mixed-race government for a short period. This would allow for a more conservative Government, where whites would still be able to influence the political playing-field to some degree. If this were possible, it would mean that the world would accept the results of the elections and the moderates would have gained power. Unfortunately, 'Op Zebra' comprised just a jumble of incidents that, ultimately, were to have relatively little effect on the outcome of the first general elections to be held in the country. The seemingly haphazard attacks on specific targets did not concentrate efforts in one place, and one could assume that the exploits of the operators were unguided and solely opportunistic.

Two teams were created, one operating from Bulawayo, and the other from Salisbury. There were to be 4 to 5 volunteers in each team. The operators were told that American passports would be available to us, should anything go wrong. The passports, and 'apparently' US$5000, were to be made available to the team members, should there be a need to vacate the country in haste. To begin with, no photographs were ever taken of any of us to create the passports. No evidence was ever made available that these facilities really existed and we all believed that we would never be caught, as 'we were too good at what we did.' Like myself, they were all veterans of many battles, over many years of conflict, both within and outside the borders of Rhodesia. 'There was no way that we would ever have to use the escape system.' Anyway, the backers of the plan were high-ranking officers in the Military, Police and Intelligence Services, who had the support of their friends in the Intelligence Services of the United States - how safe could one get? I didn't not know much about the Bulawayo Operation, except that one of their operations involved a botched effort to blow up Joshua Nkomo's car (leader of ZAPU), whilst it went over a culvert, when he was on his way to attend a rally in the Matabeleland area. Apparently the bomb was well-placed under the sand road culvert and it went off, by remote control, just behind the leader of ZAPU's vehicle. Nkomo managed to escape without injury and little was made of the incident in the press. Obviously more drastic measures would need to be taken. Rhodesians, on both sides of the military fence, were very used to minor bombings, ambushes, assassinations and the like, and an incident like this carried no weight. If Nkomo had been killed, that would have been a different story altogether.

I know more about operations in the Salisbury sector. During the time of Op Zebra, I was under the control of Special Branch 'A' Desk Projects Section, headed by Inspector Ken Stewart. Ken was not involved in the operations of Operation Zebra, nor were any of the other members of Pachedu. This was a secret operation that I joined with other men. Our base was in the northern section of Salisbury, in Borrowdale - just a few kilometres from the Borrowdale horse race course. We moved the operations for Op Zebra to a new 'Safe House', about 3 kilometres away from where I had stayed at Pachedu base, as we didn't want the rest of the guys to know what we were doing; it was just too sensitive at the time.

Special training:

The safe-house was simple, and typical of the 1950 - 1960's colonial-style constructions. A half-acre plot, surrounded by a red brick wall and a centrally-placed double garage, made up the structures and the roof was greying asbestos and unpainted. The garden was dilapidated and was typically left unattended by single men operating in the Armed Forces, who had rent agreements with the owners. The house had a few chairs and tables, a couple of foam mattresses in one room, no fridge, cutlery, or any other form of supplies or furnishing. The double garage had been made secure with the addition of a metal, pedestrian door and multiple locks, and the one and only window had been bricked-up. Inside the garage was an indoor shooting-range. The back wall was clad, from top to bottom, by old 'Yellow Pages' telephone books, piled one on top of the other. This formed an effective backstop for hand-gun bullets. There was a white, double-bed sheet hanging from the roof in front of the books. Set on the other side was a slide projector, centrally-placed on a small wooden table. A few chairs completed the remaining furnishings. Nothing of the sort had been used by me at any other training establishment. A trainee would have to stand slightly off-centre to allow the slide projector to direct pictures upwards onto the white bed sheet. A variety of pictures would be shown and the trainee had to shoot either a single or double shot, when and where required.

I remember a series of pictures that were as follows:

Exercise 1:-

- Picture 1 - 6 people, standing in a line, facing the trainee. The people were all of different heights and were wearing different-coloured clothes. Just visible behind a girl was a white man's face.

- Picture 2 - the same picture, but this time the white man's face was not visible.

- Picture 3 - the same picture again, but this time the white man's face, plus a hand-gun, was visible between two other people, but at waist height - shoot!!!!

Exercise 2:-

- Picture 1 - 4 people standing facing the trainee. One lady, in the middle, had her right arm in an arm-sling, as though she had a broken arm.

- Picture 2 - the lady's left hand enters the sling.

- Picture 3 - the lady's left hand starts to extract from the sling - a 'potential gun'.

- Picture 4 - the lady's left hand extracted completely, with a handkerchief. Don't shoot!!!!!

It was not uncommon for the trainees we had on the team, to shoot their selected target with one shot - straight through the head. The old, piled-up telephone books stopped the bullets from flying around the garage and acted, to some degree, as a sound-suppressor so that the neighbours would not complain. We only ever used hand-guns in the room, as rifles would have been too dangerous – some guys wanted to, but were stopped from doing it.

'Do it when we're not here,' was the response.

Operations and tactics:

The vehicle the team used most often was a white BMW Cheetah. It had hidden compartments for weapons storage, and the nicest item was a switch that would ignite the fuel tank and so demolish the vehicle, leaving no fingerprints or documentary evidence of the driver and occupants. This was a last-resort tactic and we never really knew if it would work – we were dying to try it out and see the car disappear in a flash of ignited petrol.

Russian TM46 land mine

One of my jobs was to supply weapons required by the operations team, as and when they needed them. In the initial stages, I was not involved in the operations. Ordinance items such as landmines, rocket-propelled grenades - such as the RPG 2 and the more modern RPG 7 - plus a variety of specialised weapons, were needed. AK assault rifles from Hungary, Russia and China were the most commonly called for, but the volunteers had Tokarev pistols. Tracer rounds were needed. Explosives such as the Russian fuses, South African Type 8D detonators, Cordtex explosive detonator cords from Russia and South Africa, Russian and Chinese landmines, plus PE4 plastic explosives were always in demand. It was understood that there would be no trace on any of the weapons and no paper-trail, whatsoever.

Blowing up the rail way tracks:

One of the operations I was involved in was to disrupt the home-coming welcome of Joshua Nkomo, the leader of ZAPU. It was March 1980. There was to be a rally in Bulawayo and we were tasked with delaying thousands of supporters travelling from Salisbury to Bulawayo by train. The idea was to show that Nkomo did not have the support he actually had, by reducing the number of people attending the rally. The second hope was that it would increase the distrust between ZIPRA and ZANLA factions. If we caused a stir, it could help to make some local folks question the real intentions of the liberation forces and encourage them to vote for a more moderate political party. A meeting of the ops team took place late one night and a decision was made to blow up the railway line leading from Salisbury to Bulawayo, the night before the rally. Lists of ordinance requirements were made and discussions were held about timing, the best place for the explosives to be placed and other related items. It was believed by the volunteers that once the railway line had been severed, there would be a signal to the nearest stations on both sides of the gap, indicating that there had been a disruption to the line.

It was said that there was an electric current running through the rails and if those were severed, the alarm would sound, showing that the line had been cut. This one bit of pure assumption by the chaps was wrong. No such signalling method existed on the railway line at that time. The date of the operation was planned for two night's hence. Nkomo was back in Rhodesia and staying in the capital - Salisbury. It was planned that the line would be broken somewhere near Hartley, some 100 kms to the south of Salisbury, as this was the only rail-link between Salisbury and Bulawayo. This would mean delays in repairs, because of the distance required for the Police, Bomb boys and railway repair teams to get to the damaged area.

The list of ordinance was simple:-

- 12 blocks of Russian TNT
  (200gram and 400 gram) (in stock)
- 2 lengths of Russian safety fuse,
  (we had about 2 metres in stock)
- Type 8D fuse detonators (plenty in stock)
- A Russian 12.5kg landmine (1 in stock)
- Russian Tokarev pistols
- The BMW with full tank of fuel
- 2 Chinese stick Grenades
- String

We would carry all our usual hand weaponry. No rifles would be needed on this trip. As a second thought, I suggested that we lay a further 'false', or unexploded, device some 100 metres from the real one. We were also to blow up any communication boxes with a booby trap, or similar device. These two additional devices were set to further delay the repairs of the line (brilliant idea). The actual explosives used were enough to blow up an entire house!

At 14h00 hours on the afternoon of the operation, we met at the safe house. I tested the Russian fuse for burn speed by cutting 2 feet off the preciously short piece we had, and then timed the burn. When we started the burn on the fuse on the rail way line, we wanted to be far enough away from the explosion to be safe and to not get caught. It was good practise to test equipment as far as possible, before any operation. We had no idea whether the fuses were fully functional, or even if the Chinese stick grenades would work. Dealing with explosives, either before or after, was never a task for the faint-hearted. If the explosives didn't go off, we would have had no choice but to leave them there and hope that if they were found, they would cause delays to the rail network.

The entire ordinance was loaded into the BMW and we headed off to Hartley to find a suitable location for the deed. We were dressed in denim jeans and dark shirts and the mood in the car was relaxed as we casually drove through Hartley and parallel to the railway line. We found a suitable location about 4 kilometres south of the town. It was ideal in that it had a long, straight open section to the road so that we could be in the middle and look both ways for approaching rail and road traffic. There were no local people living close by and, best of all, it had a communications box right next to the line. We drove back to town and spent the rest of the afternoon relaxing around the bar and swimming-pool of a local Hotel. We were not out of place, for this was a popular spot for passing Army or Police personnel. At 18:30 hours, we walked out of the hotel and left in the BMW. We drove around town until it was pitch dark and then headed off south to our bomb site. One chap drove and dropped us off, with his vehicle's lights off. The other two chaps and I jumped out and carried the landmine and explosives, etc. to the edge of the road. The driver parked about a kilometre away, positioned up a dirt road so that nobody would see him if they drove past. The road would be quiet, because it was considered dangerous to drive around at night, as there was a chance of being ambushed. Most locals were at the pub or country sports grounds, drinking.

No bang:

I found a clear area where I could work on the rail line and began to remove the granite chips supporting the line. When the hole was big enough, I planted the Russian landmine under the rail and packed half of the TNT blocks around it. I cut the Russian fuse in three pieces, attached two

detonators to two of the fuses, and set the two detonators into the primary explosives. I took the other half of the TNT blocks and piece of fuse and made up a false explosive charge, about 70 metres south of the real one. I walked across to the communications box and placed a Chinese stick grenade in it and ran an additional piece of string from the string of the Chinese grenades to a small anthill, a few metres away. Everything was set after half an hour of sweaty work. The idea was to detonate the Chinese stick grenade and then place a fresh one in the remains of the communications box, as a 'visible' booby trap - we didn't want to kill anyone. With all this, we would have created a delay so that the engineers would have to check the communications box, defuse the dummy bomb down the line and clear and re-lay the damaged rail lines. In a country like Rhodesia, at that time in its history, a delay like this could last for at least two days.

Whilst the other two waited near the road, hand guns drawn to ward off any potential threats, I took cover behind the anthill, whispered a heavy 'Take cover' and pulled the string on the Chinese stick grenade inside the communications box. Nothing happened - we had a dud grenade. I decided not to worry about it, as the existing grenade would act as a perfect 'booby trap' that the reaction engineers would have to deal with. The more delays

I cause for the repairs of the railway line, the more successful our mission. I walked across to the landmine and whispered to my companions to call the driver on the walkie-talkie to come and pick us up. We used a walkie-talkie system, which we knew had a very low transmission distance and would never be 'picked' up by any of the Security Force guys in the area. As soon as the driver was near us, I lit both fuses. I stumbled backwards in the dark, a little concerned about the Russian fuses I was using; you just never knew if they were going to work. I reckoned that we had about thirty seconds before all hell broke loose. I had used both fuses, just in case one didn't work. The driver pulled up and we all jumped in the BMW and headed off towards Hartley.

'Can't we go any faster,' I nervously urged the driver, as he drove up the road at what seemed to be a snail's pace. 'If we're too close to that bomb, it's going to take our windows out,' I said, trying mentally to speed the BMW away from the coming explosion.

We approached the outskirts of Hartley and realised that we had not heard the explosion. Doubts started to enter our minds as to whether the explosives actually had worked. Had the fuses failed me? We had a quick chat and decided to inspect the scene to be sure. After waiting five minutes behind an abandoned building, we drove back onto the road. We headed back to the site, now a lot more alert. This time I wanted to see if we had been successful, so the car was stopped whilst I ran up to the site to have a look. I couldn't see any damage from the road. My eyes had not yet adjusted to the dark, as I had been looking at the headlights of the BMW, so I found it difficult to find the site - the terrain was so flat and dark. Suddenly, my eyes caught sight of a very white area. It seemed surreal, almost as though the area had a light dusting of snow on it. The landmine and 6kgs of TNT sure enough had worked and there was a hole about 8 feet across. The white image I saw was powdered granite lying everywhere - it must have been one hell of an explosion. Just as I bent down to inspect the hole, I looked up to my right and directly into the single headlight of a train barely 50 yards away, heading right for me. I had not heard it coming.

The single, white headlight of the train lit up the area as I took off, my legs having turned to jelly, back to the waiting car. I had wild imaginings of the train derailing and collapsing in a heap on top of us. I leapt through the open car door of the BMW.

'Get the Fuck out of here,' I yelled at our driver, and we took off in great, breathless haste. Only minutes after the incident, we were questioning one another as to whether the train had derailed or not. Gee, our nerves were now well and truly frayed. Nobody could be sure; we even thought of going back again to check. However, the decision was made to get out of the area as soon as possible and head back to Salisbury and mingle back into society.

Not 20 kilometres from Salisbury, we were surprised by a row of 9 Police cars with sirens and lights going noisily past us in the direction of Hartley. We also counted 4 ambulances hurtling past us, at breakneck speed. Now we were sure that the train had derailed and that all the Salisbury rescue and emergency teams had been scrambled to handle the dead and injured. We slowed down as we got into town and headed for the area we most frequented, as we also wanted an alibi if things got nasty. We turned into Gremlins (a popular drive-in restaurant in the centre of town) and parked under some trees, to the right of the already rowdy people. There was silence amongst us. Eventually one of the chaps took the initiative.

'So what does everybody want?' he asked, in a quieter-than-usual voice, as he wrote down our food and drinks order and headed off to the serving-counter to place it. The 10 o'clock News came on the car radio and we nearly collapsed when we heard that a bus, packed with soccer fans, had crashed, just South of Salisbury on the way back from Hartley, killing eighteen people and injuring many others. That was the reason for the haste of the Police cars and ambulances, not our train crash. The train had, in fact, not derailed and had stopped some 1000 metres down the line, with no injuries.

The next day's Herald newspaper carried a small note on Page Two about the delays caused to the rail service between Bulawayo and Salisbury due to 'sabotage activities' - we had done our deed. How effective the 'gung ho' activities of the volunteers of Operation Zebra were, will never be fully known, but the risks taken by the men involved were enormous. There was no back-up of any kind, no medical assistance, or political or military support, and had anything gone wrong, the volunteers would surely have lost everything. The incidents that took place had the potential of seriously disrupting the election and the political impasse and could have spelt a prolonging of the civil war, with the loss of many lives. There is no doubt in my mind that the Rhodesian forces would have enacted immediate hell on the ZAPU and ZANU forces camped in their 'safe havens', if given half the chance. There would have been a great loss of life and the history books would have been very different today. In the end, the liberation forces won the election and Op Zebra had made no difference to the balance of power.

Spy versus spy:

New Year's Day 1981 was a day that changed my entire life. I arrived back at our Special Branch offices at Daventry House, only to find some armed members of the Police Support Unit and civilian-dressed people standing at the metal entrance door. I had to identify myself and had to raise my arms for a body search for weapons. Nothing was found so I was then allowed into our offices. I met up with all the other chaps' of the Special Branch unit called 'E' Desk, in our large meeting office. Included with those sitting around waiting for something to be explained, was Jake and a few of my work colleagues. It appeared that an investigation was taking place and the hunt was on for spies in the organisation, who were working for the South African Government or other external intelligence agencies.

Just prior to all this, there had been a bomb placed at the headquarters of ZANU PF at 88 Manica Avenue. Heads were going to roll for that one. We had no idea as to who had caused the bombing, but I had my suspicions. It had been rumoured that there were some Special Branch lads under the employment of foreign intelligence services.

In the office were various people I didn't recognise, but the names were whispered between us. Ken Flower (the head of Central Intelligence Organisation) was there, together with a number of his men and also some of the newfound 'friends' from ZANLA and ZIPRA. All were on a witch-hunt for something about which I had no idea. I was interrogated for about an hour by various people. They wanted to know about a gang called the 'Mickey Mouse Gang'. All the questions seemed absolutely ridiculous and I guessed, after a while, that I was not who they thought I was and that I wasn't involved in anything of which they suspected me. Apparently, I was Goofy from the gang. I was interrogated by Sam Magadze (CIO). Where did they come up with all this junk? After all this, I was released and told to go home. They could pin nothing on me.

Later, I found out that Jake, Phil Hartleberry and Colin Evans had been arrested on suspicion of working for the South African Bureau of States Security BOSS. They ended up in jail, in one of the worst stinking prisons in the World (Goromonzi Political Detention Centre). They went through hell, because unlicensed weapons had been found not only in their offices at 'E' Desk, but at their homes. You can read more about Jake in his book 'Sunday Bloody Sunday', which documents his and the other two chaps' troubles. The thing was that most of the chaps at Special Branch had unlicensed weapons and it was just their bad luck to have been hammered for having had stuff in their houses.

I started to become very suspicious of everybody around me. Who was working for the new government of Zimbabwe and who was on the payroll of the South Africans, CIA or MI6? I became paranoid and started to watch out for people following me. I watched who I spoke to and was very careful during telephone conversations. I would take odd routes back home, ever-conscious of anyone following my vehicle. I remembered the radio frequency we used to bug the Cubans and tried to pick up transmissions from my little flat. Were the investigators listening to my conversations? I invited nobody to my flat and whenever I left my flat, I would stick a small piece of cotton thread between the door and the door frame. If it was loose when I came back, I would know that someone had been inside and may have searched my belongings, or placed a listening device. These were very unnerving times. Everybody who had worked with me became a suspect, except of course the members of Pachedu who were down to earth, good mates. I could trust them with anything. The investigations by Central Intelligence Organisation lasted for days and they searched every bit of our offices. They found a few unlicensed firearms, but couldn't nail anybody for those as a lot of the weapons had been handed to us by the auxiliary men who had worked with Pachedu and other parts of the Special Branch network. These weapons were all in a heap at an end office next to Phil's. They were more interested in documents and files, so they ended up taking almost all of our files away. We never found out what they really were after.

Hand in your arms:

An amnesty was issued by the Government, with the idea that as many unlicensed weapons, and as much ammunition as possible, would be withdrawn from public hands. I know that many folks didn't believe this was the only issue at hand. Many of us believed that the new Zimbabwe Government, under Robert Mugabe, was trying to disarm the ex-soldiers of the Rhodesian military and one day he would wreak vengeance on us. We were told to hand in all weapons of war and I remember bringing my personal cache of assault rifles, grenades and ammunition to Salisbury Central Police Station in the back of a Land Rover. Chris Looker, one of our SB bosses, took one look at the amount I was dragging up to the mini-armoury of the station.

'What the devil is all that?' he asked, walking down the passageway toward me. With great difficulty, I was dragging my huge steel trunk that had been with me from the start of Pachedu days, up the stairs at the back of Special Branch offices.

'Well, that's all that I have, Sir,' I replied, bending down to open the large steel trunk.

'I don't know...you guys!' he mumbled, nodding his head knowingly.

'I suppose there's no paperwork with any of that?' he queried.

'Yes, Sir, my issue rifle is from Morris Depot,' I replied.

'And the rest?'

'Belongs to the Police Station, Sir,' I responded, not wanting to get more involved. There was no further discussion on all the bits and pieces. I obviously didn't get a receipt, except for my Police rifle. Everybody was burying their weapons at that stage, just in case. We were all worried about the country breaking down and civil strife being the excuse for the new government to give us a hiding. I buried an AK47 and about 500 rounds of ammunition in the garden of the place I was renting. I cut the wooden butt off, smothered it in grease and covered it in plastic film. I then covered all the ammunition in plastic film and dug a hole in the very rocky ground. I guess the weapon is still there. There was a story of one chap who had a great deal he wanted to hide, so he took off to a nearby hill and found the best place to bury his cache. Once he started digging, he came across someone else's cache and promptly lifted that and then buried all of his weapons, plus the found stuff, about fifty metres away.

The war was over and I was a wreck, both physically and mentally. With the handing in of my weapons, I was no longer an active participant in any actions. I weighed just 165 pounds and with my 6 foot 3 inch frame, I looked like a rake. I felt 'naked' and insecure.

My days in the country were over and I counted my blessings that my team and I had survived the war.

> *'Remember to use the stars, my friend...*
> *I will find you again...*
> *one day.'*

Epilogue

Pachedu closed its doors to business, with the new liberation forces taking power. We burnt every document, every map and every piece of paper or diary we could find. We were conscious of the fact that the new government would be keen to understand what went on during the war and who had been involved. We knew things were going to be a bit tough for units like ours from here on out and we were worried about the head-hunting after the war – not that we had done anything wrong. It's just that, I guess, the victor has the final laugh. Pachedu disappeared overnight. Three truckloads of weapons were sent through the Beit Bridge border-post to help fill the armoury of 5 Recce in Phalaborwa South Africa. The Recce Special Forces of South Africa were a tough unit of Special Forces soldiers.

So, what happened to some of the guys who served with me in Pachedu? Ian Suttil had one more fight with his wife and joined the elite Special Forces unit in South Africa, 5 Recce, where he was later killed in operations against South African insurgents (ANC) in Maputo, Mozambique. A grenade that he had thrown bounced off a tree branch and exploded next to him. The white, phosphorous grenade on his webbing blew up, killing both Ian and his friend, Jim. Actually Ian had sent a letter to Jake and me just before he left on that fateful operation. In the letter was a photo of him climbing into an armoured vehicle, armed to the teeth, as usual. The magazine on his shortened version of the Russian RPD weapon, had a 75 round drum on it, typical Suttil. He was a great loss to us. Jerry Webster recovered well enough from his leg injury to go into farming in Zimbabwe. Jerry is now working in Afghanistan as a hired soldier; farming ceased for him due to the land grabs that the Zimbabwe Government put in place. Ken Stewart (M/I/C Pachedu) lives in England. Ben Pretorius (2 I/C of Pachedu) left the country and joined the

South African equivalent of CIO, the Bureau of State Security or BOSS. He died recently. Our good friends, the turned ZANLA and ZIPRA terrorists like Obediah and the other instructors, who had been through so much with us and fought hand in hand with us disappeared, as best they could, into civilian life. They had a tough time. I felt so much for them and to this day wish them well. Billy Grant went to work as a saturation diver in the North Sea and now lives in South Africa. He was one tough chap. Jake Harper Ronald went to Mozambique after a while, to help establish private security companies there. He also served in Iraq as a contract soldier. He later wrote a book called "Sunday Bloody Sunday" and died recently from cancer. Jake was a career soldier through and through.

Now what

As for me, I was at the Salisbury Airport seeing off a friend to South Africa when I came across a man struggling to load dog food into his car. I just wandered up to him, grabbed the bags and threw them into his car. The man said thank you and asked for my name and telephone number, but I wasn't in the mood to give out that type of information to anybody – not during those difficult times. He persisted and eventually I did give him my name and number. At 8 o'clock the next day, I received a phone call - it was the gentleman whom I had helped the day before. He asked me to come to his office in the TAP building, the Portuguese Airlines. I pitched up at his door and he beckoned me in.

'I know things are not good for you at the moment,' he said offering me a chair, which I accepted. I wondered how he knew that!

'This is a one-way ticket to anywhere in the world that TAP flies,' he said, offering me an envelope. I couldn't utter a word for a second or two, as the offer of a new life flooded my brain. I gratefully accepted the ticket with an outstretched hand. My gratitude knew no bounds.

'Where do you want to go?' he asked, as he sat on the edge of his desk.

'Well, I can probably get into England,' I said, looking at the sealed envelope in my hands.

'Could you make the ticket out for London?' I asked, handing him back the envelope.

I bounced out of his office with a quick look back at him. He knew, deep down, that he had basically changed my life and given me a chance. I went back to my flat, grabbed my documents and nipped into the British Embassy, where the MI6 lads stamped my passport with a patriality stamp in four hours. The date was 19th February 1982. The stamp allowed me to work in England.

I finalised my rent for the flat, gave away all my furniture away to anybody who came close to me, and packed a rucksack with a few shirts and one pair of jeans. The next night, I flew out to London and a new life. I had no idea what was going to happen to me, so I'd packed my medical kit, my sleeping-bag and an emptied, plastic, saline drip. I could blow air into the plastic bag to use as my pillow. That is what I knew kept me safe. At least I could sleep in the bush - I would be safe out there in the bush. I wondered how cold it got and if there was a lot of rain. At least I wouldn't have to worry about lions, spiders or terrorists. I had never been on a jet before and the pilot called me into the cockpit, where I marvelled at all the technology. Everything was so new to me and I was one confused ex-Rhodesian.

I left Rhodesia, forever, with just Zim$16.80 in my pocket. My free spirit was released and I mentally pushed the jet faster, to get away from my mother country with all its troubles. I lost myself in new adventures in Europe and the World, and even went to church for five years to try and clear my head of all the horrors I had seen during our war – it didn't help me much.

Over the troubled times of the Rhodesian war, I endured more than 250 contacts. In every encounter, my unit was always outnumbered, sometimes up to 50 terrorists against the four of us. We never lost a man through death and for that I am grateful. Whether we were just lucky, or whether we were really good at our work, can be debated. The injuries the unit suffered were both physical and mental. The small and beautiful Country of Rhodesia is no more. It became Zimbabwe, with Robert Mugabe as its new leader. Thirty years after the battles ceased, the country is now one of the poorest in the world. The beautiful natural features of the Country are still there and the few animals and right-minded people who have managed to survive through bouts of starvation will one day build it back to what it should be – one of the most beautiful countries in the world.

We will, of course, remember it as it was.

At the end of it all, we may have lost our country but we gained the World. You can find Rhodesians in almost every corner of the World today. We still meet for reunions every year and we are still together, although we are far apart - our hearts still beat with the memories of our little Country. You can bet we will not remember all the stories, but one thing we will never forget are the true friends we made – they sure are brothers in war and we will be together ..... forever.

Looking back at the war, one can interpret it from many different angles and perspectives. There are many versions about what it was, but there is a surety, in my heart at least, about what it was not.

My ashes will lie elsewhere. But in the early morning sunrise of each new day, all I know, with conviction, is that I fought alongside Rhodesians, some of the finest and bravest people I have ever known, black and white. History will not be kind about this time, but it will also know nothing of its guts, of its essence, of what went behind the bullets and the blood. That is how it is.

So, what am I doing now? Well, I am doing all the things I always wanted to. I work amongst the wild animals of Africa. I sometimes sit up high on a warm, granite rock and gaze out across the plains and think back to the days with my buddies in war....

and sometimes I just sit......

> **'I have seen things most people
> wouldn't believe....
> All those memories washed away,
> like tears in the African rain.......'**

Glossary

- Matabele - One of the two tribes inhabiting Zimbabwe, mainly from the West and South West of the country. Bulawayo was their original capital, before they were defeated in battles with British colonial forces in the 1890s.

- Cecil John Rhodes - A well-known British expat who made his fortune in the diamond mines of Kimberley in South Africa and who was influential in much of the politics of South Africa, together with the founding of Rhodesia and the development of Bechuanaland (now Botswana), Northern and Southern Rhodesia. He died 28th March 1901.

- Shaka Zulu - The founder of the Zulu nation in the 1820s, who spread his control over vast tracts of land North of Durban in South Africa, through his aggression and development of new tactics and weapons in warfare.

- Lobengula - The son of Mzilakazi. Mzilakazi had fled the warring Shaka Zulu and moved his Matabele tribe to the Pretoria area in South Africa. He was defeated by the Boers in battles, when the Boers moved north from the Cape area in the 1820s and, later, Lobengula became King of the Matabele in 1870, when his father died. Lobengula was tricked into 'selling' land-use contracts to white hunters and prospectors. He even gave land-use away for the gift of a mirror. On the 30th October 1888, Lobengula signed the Rudd Concession, giving Cecil Rhodes mineral rights, in return for subsidies and weapons. He died in January 1894.

- Matapos - A beautiful range of hills, dominated by huge granite boulders, near Bulawayo. Cecil Rhodes gave this area the name 'Worlds View.'

- Robert Gabriel Mugabe - The winner of Zimbabwe's first free and fair election and leader of the Zimbabwe African National Union political party and Zimbabwe African National Liberation Army.

- Starbur - In Australia, it's called 'cats' face thorns. The seeds are about 5mm across and have two rather nasty spikes, which can go right through the skin of one's foot if one stands on it by mistake.

- *Mangwanani* - A Shona greeting that means 'Good morning'. The way to great a person when you first see them in a day is as follows:-

    Mangwanani (good morning)
    Mangwanani (good morning)
    Warara heri (did you sleep)
    Ndarara kana warara wo (I slept if you slept)
    Ndrara (I slept)

- Veldskoens - Shoes made from the inner part of cow hide – rather cheap, but very comfortable. This type of shoe became synonymous with the Rhodesian bush war, as many chaps wore them - without socks!

- Maize - Corn (the white variety)

- Mealie - local name for maize.

- Manyatellas - shoes made from old car tyre, similar to a flip-flop

- Bakkie - a pickup truck commonly used on farms for carrying stuff

- Duiker - a small grey-coloured species of antelope

- *Nyoka* - local Shona word for snake

- Skivying - doing chores for an older pupil at school

- Hessian - woven hemp used to make maize bags

- Thunderflash - A small charge of black gun powder, packed into an eight-inch tube, used to make a loud bang. This was often used to simulate grenades whilst training in the military. The fuse was lit and one had about three seconds to throw the device.

- Boers - Name given to Dutch settlers who had originally settled in Cape Town and moved North in the Great Trek of 1820. They spoke Afrikaans (a mainly Dutch language, which had been interwoven with words from Malaya).

- Skoff - Slang for food.

- Fanagalo - A mixture of the Ndebele, Shona and English languages. Due to the number of languages used in Southern Africa, this made-up language was useful for people to have as a common tongue in which to communicate. The language was used on farms and in the mines and is still used to this day.

- Magandangas - The Shona word for freedom fighters or Terrorists

- Gomo - A small hill

- Sadza – A thick porridge made from ground up maize

- *Mombi* - Fanagalo word for cow

- Batman - A servant who worked for officers, doing their chores

- *Penga* - Fanagalo word meaning insane

- *Impi* - The local name for a Matabele or Zulu Army.

- Tribal Trust Land - The areas allocated by the Rhodesian Government as their 'homelands' for the Black people of the country.

- Keep – Or Protected Village, where rural Black people were moved into fenced-off areas at night and allowed to run their farms outside the Keeps during the day. The Keeps were guarded by members of the Internal Affairs.

- Operation Hurricane – The Armed Forces of Rhodesia broke up the country into operational zones; Hurricane was the first to be named, as this was the area where the terrorists began their onslaught.